Football Kicking
and
Punting

Ray Guy

Rick Sang

Human Kinetics

Library of Congress Cataloging-in-Publication Data

Guy, Ray, 1949-
  Football kicking and punting / Ray Guy, Rick Sang.
    p. cm.
  Includes index.
  ISBN-13: 978-0-7360-7470-4 (soft cover)
  ISBN-10: 0-7360-7470-8 (soft cover)
  1. Kicking (Football) I. Sang, Rick. II. Title.
  GV951.7.G88 2009
  796.332'27--dc22

                              2008054204

ISBN-10: 0-7360-7470-8 (print)   ISBN-10: 0-7360-8522-X (Adobe PDF)
ISBN-13: 978-0-7360-7470-4 (print)   ISBN-13: 978-0-7360-8522-9 (Adobe PDF)

Acquisitions Editor: Justin Klug; **Developmental Editor:** Cynthia McEntire; **Assistant Editor:** Scott Hawkins; **Copyeditor:** John Wentworth; **Proofreader:** Kathy Bennett; **Indexer:** Dan Connolly; **Graphic Designer:** Joe Buck; **Graphic Artist:** Kim McFarland; **Cover Designer:** Keith Blomberg; **Photographer (cover):** George Gojkovich/Getty Images; **Photographer (interior):** Courtesy Rick Sang (p. 33, 36, 39, 48, 125, 128, 275) and Neil Bernstein, unless otherwise noted; **Photo Asset Manager:** Laura Fitch; **Visual Production Assistant:** Joyce Brumfield; **Photo Production Manager:** Jason Allen; **Art Manager:** Kelly Hendren; **Illustrator:** Alan L. Wilborn; **Printer:** United Graphics

We thank The University of Southern Mississippi in Hattiesburg, Mississippi, for assistance in providing the location for the photo shoot for this book.

Human Kinetics books are available at special discounts for bulk purchase. Special editions or book excerpts can also be created to specification. For details, contact the Special Sales Manager at Human Kinetics.

Printed in the United States of America   10 9 8 7 6 5 4

The paper in this book is certified under a sustainable forestry program.

Human Kinetics
Web site: www.HumanKinetics.com

United States: Human Kinetics
P.O. Box 5076
Champaign, IL 61825-5076
800-747-4457
e-mail: humank@hkusa.com

Canada: Human Kinetics
475 Devonshire Road, Unit 100
Windsor, ON N8Y 2L5
800-465-7301 (in Canada only)
e-mail: info@hkcanada.com

Europe: Human Kinetics
107 Bradford Road
Stanningley
Leeds LS28 6AT, United Kingdom
+44 (0)113 255 5665
e-mail: hk@hkeurope.com

Australia: Human Kinetics
57A Price Avenue
Lower Mitcham, South Australia 5062
08 8372 0999
e-mail: info@hkaustralia.com

New Zealand: Human Kinetics
P.O. Box 80
Torrens Park, South Australia 5062
0800 222 062
e-mail: info@hknewzealand.com

To Sammy Baugh, the greatest football player ever.
He made anyone who visited him feel important. We will always
remember the time you shared with us at Double Mountain Ranch.

Contents

Foreword   vii

Preface   ix

Acknowledgments   xi

Key to Diagrams   xii

Part I   The Placekicking Game 1

1   Placekicking Fundamentals 3

2   Kickoffs 29

3   Field Goals and Extra Points 53

4   Compensating for Conditions 61

5   Placekicking Practice Drills 77

Part II   The Punting Game 105

6   Punting Fundamentals 107

7   Situational Punting 131

8   Coverage Recognition and Pickup 145

9   Punting Practice Drills 155

Part III Countdown to Game Day. 185

10 Snaps, Holds, and Recovery Plays 187

11 Pregame Program. 207

12 Special Teams Preparation 231

13 Coming Through in the Clutch. 243

14 Conditioning for Kickers and Punters 249

Index   269

About the Authors   274

Foreword

Ray Guy is something very special as a person and was something very special as a football player. I remember when we drafted him with the Oakland Raiders and took him number one. Everyone wondered how we could draft a punter number one. Our response was that we drafted him number one because he was not only the best punter in the draft, he was the best punter who ever punted a football. And you know something about that draft—that was the least amount of arguing we had of any draft I can remember. We had a consensus of everyone in the room. Al Davis, the owner; Ron Wolf, the director of personnel; all the coaches—everyone agreed that Ray Guy should be the number one pick. Then he went on to prove it.

He could do everything. Not only was he a punter, he was a great athlete. He could kick off, he could catch the ball, he could throw, he could do all those things that the great ones had to do. It helped us so much. After we had Ray Guy, I would tell our quarterback that if it gets to third down to just throw the ball away, if necessary; the worst we'd have to do is let Ray kick it, and that was pretty good. Then Ray would punt the ball and help our defense.

During all those years with the Raiders, Ray was one of our most valuable players. He had a tremendous work ethic and he never missed a game. He contributed to our team in so many ways. In practice, Ray would work with the defensive backs, pass to the receivers, throw as our scout team quarterback, whatever he could do to stay involved and be part of the team. He popularized the term *hang time* by keeping his punts in the air as long as six seconds sometimes. He would complement his skill with placement to best benefit the team. He didn't care about his statistics as long as we won the battle of field position. He was so effective that he never had a punt returned for a touchdown in his entire career.

Ray Guy has proven he is the best punter to ever punt a football. His career accomplishments are the inspiration for this book. His contributions to his team are an inspiration to all. The skills he developed and the methods he used are timeless. Any athlete anywhere—especially young players today—who takes the initiative to learn about him can share in his success. By reading his book, you have that opportunity.

John Madden

Preface

Football Kicking and Punting is your guidebook to kicking more accurately and punting more effectively. This invaluable resource serves as a blueprint for a career of practice and improvement for kickers, punters, and kicking coaches. The step-by-step progression of each technique enables kickers and punters to learn quickly and remember the biomechanical principles that will most effectively guide them throughout their careers. These proven techniques and innovative learning concepts not only produce immediate results, they enable kickers and punters to coach themselves.

To perform effectively, kickers and punters must become self-reliant and learn the fundamentals and techniques that lead to success. The proper mechanics of kicking and punting are not complicated; any athlete or coach dedicated to studying the principles can learn them. The key to applying these principles is for each athlete to develop the skills and techniques in a way that are most natural for him.

Football Kicking and Punting is for kickers and punters at all levels of play. Although football fields are the same size, hash mark widths, kickoff distances, and the measurements of goal posts are adjusted for the high school, college, and professional games (figure 1). In the National Football League (NFL), the hash marks are narrow, 70 feet, 9 inches from the sidelines and 18 feet, 6 inches wide. In college, the hash marks are 40 feet wide and start 60 feet from the sidelines. In high school, they are 53 feet, 4 inches wide and 53 feet, 4 inches feet from the sidelines. The dimensions of the uprights vary from level to level as well. In professional and college football, the uprights are 18 feet, 6 inches wide. In high school football, the uprights are 23 feet, 4 inches wide. At all three levels the crossbar of the goal posts is 10 feet high. The height of the uprights varies from 20 to 30 feet for amateurs and 30 feet is the standard height in the NFL.

Football Kicking and Punting contains the techniques, training routines, and practice drills necessary to succeed in the kicking game. This valuable resource will empower the kicker and punter to take the initiative to thoroughly study and implement the training methods into their personal practice routine.

Part I covers every aspect of placekicking: the fundamentals of placement, alignment angle, approach, impact, and follow-through; the basics of kickoffs, field goals, and extra points; the best way to adjust to game conditions; and drills to develop and fine-tune a placekicker's skills. In part II, coverage switches to the punting game. Fundamentals covered include the stance, reception, alignment, approach, drop, impact, and follow-through; situational punting and game-day strategy; coverage recognition and pickups; and drills to increase hang time, eliminate returns, and win the battle of field position. Finally part III brings it all together by advancing the kicker and punter's preparedness for competition. The kicker and punter will learn ways to practice through the countdown to game-day, and the importance of working with the snapper and holder; game-day readiness; special teams preparation; and coming through in the clutch.

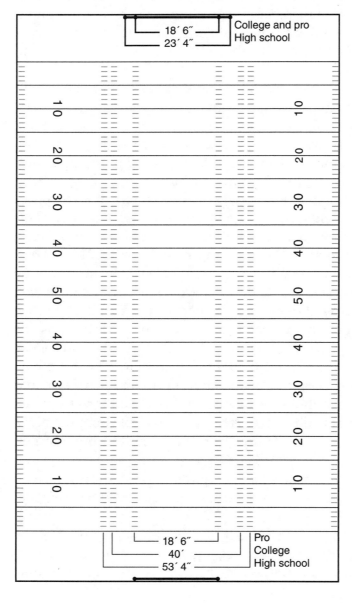

Figure 1 Upright and hash mark dimensions for high school, college, and professional football.

Acknowledgments

Thanks to the staff of Human Kinetics, Inc., especially Justin Klug for the opportunity, guidance, and encouragement and for believing in us; Cynthia McEntire for her patience, professionalism, and amazing organizational skills; Neil Bernstein for his talent and ability to capture pictures of athletic movement that educate at a glance; Scott Hawkins, who masterfully brought many months of work together in order for our message to flow effectively on the pages; and Alexis Koontz for her challenging task of sharing our work with the world.

Thanks to Ben Fuller, Alan Mayo, J.B. Gibboney, and David Hood for their behind-the-scenes help and support. Thanks to Richard Giannini, director of athletics at the University of Southern Mississippi for providing us the opportunity to conduct our photo session at a remarkable facility. Thanks to coach Bob Sang, coach Paul Leroy, coach Bill Tom Ross, coach Herb Conley, and coach Roy Kidd—you lead the charge of all of the coaches who have inspired us to teach, coach, and inspire others. Your message lives on through this book.

We also would like to thank all the staff at prokicker.com and the athletes who have been involved with our national kicking, punting, and long snapping camp program over the past 29 years as well as the thousands who continue to attend annually. Because of you we can continue to learn, teach, and help others. To all of the coaches—your experience, knowledge, passion, and devotion to personally coach and develop each athlete individually continues to be the key to our success. We are very thankful for the time we share together.

Special thanks to all of the past and present kicking specialists who provided us the opportunity to learn from their accomplishments and skills. Extra special thanks to Dewain Akerblom, Ian O'Connor, Jonathan Ruffin, and Nick Harris for allowing us to share photos of your God-given talent on the pages of this book so that it may help others learn and aspire to achieve success.

Key to Diagrams

R   Returner

V   Kick-return team

◯   Kicking team

●   Snapper

K   Kicker

⟶   Player's running path

--------▸   Ball's path

(L1)   Coverage player on kicking team

X   Target

◖   Football

I

The Placekicking Game

1

Placekicking Fundamentals

The prepared placekicker eagerly awaits the command of his coach for the opportunity to run into the game and perform what he does best—kick the football. When the moment arrives, he confidently joins his team onfield, aligning in position in concert with his teammates on the kicking unit. His approach to aligning for the kick is so consistent and methodical that it has become automatic. His natural kicking abilities have become highly successful habits that translate into confidence—a key component of successful kicking.

In this opening chapter we present the fundamentals of kicking in a systematic order that matches the sequence in which the skills are executed in games. Using a step-by-step approach, we cover every facet of placekicking the football. This methodical approach allows placekickers to learn every detail of the kick, promoting faster learning and deeper retention. This approach also makes for effective progression, with each technique being well learned before the athlete advances to the next. Once perfected, the skills become automatic and create a self-reliance that allows the kicker to become his own coach.

Soccer-style kicking is prevalent in American football today. Many athletes learn to play soccer at an early age and are introduced to the basic fundamentals of approaching the ball from an angle and striking it with the front instep of the foot. By approaching the football at an angle, the kicker enhances both power and control of the kick—accomplished through a torque effect created by the body as hips quickly twist to align squarely to the target as the kicking leg moves through the football. The twisting movement of the hips accelerates leg speed, increasing power as the entire momentum of the body directs the flight of the football. Control is accomplished by contacting the football with the solid bony area on the top inside of the kicking foot. This part of the foot provides a broad surface that maximizes the impact point, allowing more of the foot to compress the football, making for a more accurate kick.

Although the straight-on kicking approach remains a sound way to kick a football, few kickers learn this style early enough for it to become their preference. In fact, straight-on kicking is virtually extinct at the college and professional levels. A benefit of the straight-on kicking style is that the kicker takes a straight approach to the football and to his target. A disadvantage is that this style does not produce the body torque for increased leg speed and power. Another drawback is that because contact is made with the toe rather than the top of the foot, the impact area is not as great. Thus, the straight-on kicker has less room for error—he must contact the football precisely to achieve accuracy. We'll discuss both types of kicking in this book but will emphasize soccer-style kicking.

Figure 1.1 Target zone.

Target Zone

Before a kicker aligns in preparation to kick the football, he must know precisely where he wants to kick it. Before kicking an extra point or a field goal, the placekicker focuses attention on the region above the crossbar, beyond and between the uprights. This area is called the target zone (figure 1.1).

The natural frame effect created by the crossbar and uprights helps the placekicker narrow his focus and identify an even more precise stationary target, such as a flagpole or part of the scoreboard. Establishing a precise target zone is crucial and should be done before the game starts, during the pregame warm-up.

Point of Placement

Once the kicker has established his target zone, he determines the exact flight path the ball needs to travel by positioning himself at the point of placement, generally 7 to 8 yards behind the snapper. At this point, the kicker marks exactly where he wants his holder to set the football (figure 1.2). He does this by facing his target directly and aligning the kicking block (for high school) or his kicking foot (for college and pro) toward the target and allowing the holder time to place the fingers of his holding hand on the exact spot determined.

By establishing two points of reference—his point of placement and his target—and visualizing an imaginary line between them, the kicker creates a benchmark for proper alignment that serves as a natural guide for the direction of every kick.

The typical point of placement for an extra point or a field goal is 7 yards behind the line of scrimmage. Many teams are adjusting to a distance up to 8 yards to increase ball elevation, which is a must for good placekicks. By adding up to 1 yard from the line of scrimmage to the point of placement, the kicker can dramatically increase ball elevation before the ball passes the line of scrimmage and thus minimize the chances of the kick being blocked. This simple adjustment allows the kicker to perform the same kick with the same trajectory but resulting in a higher kick as it reaches the line of scrimmage.

Figure 1.2 The kicker marks where he wants the holder to set the football.

Alignment

A kicker can align in many ways. Most important is to develop a consistent method to mark off his steps and thus achieve proper depth and alignment. He should mark off his steps the same way every time.

One of the most common and recommended ways for a soccer-style kicker to align is by marking off his steps with the three-steps-back-and-two-steps-lateral method (figure 1.3). This method was developed by Ben Agajanian, pro football's first kicking specialist and kicking coach. He devised this method to enable soccer-style kickers to position themselves consistently at the correct distance and angle to the football. This method enables each kicker—whether he is 6 feet 4 inches or 5 feet 8 inches—to position each step consistently at a precise distance that is the most natural and relative to his size.

Figure 1.3 The three-steps-back-and-two-steps-lateral method of marking off: *(a)* step one; *(b)* step two;

Figure 1.3, *continued*   The three-steps-back-and-two-steps-lateral method of marking off: *(c)* step three; *(d)* step four; *(e)* step five, toeing the line; *(f)* step six, feet together again.

Using this method, the kicker simply marks off his steps to form a 90-degree angle from the target line. The target line is determined by positioning three steps back and aligning the kicking foot, point of placement, and target on the same imaginary line.

Three Steps Back to Determine Depth

The kicker first positions at the point of placement (the kicking block or the spot at which the ball will be held) and locates the target zone. From this position, he begins marking off his steps by taking full, comfortable strides backward, taking the first step with the kicking foot. These steps should be effortless and consistent. The kicking leg, point of placement, and target zone should all stay in line as he takes each step.

When the kicker completes his third step, which is with his kicking foot, he must keep this foot in the exact same position in order for it to serve as the anchor to the vertical and lateral alignment steps. This same anchor point determines where the lateral steps will be taken to form a 90-degree angle from the target line and determine the precise distance from where the football will be positioned for the kick.

When taking the last step back, the third step, kickers may show a tendency for this step to be not as consistent as the preceding two steps because it has become a stopping point. Since the last step determines the exact distance back from the football, it is crucial that the positioning be very precise and consistent. By temporarily adding an additional step, a fourth step, the kicker can divert the stopping point to the fourth step and ensure all three preceding steps are identical. Thus, the kicker can consistently keep his body at a more precise distance from the point of placement.

This fourth step does more than promote consistency of the first three steps—it also becomes a stopping point that allows the kicker to lean back slightly and view the position of his kicking foot in relation to the point of placement and the target zone. This is called *toeing the line* and allows the kicker to use his kicking foot as a natural guide to create a line of sight directly to his target, ensuring he has aligned in a straight and precise path.

Once he has toed the line and confirmed proper alignment, the kicker steps forward with the nonkicking foot, placing it alongside his kicking foot. He's now precisely three steps back from the point of placement, directly facing the target and in position to begin the two lateral steps that create the 90-degree angle from the vertical alignment mark (toeing the line).

Using this technique, the kicker can adjust his alignment if he drifts from the correct line as he steps back. Remember that he must be consistent with his steps in order to align at a proper depth from the ball.

For a more compact and controlled approach to the ball, some kickers prefer to take only two steps back, though this is rare. By taking only two steps back, the kicker shortens his approach and aligns tighter to the football. Because he's positioned a minimal distance from the ball, he eliminates the jab step and takes only two concise steps during the approach.

Two Steps Laterally to Create Angle

Once the kicker is three steps back, his entire body is directly facing the target, and his feet are beside each another, he takes two comfortable and controlled steps to the side opposite the kicking leg. As soon as the first lateral step is taken with the nonkicking foot, the kicking foot immediately positions alongside the nonkicking foot via a basic sidestep that spreads the legs followed by a gather step that brings the legs back together. These steps should be precise and in a straight line to form a 90-degree angle.

By keeping his body directly facing and square to the target, the kicker can keep his lateral steps consistent and in a straight line from any position on the field.

The second lateral step taken by the nonkicking foot is the last one needed to complete the alignment phase. This step is taken in exactly the same way as the first step, staying precisely in line with the first step and maintaining the exact same distance. Once the nonkicking foot is placed on the ground, body weight shifts to the side of the nonkicking foot, which allows the kicker to begin pivoting clockwise (for a right-footed kicker) directly toward the point of placement.

As the nonkicking foot pivots, the kicking foot gathers toward the nonkicking foot as before. As the kicking foot approaches, instead of positioning alongside the nonkicking foot as before, it slips behind the nonkicking foot and is placed behind the body, as in a drop step, to produce a stagger effect. The nonkicking foot simply remains in front on the exact same spot at which the pivot was performed.

At this point, the nonkicking foot is directly in line with where it will be placed during the plant, whereas the kicking foot is aligned directly with where the ball will be set for the kick (figure 1.4).

Pivoting the Foot

It's important that the nonkicking foot pivots only and doesn't alter position. The spot at which the foot pivots determines the kicker's exact alignment prior to his approach to the ball. His goal is to find this precise area every time. This develops confidence as well as consistency.

Figure 1.4 The nonkicking foot is aligned with the spot for the plant; the kicking foot is aligned with the spot for ball placement.

The kicker must be disciplined and create the 90-degree angle based on his alignment toward the target and not on the stationary lines of the field. In other words, if he's kicking from the area on the left hashmark, his steps back from the point of placement will angle slightly to the left of the hashmarks so that he can align directly with his target. Thus, when he begins his lateral two steps toward the sideline to complete the 90-degree angle from the target line, he'll appear to be going slightly up to the left (judging by the horizontal yard lines). Of course the opposite will occur at the right hashmark.

In a possible variation, once the kicker has toed the line, he might desire to start his lateral steps immediately from this position by bringing his nonkicking foot up at an angle and placing it directly away from the kicking foot in the first lateral step position, eliminating the motion of placing it alongside the kicking foot before taking the lateral step. Typically, this variation is chosen only by more advanced kickers who are extremely accurate with their lateral steps and confident of their body position while taking their steps.

The three-steps-back-and-two-steps-lateral method establishes a mental blueprint for the kicker to use to line up directly at his target from any position on the field (middle, right hashmark, or left hashmark). Thus, regardless of field position, each kick can be executed with the exact same alignment, which is crucial in developing consistency and confidence. This method also establishes a mental advantage for the kicker—although field position might change, every kick is executed in basically the exact same way. The only difference is that the goalposts become gradually narrower as the angle of the kick increases toward either hashmark. So when a coach asks a kicker from which side he kicks best, the kicker can respond, "It doesn't matter which side." Because it's the same kick from anywhere on the field. Developing this type of mentality minimizes the thinking process and enhances the kicker's ability to respond successfully in any situation.

Ready Stance

In preparation for the stance, the front (nonkicking) foot is flat on the ground with toes pointed directly in line with where the foot will be placed during the kick. Meanwhile, the back (kicking) foot is either flat on the ground or slightly up on the toes with toes turned out away from the body. Although the toes of the kicking foot are turned out during the stance, the foot itself must be in a direct line to the football in preparation for the approach. With the nonkicking foot in line with where it will be placed during the kick, and the kicking foot in a direct line with the football, the borders of a narrow approach path have been created (figure 1.5). At this point, all the kicker needs to do when approaching the ball in preparation to kick is to follow this natural guide that's within the framework of his body.

The spacing of the feet from the heel of the nonkicking foot to the toe of the kicking foot is minimal—about half a step. The feet need to be in a narrow prestance position, slightly apart, as if the kicker is taking a stride while walking. Positioning his feet this way, he creates a natural path to the ball.

Figure 1.5 Narrow approach path.

The kicker's entire body leans forward, with weight primarily on the front foot (figure 1.6). He must not bend only at the waist. He either keeps his entire body on the same plane and leans slightly forward or leans his upper body slightly more forward, whichever allows him to get the ball off quickly and accurately. Arms are relaxed and hang down to the sides. By moving or shaking the fingers quickly, the kicker can help relax his arms. If he prefers, he can position his arms slightly out in front of the body in the direction of the approach. This gives him a little more weight to abet the initial approach and forms an outer frame of his approach path. Regardless of how he positions his arms, he ensures they're not swinging back and forth as he anticipates the snap. Swinging the arms leads to inconsistency and prevents a fluid approach because the snap might begin when his arms have swung into a back position for one kick and into a front position for another.

The knees are bent slightly, allowing the entire body to lean forward with the back flat. The entire body is in a straight line, beginning with the back of the ankle of the front (nonkicking) foot and extending all the way through the back of the head. The kicker is simply positioning and holding his entire body at a point of forward lean. When any additional lean is applied, forward movement is initiated and a jab step or full step is needed to maintain balance. Leaning forward puts the kicker in the

Figure 1.6 Body lean: *(a)* entire body leans slightly forward on the same plane; *(b)* upper body leans slightly more from the waist.

most economic position to initiate forward movement. The objective is to develop a stance that eliminates any wasted motion as he begins his approach. This translates to a smooth and fluid movement that enables optimal timing of the kick. The purpose of the body lean is to build forward momentum while anticipating the holder's placement of the ball and creating a need for an initial step. The amount of body lean is determined by the individual kicker.

After the kicker checks the target zone, he lowers his head comfortably, putting his eyes in position to focus on the point of placement. His head and eyes remain in the same position throughout the kicking motion. Total concentration is a must.

Direct Path to the Ball

From this position, the kicker can employ an important aspect created when he formed a 90-degree angle from the target line that will help him check his alignment and guide his step approach. By simply visualizing an imaginary line that connects the two points of the right angle (the kicking foot and the point of placement), the kicker forms a triangle (figure 1.7). This imaginary line is identified as the hypotenuse and serves as an important guide for the kicker's kicking leg to follow as he approaches the ball.

Figure 1.7 Triangle formed by the placekicker, the target line, and the point of placement.

Center Controls the Snap

The center (the snapper) must control the precise timing of the snap. He should not be forced to deliver the ball on cadence. His controlling the timing ensures that he delivers a consistent snap that's both timely and accurate.

It's common to teach the kicker to step down this imaginary line and not across it. If he steps across the line and into the triangle, he rounds his steps as he approaches the ball. This type of approach forms a banana-like stepping pattern that takes him out of proper alignment and drastically affects his kick. One of the main purposes for aligning to the side for a soccer-style kicker is to enhance the torque of the body. When the angle is decreased, the torque effect is minimized.

The direct path (hypotenuse) approach gives the kicker a visual to guide him as he begins his approach. With his eyes focused on the holder's hand, which is on the point of placement (the kicking block or the ground), the kicker uses his peripheral vision to acknowledge to the holder that he's ready as the holder looks back for approval. A quick nod is generally all it takes for the kicker to let the holder know he's in position and ready for the snap. At this time, the holder delivers a ready call to alert the kicking team to get set in anticipation of the snap. The moment this call is made, the holder raises his front hand; his back hand (the hand away from the snapper) remains at the exact point of placement.

The kicker keeps his body in position with eyes focused on the holder's hand at the point of placement. At the exact moment the ball is snapped, two precise movements occur simultaneously. The holder's back hand moves from the point of placement and joins the other hand to catch the ball (figure 1.8). As he sees the hand rise, the kicker immediately leans forward, leading with his chest, to create the need for the initial step. The entire sequence of events—snap, rise of the holder's hand, and the kicker's forward lean—should all happen as close to simultaneously as possible. This orchestrated movement is key to the optimal timing of the kick.

Approach

The steps of the approach are taken on a direct straight path in line with the point of placement and the spot where the nonkicking foot will plant. Body weight is on the balls of the feet. The body maintains the same forward lean initiated as the approach began. The back remains flat; head and shoulders remain on the same plane throughout the kick.

Figure 1.8 The holder's back hand moves from point of placement to join the other hand and catch the ball. The kicker simultaneously leans his entire body forward.

The two basic stepping patterns used by soccer-style kickers are the two- and the two-and-a-half-step approaches. The recommended pattern, and the one that's most common, is the two-and-a-half-step approach.

Two-and-a-Half-Step Approach

The two-and-a-half-step approach features a jab step, a drive step, and a plant (figure 1.9). The approach is initiated as the kicker begins to lean forward as he sees the ball has been snapped. Prior to the snap, he focuses on the holder's hand at the point of placement. Once he sees the holder move his hands together to catch the ball, the kicker immediately begins to lean his entire body. The lean needs to be nearly simultaneous with the snap and the lift of the holder's placement hand. The kicker leans his entire body to naturally create the need for steps as he approaches the ball. He doesn't only bend at the waist as the body leans forward. He keeps his back flat and maintains his lean all the way to the point just prior to the kick.

Jab Step

The jab step, taken with the nonkicking foot, sets the direction of the approach. During the jab step, the nonkicking foot is placed in direct line to where the plant foot will be positioned when the football is kicked. The jab step is a very short step taken as the kicker initiates forward body lean when the ball is snapped. As mentioned, the body lean naturally creates the need for the initial step as well as the steps to follow. By leading with his chest, the kicker flows right to the first step. This specific movement,

Figure 1.9 The two-and-a-half-step approach: *(a)* jab step; *(b)* drive step; *(c)* plant step.

leaning to the jab, starts the momentum toward the point of placement, enabling the steps to be fluid and quick, enhancing leg speed through the football. The jab step is the step that's omitted in the two-step approach.

Another important aspect of the kicker's body lean is that it allows the drive step (the first full step) and the plant step (the final step) to occur quickly and naturally. The lean is an extremely critical motion that enables the kicker to begin his approach with a smooth, rhythmic motion that lasts throughout the kick. Most important, the lean helps the kicker develop the precise timing necessary to master getting the ball over the oncoming rush.

Stay Square and Focused

As the steps are taken, the body maintains forward lean while staying square as the kicker heads directly down the path, the hypotenuse, to the point of placement. The eyes remain focused on the point of placement throughout the kick.

Drive Step

The drive step, taken with the kicking foot, is a full step that builds momentum in preparation for the plant step. During the drive step, the left arm (for a right-footed kicker) comes forward naturally, parallel to the ground, as if to point downfield in the direction of the target. This arm movement is a preliminary body adjustment in anticipation of the pivot of the plant foot.

As soon as the drive step is completed and the body momentum continues forward, the left arm begins to move laterally, maintaining a parallel position to the ground as the final step (plant step) begins its descent to the ground, heel first, alongside the ball. The right arm is extended out and slightly down, away from the body in a position to aid in balance.

As the left arm nears a direct lateral position away from the body, the kicking leg simultaneously draws back and bends at the knee, positioning the kicking foot directly behind the right gluteus. This positions the lower leg in an above parallel position to the ground.

The kicker must be flexible to enhance the drawback of the leg prior to contacting the ball. The drawback of the leg should not be exaggerated. If the leg is too far back, the kicker might have difficulty timing the leg lock on the ball. The kicking leg reaches back in preparation of snapping forward quickly to kick the ball. This motion must be natural and fluid. By improving flexibility and performing proper technique, the kicker will naturally develop optimal leg positioning.

During the drive step, and as the heel of the plant foot touches the ground, the body gradually adjusts from leaning forward to leaning slightly back. This natural effect enhances leg speed as the weight and the forward motion of the body transitions to the plant foot as the heel lays the foot down and the foot rolls to the toes during the kick.

Plant Step

The plant step provides support and gives direction to the kick. As the plant step is made, the foot gradually pivots and is placed heel first beside the point of placement in the general direction of the target. The exact distance of the foot plant from the football varies from kicker to kicker and is often influenced by the kicker's foot size.

When a kicking tee is used, the middle of the foot typically aligns with the football and is 6 to 10 inches to the side of the ball. The distance of the plant foot from the ball is based on personal preference and can be determined by the use of a lower tee or even by spotting the ball on the ground (figure 1.10).

If the ball is spotted on the ground, the plant foot should be placed slightly forward and tighter to the ball to compensate for the lower football. When the ball's on the ground, the kicker really needs to dig to lower the kicking foot and get the ball up high enough to avoid the oncoming rush. Note that the plant step lands initially on the heel. This aids balance and helps distribute body weight.

At the precise moment the heel of the plant foot touches the ground, the kicker is in position to bring together all the necessary body mechanics to perform the kick. The pivoting of the plant foot to the direction of the target creates a natural guide for the rest of the body to follow.

As described earlier, by approaching the ball from an angle, the kicker naturally creates torque (twisting of the body) that increases leg speed as the leg swings through the ball. The torque effect created by the angle of

Figure 1.10 Plant step: *(a)* when ball is on the ground; *(b)* when ball is on a 1-inch tee; *(c)* when ball is on a 2-inch tee.

approach is supplemented by the body lean as the body pulls through the kick to naturally maintain balance and transfer energy.

Two-Step Approach

In the two-step approach, which leaves out the initial jab step, the kicker still leans, leading with his chest, as the holder's hand rises from the point of placement to receive the ball. But because there's no jab step, he may choose to delay his forward motion and begin his movement just as the ball hits the holder's hand. Again, the forward lean of the body creates the need for a first step. In the two-step approach, the first step (drive step) is taken with the kicking foot.

Although there's no initial jab step, the knee of the nonkicking leg creates a similar action. This action is initiated when the kicker leans his body forward as the ball is snapped or as it's being received. As his weight shifts forward, creating the need for a step, he raises the heel of the nonkicking foot off the ground, bending the knee slightly and moving it forward in anticipation of the first step, which is taken with the kicking foot.

Ball Position and Hold

Proper ball positioning is developed through repetition. The snapper, holder, and kicker work together to develop consistency and confidence in one another. Inevitably there will be a bad snap, a mishandled ball, or a combination of the two. When this occurs, the kicker adjusts his approach, or continues on his normal approach, confident that the holder will recover and position the football at the point of placement in time for the kick. By working regularly with the holder and snapper, the kicker can learn to adjust at the last second, allowing for a successful kick.

The holder positions the football straight up and down with the laces facing the target (figure 1.11). The laces should not face the kicker. Some soccer-style kickers might want the top of the football to tilt slightly away from the plant foot (that is, slightly toward the holder) to obtain better contact (figure 1.12). Because the kicking foot is angled slightly at impact, a slight tilt of the ball creates an ideal spot (a sweet spot) for ball compression and control. This simple adjustment allows for a more powerful vertical rotation of the ball, which promotes a truer flight path.

When tilting the football back, the holder decreases the exposed portion of the sweet spot. An erect placement (straight up and down) allows the kicker to see the entire football, enabling him to hit just under the ball's middle to get maximum height and distance. In some cases, kickers are so proficient in hitting the sweet spot that they might ask

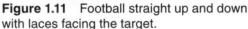

Figure 1.11 Football straight up and down with laces facing the target.

Figure 1.12 Football slightly tilts toward holder to allow better contact.

their holders to lean the football forward slightly to expose even more of the area of the ball at which they can obtain the most compression.

Leg Swing and Foot Position

As the kicking leg and foot start in the downward arc toward the ball, the upper body pivots (torques) in the direction of the plant foot. The plant foot establishes the direction and alignment for the body to follow at the moment of impact. The plant foot provides stability and guidance as all the mechanics used in kicking the ball come together as the foot compresses the ball. The left arm counterbalances the kicking leg. As the foot moves to the ball, the left arm simultaneously moves forward to coincide with the kicking leg's movement to maintain balance and control the torque effect. The kicker's leg swings in a sweeping motion from the hip. He minimizes any lean forward or backward during the kick so that the kicking leg can move quickly and fluidly.

Right at impact, the kicking foot aligns to the football with the ankle locked and the toes pointed down and out in the general direction of the holder. The kicking leg and foot begin to form a straight line in preparation for the leg lock at the knee (figure 1.13). Positioning his foot this way, the kicker can contact more of the ball. By contacting the ball with the hard bony area of his foot, he creates a solid impact that transfers power to the kick.

The position of the kicking foot will vary from kicker to kicker. The inside lace area of the shoe on the kicking foot (the inside top of the foot) should be in position to impact and compress the football. Rarely, kickers use more of the side of the foot or the instep, which is sort of like contacting the football with the foot in a golf-club position. This is an uncommon way to kick a football and not a practice that young kickers should learn. It's more natural to contact the ball with the top inside of the foot, allowing the kicker to use the more powerful muscles of the leg to swing and pull the kicking foot up through the ball.

Figure 1.13 Kicking leg and foot begin to form a straight line right at impact.

Impact With the Sweet Spot

For a soccer-style kicker, the sweet spot of the ball is about 1 ½ to 2 ½ inches down from the ball's widest segment (figure 1.14). Contacting this area of the ball on the kick is most effective to achieve the optimal height and distance. When the holder positions the football in a straight up-and-down position, the kicker has a greater opportunity to strike the sweet spot.

Because the ball is a prolate spheroid shape, its axis of symmetry is longer than its other axes. This means the ball has a natural curve from its midsection that continues inward and to both points of the ball. When the football is positioned for placement—vertically for maximum sweet spot exposure—the inward curving of the ball from the midsection down to the point of placement on the ground provides the ideal surface area for contact on the kick. When the kicker strikes the ball as the kicking foot ascends, the ideal impact surface of the football and the top of the foot are more likely to meet, making for optimal impact and compression.

Figure 1.14 A football's sweet spot.

On contact with the ball, the kicker's upper body is angled back slightly and away from the ball. Contact occurs at the exact moment the kicking foot begins to ascend. The kicking leg is rotated inward slightly as the kicking foot remains locked at the ankle with toes pointing down and out. The kicking leg should be in a nearly locked position.

The inward rotation of the kicking foot allows contact to occur at the top of the foot. This motion enables the leg to rotate slightly, allowing the knee of the kicking leg to move forward and face the direction of the target. At the moment the ball begins to compress, the impetus of the body—including the plant foot, hips, and leg swing—comes together to maximize the energy transfer through the football. At this moment, all the mechanics of the kick coordinate with the direction of the plant foot, which has transitioned to a firm and flat position, and come together to focus all energy directly toward the target.

At the very moment the football is compressed, the kicking leg locks. The kicker's hips are square to the target and should continue forward in a thrusting motion, allowing for optimal power through the football. The left arm begins to sweep forward to counterbalance the anticipated swing of the kicking leg and provide stability as the body's energy becomes concentrated toward the target. The right arm is slightly behind the body as it counterbalances the plant foot and the swing of the left arm.

The lean of the kicker's body positions his head at an angle above and almost directly over a spot slightly behind and to the outside edge of the plant foot. This natural positioning of the body provides an optimal viewpoint. As the body continues the slight lean, with chest, hips, and kicking leg in a direct line to the kicking foot, the kicker looks down his body with eyes focused intently on the ball.

Optimal Trajectory

On impact, the kicker's body is slightly back and angled away from the ball, which allows him to kick up and through the ball, gaining immediate elevation to clear the ball over the oncoming rush. This is the kicker's natural way of adjusting his center of gravity to get a quick lift on the ball.

Optimal trajectory means obtaining maximum height and distance on the football to clear 10 feet easily from a 7-yard distance. An extra point or field goal is kicked 7 yards behind the line of scrimmage, where the potential blockers are swarming. Oncoming rushers can jump about 10 feet in the air. Thus, once the kick is on its way it must immediately climb above 10 feet before it travels 7 yards.

Optimal Timing

Kickers should be timed frequently to make sure they get the ball away quickly and to help them develop proper rhythm and improve consistency. The total time from snap to kick should be 1.3 to 1.4 seconds for high school kickers and 1.25 to 1.3 seconds for college and professional kickers. The best way to develop consistent timing is to have the snapper, holder, and kicker work together so they can develop optimal timing and tempo. It's also important to chart snap-to-kick times because charting promotes keener focus among the snapper, holder, and kicker.

Optimal Time Versus Fastest Time

Kickers and coaches must understand the difference between optimal time and fastest time. Coaches particularly can develop a track meet mentality when it comes to timing kickers, trying to make get-off times faster and faster. This kind of approach can be detrimental to the kicker as well as the team. There's a point at which the kick becomes too fast. When this happens, the mechanics of the kicker and the holder become rushed, and performance suffers.

A professional kicker's get-off time is in the 1.25- to 1.3-second range. There's no reason a college or high school player needs a faster time. If kicks are getting close to being blocked, and the kicker has get-off times in the appropriate range, the protection must improve.

Another alternative is to consider backing up the point of placement from 7 yards behind the line of scrimmage to 7 ½ to 8 yards. This adjustment enables the kicker to dramatically improve his trajectory because he has up to 1 yard extra in which to gain elevation over the oncoming rush. (And moving the ball back slightly is not going to make it any easier for the outside rushers to get to the block point.) This minor adjustment goes virtually unnoticed by the snapper but it makes a tremendous difference in increasing the ball's elevation as it climbs above the line of scrimmage. More important, the kicker simply performs the same kick as he did before, and the added distance from the line of scrimmage takes care of the rest.

On game day, a stopwatch comes in handy to assess the special teams. By timing every kick during the game, coaches can confirm consistent get-off times and identify protection problems. For instance, if a field goal was almost blocked but the kicker's get-off time was ideal, the problem is the protection. This information is relayed to the coaches and players involved, ideally leading to a quick solution.

Follow-Through

The follow-through is the culmination of the entire kicking motion, aligning the mechanics of the body with the direction of the football as it travels toward the target.

At the exact point of impact, the force created by the controlled momentum of the approach, the torque of the body, and the speed of the kicking leg drive the foot into the football, causing it to compress. At the very moment maximum compression of the football is reached (as the kicker continues to kick through the ball), the football will immediately begin to decompress in the area of impact. These two combined forces cause the speed of the football to dramatically accelerate as it separates and rises from the kicking foot. This is the exact point at which the leg locks and the follow-through of the kick begins.

In an optimal kick, the kicker imparts the entire energy of his body through proper mechanics to a concentrated area of the football in such a way that optimizes elevation, distance, and direction of the kick. A correct follow-through is required for this to happen consistently.

As the football leaves the kicking foot, the foot continues to ascend as if it were uninterrupted by the impact with the football. By kicking *through* the football, the kicker imparts maximum power, allowing the leg to momentarily maintain the same speed as it had at the point of contact.

While the kicking leg continues to rise, it moves on an upward course, coming slightly across the body as it heads in the direction of the left shoulder. This is caused by the torque effect of the body that's created by the angle of approach. By approaching the football at an angle and placing the plant foot toward the target, the kicker creates the need for the upper body to lean away from the ball as the plant is made, eliciting the torque effect.

Remember that the plant sets the direction of the kick. Thus, as the kicker approaches the ball, leans, makes his plant, and begins to torque his body, his kicking leg swings down from its drawn-back position behind the right buttocks and directly toward the football. As the kicking foot levels out just above the ground and begins to ascend, it makes contact with the football. At the moment contact is made and the football becomes compressed, the kicking foot is on a direct course to the target.

As the football accelerates and separates from the foot, the kicking leg continues to rise. It moves slightly across the body to the shoulder opposite the kicking leg (the left shoulder for a right-footed kicker). The leg swing creates an arc as the kicking foot moves from the right buttock area down to the right as the foot approaches the ball, up through the football directly toward the target, and then toward the left shoulder.

The upper body moves very little. It leans back slightly during the kick then moves to a vertical position as the momentum of the body continues forward. During this time the arm opposite the kicking leg continues to move forward, gradually coming across the chest in a parallel to upward motion.

By maintaining his upper-body position, the kicker enables his kicking leg to maximize the follow-through. If the kicker leans forward at the waist only, he inhibits maximum follow-through because the kicking leg stops sooner. Leaning back affects balance and minimizes leg power. Maximum follow-through equals maximum leg speed and power, not to mention a more fluid and rhythmic motion.

High or Low Follow-Through

Not all kickers have a high follow-through. For some kickers, maximum follow-through is to swing the leg just above the waist. The key is for the kicker to learn what feels natural to him. He must be consistent and smooth with his kicking motion to enhance leg speed and control.

During part of the deceleration process, the follow-through of the leg generates enough power and energy to lift the kicker off the ground slightly and in a forward and outward motion (figure 1.15). This is called the *skip*. The name is derived from the appearance of the plant leg skipping forward and slightly away with very little elevation as it moves. The plant leg practically brushes off the top of the grass for the brief moment it's off the ground.

This simple process of skipping through the ball has tremendous effect, making for an optimal transfer of energy through the football by allowing the body to maintain balance as it becomes momentarily airborne. By using proper mechanics and a concentration of power through the football and on toward the target, the body generates so much energy at the point of impact that it naturally needs a way to quickly decelerate and maintain control and balance. By allowing the plant foot to skip through naturally, the kicker provides himself a great advantage. He can effectively transfer all the energy of his body in a fluid motion, maximizing power and control.

Figure 1.15 Follow-through of the kick.

Remember that when the kicker initially places his plant foot on the ground during his approach, he places it heel first. Just before the kick, the plant foot quickly transitions to a firm, flat position on the ground, stabilizing the leg as the body's momentum continues and the kicking leg swings through the ball. As the kicking leg begins to ascend just past the knee of the plant leg in route to maximum follow-through, the plant foot begins to rise to the toes in preparation for the skip step.

Note: Because of the torque effect of the body and the plant, body lean, momentum, and direction of the leg swing, the skip step of the plant foot will not only go forward but will align and return to the ground slightly out and away from the target line. It repositions on the ground in the exact direction of the swing of the kicking leg, with toes pointed in the same general direction that the skip traveled (slightly outward in relation to the target line). The exact distance and position varies from kicker to kicker.

After impact, as the football accelerates and separates from the kicking foot and the kicking leg begins to ascend, the momentum of the leg swing shifts the body's momentum as the energy transfers from the direction of the target to the direction of the follow-through, which is toward the opposite shoulder.

Recall that the kicker approaches the point of placement from an angle to create the torque effect with his body as his leg kicks the ball. As the body twists during the kick, it needs to continue turning in a controlled manner as the follow-through begins to rise toward the opposite shoulder. As the follow-through begins, the left arm simultaneously sweeps across the front of the body in a parallel to upward motion, counterbalancing the skip.

The counterbalance movement of the opposite arm ensures the body maintains proper balance as the energy of the kicking motion is concentrated toward the target. The counterbalance is the key to controlling the degree of torque and slowing the motion, thus bringing the body and kicking leg to a position square to the target as the kicker completes his skip step.

Postkick Check

The postkick check is the confirmation point at which all the proper mechanics performed by the kicker come together to accomplish the goal of kicking the football as well as he can. This confirmation point includes a self-coaching strategy that every kicker can use to ensure the football is traveling the intended course based on the exact position of the kicker's body. The dedicated and focused kicker develops this technique until it's a habit. When he kicks the football, he knows exactly where it is by simply evaluating his mechanics and identifying his body position on completion of his kicking motion. He doesn't need to look at the flight of the ball.

If a kicker both starts and finishes his kicking motion correctly, his entire kicking motion will be correct. The postkick check is a form of learning backward. By learning the finish, the kicker focuses on what he wants as the end result, providing a tremendous mental and physical advantage that allows his body to perform the skill automatically.

In order to have proper mechanics (or even to determine if he does), a kicker must kick toward a specific object or area. Every phase of kicking the football—setting the point of placement, marking off the steps, making the approach, planting the foot, getting in position for impact, and following through—is aligned and directed toward a predetermined target.

Stay Focused

Throughout the kick and follow-through, the kicker's head is down with eyes focused on the position of his kicking leg to ensure alignment and proper body mechanics. He raises his head the moment the kicking foot is securely on the ground after the skip step and his body weight begins to shift to the kicking foot. This is when the placekicker needs self-discipline. Most kickers want to look up at the ball the moment they kick it, but this causes consistency problems and takes the kicker's mind off his mechanics prematurely. In essence, the kicker becomes merely a spectator because he's now watching and no longer performing.

Each phase of the kick has reference points that the kicker can identify to determine at any point if he's aligned correctly or not.

Once he understands the importance of checking his alignment as it relates to the reference points of each phase of his kick, the kicker can become his own coach. Once he is his own coach, he can learn even more, advancing until his kicking skill develops into a combination of great habits. Once he has developed great habits, he can identify any challenge he faces and respond accordingly.

The kicker focuses on the exact way the mechanics of his kick finish in relation to the flight path of the football. What he learns here is a great resource in regard to developing visualization skills. By focusing on his mechanics and exact body position, he can anticipate exactly where the ball is in flight when he looks up at the right time.

The postkick check begins as the plant foot returns to the ground after the skip and lands in a firm, flat position, supporting the entire body as the momentum slows. The kicker lands on his plant foot balanced and in complete control of his body as his body remains square to the target.

As his kicking leg returns to the ground, the kicker controls the leg so that the toe of the kicking foot touches down comfortably out in front of the body and in line with the target. The left arm comes back naturally to his side as his right arm extends slightly as his body weight transitions forward.

Once the kicking foot is securely on the ground, the weight of the body shifts forward to the kicking foot. The right arm slowly swings forward, aligning with the outer edge of the kicking leg. As the kicker slowly raises his head to check the alignment of the ball in relation to his kicking leg and his arm, his body remains square to the target with the majority of body weight shifted to the kicking foot. He might want to continue the motion of his right arm by lifting it high enough so he can point in the direction of the target. He might even be so precise with his mechanics that, as he lifts his arm, he acts as if he touches the football in flight as it heads for the intended target.

The kicker always kicks through the football. The key to the follow-through is to finish with hips and kicking foot aiming toward the target. The kicking foot finishes out in front and right of center of the body. By concentrating on proper body position after the kick, the kicker promotes the correct plant, body position, and leg swing prior to and during the kick.

2

Kickoffs

Before any football game can start, there must be a kickoff. A kickoff begins the game, begins the second half, and is used to resume play after a touchdown or field goal. On some levels of play, a kickoff begins the overtime period, if there is one. The opening kickoff is one of the most photographed plays during the Super Bowl and yet remains one of the least practiced skills. One reason the kickoff is not practiced more is the intense physical demands placed on the placekicker's body when he drives the football downfield. A kickoff culminates with a violent kicking motion that applies wear and tear on the kicker, especially when the kickoff is not practiced properly.

The kickoff has become more significant in recent years because of new rules implemented to make kickoff returns more likely. Some of the more notable rule changes were at the college level to make play more exciting for spectators. College placekickers must now use a 1-inch kickoff tee and kick off from the 30-yard line, the same rules used at the professional level. These rule changes make it tougher for kickers to achieve the hang time and distance needed to minimize an effective return. With the increased chance of a successful kickoff return, coaches now place even more emphasis on covering and defending kickoffs.

In this chapter we teach the fundamental techniques that enable the placekicker to develop a kickoff style that's effective for his team. Kickers will learn the subtleties of the kickoff and how and why to kick for position, which is a key part of team strategy and to winning football games.

Target Zone

Before the placekicker aligns to kick the football, he must know precisely where to direct the flight of the ball. This is called the target zone. Once he has been instructed by the coach on the type of kick for the kickoff (angle, drive, squib, etc.), the kicker selects the exact area of the field that he wants to place the ball. This selection determines both his target zone as well as an even more specific target within that zone.

When kicking extra points and field goals, the placekicker focuses on the area above the crossbar, beyond and between the uprights. When kicking off, he generally focuses on a specific area of the field. For instance, the kickoff team might want to direct the kick to the corner of the field in order to pin the return man near the sideline. When kicking from the near hashmark, the specific aiming point can be between the hashmark and the sideline toward the top of the numbers (figure 2.1). This positioning

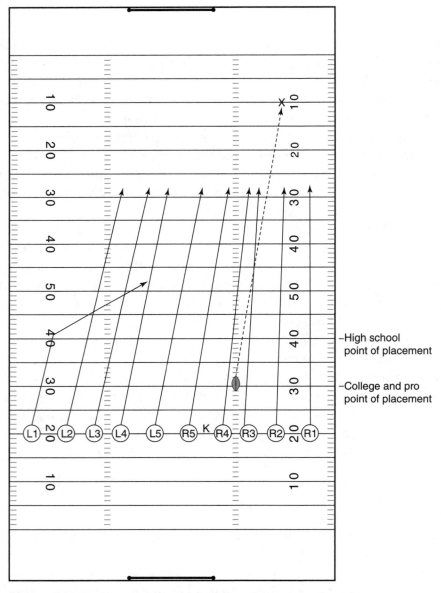

Figure 2.1 Target zone for a kickoff from the near hashmark.

minimizes the options of the return man, forcing him to head either upfield or across the field. The proximity of the sideline negates the option of running in that direction (because he would immediately run out of bounds). The more limited the options for the return man, the easier the job for the coverage team.

College and professional kickers commonly consider placement of the kick on the kickoff, whereas younger players focus on distance (mainly because they can't kick as far and want to make the return man run as far as possible to earn his yards). Placement is important in college and the pros because, when kicking from the 30-yard line, it's more difficult to kick the ball into the end zone for a possible touchback—especially when kicking into the wind. In addition, kickers want to avoid kicking to a return man such as Devin Hester of the Chicago Bears, who specializes in running kicks back for long yardage or touchdowns, even when the kick reaches the end zone. So it has become more strategic to place the football in a particular area of the field to increase the coverage team's effectiveness. Then again some teams simply kick straight down the field, using the hashmarks or goalposts as their guide. Their philosophy is to kick the ball as high and far as possible to provide ample coverage time and maximize the distance the returner has to travel. They feel they can attack and converge on the returner just as well in the open field to gain an advantage in field position.

Point of Placement

When the placekicker is teeing up for a kickoff, his point of placement (the point from which he kicks off) is a predetermined yard line. In high school football, the line of scrimmage for a kickoff is the kicking team's 40-yard line; at the college and professional levels, the point of placement is the 30-yard line (figure 2.2). These yard-line positions will vary if penalties are applied.

Determining the exact position on the field to tee up the football for a kickoff in relation to the hashmarks is based on several factors, including the abilities of the placekicker, weather conditions, and the return abilities of the opponent. For example, a kicker who lacks a strong leg focuses on placing the kick to a particular area on the field with maximum hang time to allow effective coverage. This can be accomplished simply by teeing the football on the hashmark nearest the direction of the kick. For instance, if the kick is to be directed toward the deep left corner of the field on the numbers, the tee is placed on the left hashmark. This approach provides the not-so-strong kicker the advantage of directing the flight of the football down the straightest and shortest line. This same strategy is

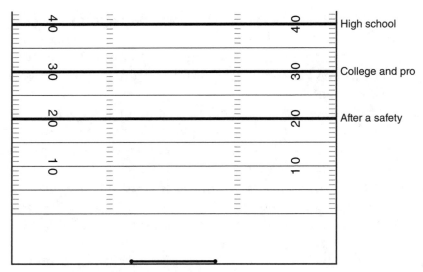

Figure 2.2 Point of placement for kickoffs.

effective for a kicker with a powerful leg who is facing a strong headwind or who wants to maximize hang time to minimize the return threat of a talented return man.

After all factors are evaluated, the decision on where to kick is made through coaching and team strategy. Once coaches communicate the kick they want, the placekicker knows exactly where to position the football for the kickoff.

Teeing Up

Up through high school, placekickers are allowed to use a 1- or 2-inch elevated kickoff tee. At the college and professional levels, placekickers use a 1-inch kickoff tee. Young placekickers should start with the 2-inch tee to take advantage of the higher elevation to get more lift on the ball. Most playing surfaces at the younger levels of play (middle school and high school) are not as nicely manicured as the playing surfaces at the college and professional levels, so the higher tee comes in handy.

Once the high school kicker moves on to the college level, he's no longer allowed to use any sort of placement tee for extra point and field goal kicks. For kickoffs, he must adjust to using the 1-inch tee. This necessary adjustment from high school to college football can create a misconception for kickers still in high school. It's common for high school kickers to think it serves their best interest to progress to a lower tee, or even to kick off the ground, in order to attract the attention of college teams. This is inaccurate and no way to impress the scouts. What does impress them is a powerful kickoff leg—not kicking off the ground. Although the kicker will have to kick off the ground when kicking extra points and field goals and kick off a 1-inch tee on the collegiate level, this doesn't mean he should begin doing so while still in high school. If he does, he's putting his own interests ahead of the team's—because the fact is that young players kick more effectively off the tee. In football at all levels, the emphasis needs to be on the team, not the player (despite what the high school placekicker might read on Web sites or hear about in camps).

When positioning the football on the kickoff tee, the placekicker should place the ball so the laces face downfield and directly at the target. This positioning keeps the laces on the side of the ball opposite the foot, allowing for optimal compression of the ball on contact. Kicking the laces minimizes compression because the more concentrated material (the laces) adds tightness in this area. If the laces point to either side of the field, a drag effect tends to pull or push the ball in either direction. When the ball is kicked just below its center mass, it's propelled in an end-over-end trajectory with an ideally slow backspin. If the laces are turned to either side of the field, when the ball is kicked the air will travel smoothly over one side and be disrupted on the other side, causing a drag effect.

From the back, the ball may appear to be in a vertical position, perpendicular to the ground (figure 2.3a), although soccer-style kickers might want the top of the football to tilt slightly away from them (figure 2.3b) to obtain better contact and rotation by matching the angle of the foot with the angle of the ball.

The side view reveals the football is almost vertical with a slight backward lean. This allows the football to stabilize on the back portion of the tee, which is designed for support. Otherwise the football needs to be as close to vertical as possible.

Figure 2.3 Football set on the tee: *(a)* vertical position; *(b)* slightly offset position for soccer-style kickers.

Maximizing Hang Time

If the objective is to maximize hang time, the kicker must sacrifice some distance. This can be done by leaning the football back slightly from its near vertical position. The kicker kicks more up and through the football. As is true with any other kick, this kick needs to be practiced until the kicker learns the best positioning of the football. It is important to emphasize a slight lean. Any more than a slight lean minimizes the impact surface and disallows optimal ball contact on the kick.

Because the football curves slightly from end to end, the more vertical positioning gives the placekicker the best opportunity to contact the area of the football where the curve of the ball best matches his foot, maximizing compression of the football and optimizing distance, hang time, and direction. Leaning the football back too much shortens the height of the football from the ground, minimizing the area of impact.

Alignment

The main objective for alignment on kickoffs is to determine a spot that's comfortable for the kicker and allows for a consistent approach to the football. When aligning for kickoffs, the placekicker should use the same basic procedure that he uses to align for extra points and field goals. This keeps things simple. He'll develop more self-confidence and consistency. Remember that placekickers can have success using a variety of styles and approaches. So much depends on the individual's natural abilities. That said, every placekicker should follow the basic fundamentals of kickoffs as he develops his personal technique.

When you think about it, all kicks are basically the same in regard to direction. The determining factor that specifies which direction the ball will go is based on the alignment used to perform the kick.

As mentioned, the placekicker should approach kickoffs with the same approach angle he uses for extra points and field goals. Once he determines his approach angle, he chooses the exact depth he needs to align from the football.

First, he determines the point of placement for the kickoff. He then picks a target at which to direct the flight of the ball. He marks off his steps to align exactly the way he would for an extra point or field goal. When preparing for an extra point or field goal, his target is the area above the crossbar, beyond and between the uprights. When preparing for a kickoff, his target might be a very specific area of the playing field, such as the number 5 on the 5-yard line. Picking a precise target is extremely important for the placekicker to improve accuracy and align properly every time.

Once the placekicker establishes a visual reference, he positions himself at the point of placement and visualizes the exact flight path the ball will travel. He directly faces his target and aligns the kicking tee toward the target. This establishes two points of reference and creates an imaginary line toward the target. This line serves as his guide to direct his kick. Now he is ready to mark off his steps and align himself for approach.

There are many ways a placekicker can align properly on kickoffs. He should first develop a consistent method to mark off his steps so he achieves proper depth and alignment. Once he determines these steps, he should mark them off the same way every time and at the same approach angle that he uses when kicking extra points and field goals.

The recommended way for a soccer-style kicker to mark off his steps in preparation for a kickoff is by using the three-steps-back-and-two-steps-lateral method. Using this method, the kicker simply marks off his steps to form a 90-degree alignment angle from the target line, the same angle he uses when kicking extra points and field goals.

Once he's in his stance and in position to kick, he places a marker such as tape or a coin on the exact spot where his feet are aligned on the ground. This spot represents the 90-degree alignment angle. Once the proper alignment angle is marked as a reference point, he's ready to determine the exact depth he needs to align from the football.

He can use several ways to determine the depth of his alignment. One way is to position at the point of placement with his plant foot aligned to the side and slightly back from the point of placement. This is essentially the same position in which his plant foot will be during the kick.

The kickoff is nearly the same kick as an extra point and field goal except the body needs to adjust naturally because of the increased momentum to the football during the approach and the desired trajectory of the kick. The adjustment is that the plant foot is slightly back in relation to the tee from where it would normally be placed during an extra point or field goal.

While at the point of placement, the kicker pivots on his plant foot, turns nearly in the opposite direction, and faces back toward the direction of his anticipated approach path. From this position, he looks directly over the spot he marked when he determined the proper angle using the three-steps-back-and-two-steps-lateral method. From this vantage point, he can visualize two reference points that form a straight line extending from his plant foot where he's standing (the point of placement) and through the spot he marked (where he was in his stance) (figure 2.4).

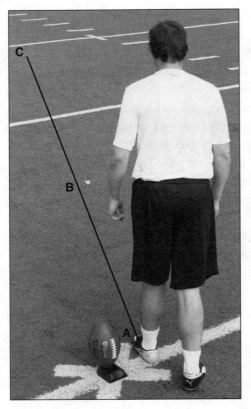

Figure 2.4 Two reference points.

Once he has established these two points, the kicker extends the straight line to an area 8 to 12 yards away. A coach or teammate stands in this general area to help mark the spot where the kicker's plant foot will land during a simulated kick. This area represents the approximate distance the kicker will be away from the football while in his stance in preparation to approach the football for a kickoff. To determine the exact distance, he needs to identify the approach and the number of steps that feel most natural, allowing him to be more precise in approaching the football for the kickoff. This is where the three reference points he has just established come into play.

When determining the exact distance, the kicker remains at the point of placement and faces the area 8 to 12 yards away that's directly in line with his plant foot and the point where he was aligned in his extra point and field goal stance. As he faces this area, he visualizes a spot straight down this line within the 8- to 12-yard distance that he feels is about where the football would be positioned for him to kick.

If the placekicker is confident in knowing his approach angle, he might want to go in a direction that feels most comfortable to him as he determines his step approach and identifies the exact spot for alignment. He simply heads directly from the point of placement to a spot that feels most natural instead of going on a straight line from point A to point B to point C. He goes directly from point A to point C, bypassing point B.

Note that no football is being used yet. This is only a simulated kick to help the kicker determine the flow of his approach and the number of steps he feels most comfortable taking. The goal is for the kicker to take several practice runs with a coach or teammate marking the spot of the exact distance needed for the placekicker's alignment. This exact spot promotes a natural stride in the approach to the football, optimizing the entire motion of the kick.

From a comfortable stance, with legs slightly flexed and nonkicking foot forward, the kicker begins his approach by taking a short step with his nonkicking foot. This first step simply initiates a walking step with his kicking foot. As the next steps follow quickly, he transitions into a jog, gradually building speed to a controlled run as he approaches the spot he has visualized as the point of placement (where the ball would be teed up).

If he uses a two-and-a-half-step approach for extra points and field goals, he should take his first step with his nonkicking foot. If he uses a two-step approach, he starts his approach with his kicking foot. This keeps his initial start for kickoffs the same as for extra points and field goals. He develops a consistent number of steps as he approaches the football. A six- or eight-step approach is common, although some kickers may want to align even deeper. If he uses a jab step, as he does for extra points and field goals, his approach would be considered a six-and-a-half- or eight-and-a-half-step approach.

As he reaches his visualized point of placement (the spot where the ball would be), he gradually builds enough speed and momentum to explode through the football. Again, the approach angle on the kickoff is very similar to the angle for extra points and field goals.

It is a challenge for a placekicker to master both kickoffs and field goals. Although the approach angles are similar, the execution of each skill is considerably different. For instance, the action for the kickoff tends to be violent and explosive as the kicker tries to generate enough power to drive the ball downfield for maximum distance. Extra points and field goals require a more controlled power that relies on smooth and fluid motion; the focus is more on accuracy than on power.

There are other basic differences between kickoffs and extra points and field goals:

- On kickoffs, the placekicker starts his approach much slower than he must for extra points and field goals.
- The longer approach of the kickoff enhances the placekicker's speed to the ball.
- On kickoffs, the plant foot needs to be slightly back, a natural adjustment caused by the increased momentum toward the ball and the slight change in mechanics as the body positions to drive the football downfield.
- The kickoff is more explosive through the football, driving the ball upward and downfield.
- A kickoff requires more upper-body lean at the moment the foot contacts the ball because of the need to drive the football downfield.

- The biggest difference is in the plant foot after the kick. As the nonkicking foot plants and the placekicker kicks through the ball, instead of skipping with his nonkicking (plant) foot as he does on an extra point or field goal kick, he kicks up and through as if hurdling, landing on his kicking foot instead of his plant foot.

Understanding these basic differences helps the kicker determine his alignment through practice runs that simulate his approach to the football.

As the kicker explodes through the football, a coach or teammate focuses intently on where the plant is made. Once the kicker completes his simulated kickoff, the coach or teammate marks the spot where the plant occurred. After several runs back and forth through the entire kicking motion, the kicker will notice a consistent spot that produces a precise distance from the point of placement. After identifying this spot, he can determine how he'll align in relation to the point of placement and the direction of the kick.

Now that he has identified reference points and determined the exact angle and distance he'll use to approach the kickoff, the kicker creates a stepping pattern and alignment to match. Standing just behind the football, which is on the kickoff tee, he places his nonkicking foot comfortably at the spot that he anticipates planting it. From this position, he begins to mark off his steps by walking back, starting with his kicking foot. He backs up directly away from his target, counting his steps to a depth that aligns with the spot he previously marked. This spot precisely determines his approach angle, his exact distance from the point of placement and his exact step approach to the point of placement.

As he walks back, he keeps his shoulders square to the target to ensure he's in a more precise position in relation to the target once he reaches the proper depth, which is generally 8 to 12 yards. Once he reaches the depth that's best for him, he remains square to his target with his shoulders

Stepping Back

Generally a placekicker takes 8 to 12 steps back from the point of placement, depending on the kicker. The number of steps taken also depends on which foot the placekicker starts with. The kicker might choose to walk back by turning and walking away from the point of placement. Once he completes his steps back, he turns, toes the line to check his alignment, and takes his lateral steps. Whether he chooses to face the target or not when stepping back, the important thing is to take consistent steps.

and hips. His kicking leg is in direct line with the football on the kickoff tee and through to the target.

He is now at a stopping point, similar to aligning for extra point and field goals, which allows him to view the position of his kicking foot as it relates to the point of placement and the target zone. Again, this is called toeing the line and allows him to use his kicking foot as a natural guide to create a line of sight directly to the target, ensuring he has aligned in a straight, precise path.

Once vertically aligned, he's ready to move laterally. He walks to the marked spot that determined his approach angle and distance to the football. To walk laterally, he lifts his nonkicking foot while pivoting on his kicking foot and turns his body to face laterally as he takes walking steps (usually four or five) directly toward the spot. Once at the marked spot, he pivots on his nonkicking foot and turns his body to look down his path of approach to the football while slipping his kicking foot behind his nonkicking foot. This is a sort of drop step behind the body that produces a stagger effect with the feet, similar to the technique used for extra points and field goals.

The kicker has formed a 90-degree angle between his position, the target line, and the football (figure 2.5). Essentially, this is an extension of the approach he uses for extra points and fields goals. He's now ready to get into his stance and begin his approach to the football.

The sequence of steps kickers use to determine alignment varies from kicker to kicker. One kicker might take 10 steps back and 5 steps over to determine his alignment, whereas another might take a 9-step and 4-step approach. This individual preference must be worked on so the kicker develops consistency and gets in position in the precise location every time.

Figure 2.5 Aligning at a 90-degree angle to the football.

Stance

Once the kicker completes his steps to determine his alignment, he gets into his stance and positions in the exact same way he does for kicking extra points and field goals—shoulders and hips square and facing the football. The front, nonkicking foot is flat on the ground, toes pointed directly in line with where they'll be placed during the kick. The back foot (kicking foot) is either flat on the ground or slightly up on the toes, with toes turned out away from the body. Although the toes of the back (kicking) foot are turned out during the stance, the foot itself is in a direct line to the football in preparation for the approach. This alignment creates a natural guide within the framework of the body for the kicker to follow all the way to the football.

The biggest difference between kickoffs and extra points and field goals is that the placekicker starts his approach much slower on the kickoff. He doesn't need the quickness required to beat an oncoming rush. For the kickoff, his body position can be slightly more relaxed, with a very slight lean, allowing him to start his steps slowly and controlled. He gradually builds up speed as he approaches the football.

Approach

The approach for a kickoff starts out slowly and gradually builds up speed and power as the kicker approaches the ball. This gradual build-up of speed provides consistency and gives the kicker more control of his body. Consistency is the key.

The placekicker's alignment and stance position him directly toward the football. His nonkicking foot lines up to the spot where his plant foot will contact the ground, and his kicking foot is lined up with the ball. Both feet border a direct path and a straight approach to the ball.

Because the placekicker is in a more relaxed stance, his initial approach can be more controlled, and he can use walking steps. For example, a successful stepping approach starts with the kicker taking a short step with his nonkicking foot and following with two normal walking strides. By the time he finishes the second complete walking step, he'll have built up enough momentum to transition into a slight jog. After three jogging steps, his speed transitions into a controlled run of three steps to the football in preparation for the plant step. The total number of steps in this approach is eight and a half. Remember that kickers vary in their approach. A six-and-a-half-step approach can be effective as well. The kicker finds the approach that works best for him, sticks with it, and constantly fine-tunes it.

Plant Step

During the plant step the foot contacts the ground in a similar way to the plant for an extra point or field goal. The foot gradually pivots and is placed heel-first beside the point of placement in the general direction of the target. The exact distance of the foot plant from the football varies from kicker to kicker. For kickoffs, the plant foot is slightly back. This natural adjustment is caused by the kicker's increased momentum toward the ball and the slight change of mechanics as his body gets in position to drive the ball downfield.

With a 2-inch tee, the plant foot is generally 10 to 12 inches from the football, depending on the individual, with toes lined up with the middle of the ball. With a 1-inch tee, the plant foot naturally needs to move up slightly and be tighter to the ball to compensate for the lower football.

Impact With the Ball

The impact of the foot on the ball on kickoffs is similar to the impact for extra points and field goals. The difference is that now the ball is contacted in a way to drive it downfield, so the body's mechanics adjust naturally to get the desired result so the football can be compressed at a slightly higher spot, changing the trajectory to maximize distance and hang time.

At impact and during compression of the football, instead of the kicker's body being slightly back and angled away from the ball as during extra points and field goals, it leans forward more as the body unleashes its full power (figure 2.6).

Figure 2.6   Impact during a kickoff. Kicker leans forward as he unleashes his power on the ball.

The forward lean is also a natural way that the body positions itself for what's to come. Because the placekicker has considerably more momentum going through the football as a result of the longer, controlled approach, the body is preparing to lean even more as the football leaves the foot. This is sometimes called crunching forward and is a normal adjustment for a placekicker during a kickoff. It's simply the culmination of power as the kicker drives through the football and begins his follow-through.

Follow-Through

During a kickoff, the placekicker focuses on driving the football downfield, maximizing distance and hang time. To do this, he needs to get his whole body into the kick. This is where the longer approach to the ball comes into play because a longer approach increases momentum.

As the kicker follows through after the kick, he kicks up and through the ball, raising his hips toward the angle of trajectory as he heads directly downfield to his target. His upper body leans more than usual and tends to crunch to abet the forward motion of the body and maintain balance.

By kicking up and through and getting his hips up, the kicker maximizes distance and hang time. He can tremendously enhance this motion by lifting his kicking leg high, as if jumping over a hurdle (figure 2.7a), allowing his entire body to explode through the ball and thus optimizing the kick. The motion of the body might be explosive through the football yet remains fluid and rhythmic because of the gradual build-up of speed during the approach.

Once the kicking leg begins to descend, the momentum of the body continues forward, and the kicker continues directly toward his target. This is a major difference between kickoffs and extra points and field goals. As he returns to the ground after his follow-through, he lands on his kicking foot instead of his plant foot (figure 2.7b). Because kickoffs are more about driving the ball downfield for distance and hang time, he can be more aggressive to the football. Accuracy is still important, but accuracy on a kickoff is more about placement and field position.

Although the mechanics of the kick and the motion of the kicking leg shift the kicker off the target line and slightly past the plant foot, he still needs to finish his follow-through square to and facing his target. If at any time he is off balance after the kicking motion is complete, he might be approaching the football too aggressively or too fast.

The decision to kick off from the middle of the field or from either hashmark is based on the placekicker's ability and team strategy. Traditionally, the ball is positioned between the hashmarks and kicked straight down the field. More and more kickers position the football on the hashmark

Figure 2.7 *(a)* After kicking up and through the ball, *(b)* the kicker slightly bends his leg as he "hurdles" forward (and downward) in preparation to land on his kicking foot.

and direct the football to the same side of the field, allowing them to kick the ball a shorter distance while positioning the kick for more effective team coverage.

Generally, the further the football is away from the middle of the field, the more likely the kicker is to kick the football down the same side of the field he has favored. In other words, if he kicks on or near the left hashmark, he'll tend to kick the football down the left side of the field. However, by keeping the football in the center of the field, he maintains the element of surprise and is less predictable.

Kickoffs can be executed effectively on or anywhere in between the hashmarks. What's most important is that they are executed in the way that most benefits the team.

Kickoff Hurdle Drill

Objective
The kicker practices kicking up and through the football to provide optimum power and trajectory for kickoffs.

Equipment
A kickoff tee, two 12- to 18-inch cones, and a 3-foot foam crossbar are needed.

Progression
1. The placekicker determines the point of placement and tees up the football at midfield or near the yard line from which he will kick off (college and pro, 30-yard line; high school, 40-yard line).

2. He places two cones 3 feet apart and approximately 3 feet in front of the point of placement, slightly favoring the plant-foot side. He places the foam crossbar across the tops of the cones to create a hurdle.

3. Once the hurdle is in position, the placekicker aligns to perform a kickoff. He performs the kickoff using his normal approach.

4. The placekicker focuses on kicking up and through the football in order to clear the hurdle with his kicking leg (figure 2.8). This up-and-through motion is similar to hurdling over an object. It allows the kicker to perform a more natural motion and land on his kicking foot instead of his plant foot to maintain balance, especially important because of his increased momentum due to the longer approach.

Figure 2.8   Kicker clears the hurdle with his kicking leg.

Tips From the Coach
- The placekicker must use his normal kickoff motion.
- The placekicker kicks up and through the football in a hurdling motion so he clears the hurdle and lands immediately on his kicking foot.
- Once the placekicker lands on his kicking foot, his momentum continues down the field in the direct line of the kick as he remains balanced and in control.

Variations
Initially the placekicker can perform this drill without a football. He aligns for a normal kick-off, approaches the point of placement, and simulates his kicking motion in order to focus more on his hurdling ability.

Hang Time on Kickoffs

To obtain distance on a kickoff, the kicker must get a certain amount of hang time on his kick. He might be able to drive a football deep, but only if he has kicked the ball with the right trajectory. Kickoffs of the greatest distance are complemented by an optimal amount of height to be most effective. If a kicker attempts to drive the ball deep but kicks it too low, gravity pulls the ball to the ground before it can travel far. Performing the optimal kickoff requires kicking the ball with the trajectory that allows it to carry a great distance.

Hang time is defined as the amount of time a kicked football remains in the air. The benefits of hang time in regard to field position are monumental. Hang time not only allows the football to maintain flight longer, and thus travel farther, it also determines the amount of time the coverage team has before the returner catches the ball and heads upfield.

A low, line-drive kick with minimal hang time may travel a good distance, but it gets to the returner's hands quickly. The speed at which the returner gets the football means two things to the coverage team: more distance of separation from the returner and less time to get to him, both of which increase the likelihood of a great return. Even if the kicking team does a good job covering the return and making the tackle, the return team retains the advantage because of the limited hang time. Optimal hang time for a kickoff is 3.8 to 4.0 seconds or more for college and professional players and 3.6 seconds or more for high school players.

Situational Kicks

Coaches often refer to the different types of kicks required during a game as directional kicks. Although this terminology is correct, the truth is all kicks are basically the same in regard to direction. What determines direction is the placekicker's alignment. To align properly to perform the kick, he must use proper mechanics. To perform proper mechanics on every kick, the placekicker must determine a direction. It's that simple.

Situational kicks are not only about direction. They are also about where and how the placekicker contacts the football. The kicker still uses proper mechanics, but he makes natural body adjustments so that he makes contact with the football to get the trajectory he wants.

Kicking With Purpose

The placekicker must have a purpose for every kick. Every time the football is kicked during practice or a game, the ball needs to be directed toward a particular target. Only then can the kicker develop truly consistent and accurate control and placement.

Directional Kicks

One of the more advanced approaches to kicking off is placing kicks to the right or left side of the field. These are commonly called directional kicks. A placekicker who can consistently place the football in either corner is a valuable asset to a team. This type of placement allows the coverage team to focus on a specific side of the field to limit the returner's options. When the kick goes to an area just outside the numbers, the returner has no choice but to bring the ball straight upfield or back toward the middle. He has no room to run outside because he's closed off by the sideline.

The kick is executed from the middle of the field. It's identical to a straight-ahead kickoff except that the alignment is in the desired direction of the kick. It's similar to lining up for a field goal or an extra point except the kicker uses the alignment and approach used for kickoffs. The directional kick is ideal for a kicker who's not strong enough to kick deep into the end zone. Another advantage of the directional kick is the increased hang time and ball placement (in a specific area and not as deep) give the coverage team less distance to travel.

Another way to execute the directional kick is to tee up the football on the hashmark and kick it straight downfield or slightly outside the numbers. This positioning requires a precise kick. The flight of the ball is still directed to a very particular area of the field. The coverage team has the advantage of knowing where the placekicker is placing the football.

Although this technique virtually eliminates the element of surprise, it might give the not-so-strong placekicker an advantage by allowing him to kick at less of an angle and for slightly less distance. A kicker with a more powerful leg can take advantage of the shorter distance and translate it into even more effective hang time.

Surprise

The placekicker should develop each variation of his kickoffs so that the start of all his kicks looks about the same. The better he can disguise his kick from the return team, the more effective his kick will be.

Keeping the ball in the middle helps maintain the element of surprise for the return team. An advanced placekicker who's comfortable with the directional kick can approach the football the same as he usually does and then quickly adjust his steps to kick it to either direction, thereby disguising the kick from the return team so they don't know what's coming until the last minute.

Deep Kicks

When first learning to kick off, the placekicker focuses on the body mechanics that drive the football deep downfield. He uses a longer approach to build up controlled momentum to the ball. He explodes through the football, driving it downfield with the entire momentum of his body going through to the target. He has so much controlled momentum built up that as he returns to the ground he lands on his kicking leg and quickly transitions to a run toward the target in order to maintain balance and body control. Thus the entire kickoff motion is designed to optimize the flight of the football and the distance the ball will travel.

A kick for distance is also known as a deep kick. The deep kick is one of the most common types of kickoffs, although it's probably not the best choice for every team or every situation.

In college and professional football, the placekicker kicks off from the 30-yard line. It's difficult for many kickers to kick a football more than 70 yards, so kicking at this distance promotes more kickoff returns. This can be fine if a team has an extremely strong coverage unit; otherwise, it might be wise to try a different strategy, depending on the ability of the placekicker. If a team has a very strong placekicker and the coverage team is good, the deep kick can be the best choice, especially when the kick is aided by the wind.

High school players kick off from their own 40-yard line, which allows strong kickers to help their team tremendously in regard to field position. Some high school rules don't even allow the return of a kickoff that travels into the end zone.

The optimal distance to strive for when kicking off is 65 to 75 yards for college and professional players and 60 to 65 yards for high school players. Rare, exceptional kickers may be able to kick it even further consistently.

When kicking the football for distance, the kicker is executing the skill in the most optimal way. Kicking for distance is simply kicking the football at a trajectory that allows maximum hang time and maximal distance. This combination determines how far the football will travel.

Onside Kicks

An onside kick can be a surprise kick or a kick that everyone in the stadium knows is coming. The kicking team executes the onside kick with the intention of obtaining possession of the football. An onside kick can be used at any time to create a big play, but usually these kicks are employed when the game is on the line and the kicking team desperately needs the ball in the hands of its offense.

Kicks are considered onside kicks if they go at least 10 yards (enough to be legally recoverable) and provide the kicking team an opportunity to recover the kick and secure possession of the ball. Kicks that can be used for onside kicks include the high-bounce kick, the classic drive kick, and the drag kick.

High-Bounce Kick

The high-bounce, or lob, kick is angled toward the sideline, bounces off the ground, travels high in the air, and comes down at a point just beyond 10 yards. This kick gives the coverage team an opportunity to catch the ball before it hits the ground.

To get the high bounce, the placekicker positions the football in the same way he normally would tee up the ball for a kickoff, with the exception of turning the tee backwards. This allows the football to immediately hit the ground without making any contact with the tee. He takes a position to the left side of the ball (for a right-footed kicker), about two and a half steps away. From this position, he faces down a line that connects his plant foot, the ball, and the spot he's kicking to—a spot 10 yards away.

The approach is similar to that for an extra point or field goal. The placekicker leans, jab steps, steps, and plant steps past the ball, allowing the kicking foot to strike down on the upper third of the football with the inside tip of his toe. He sweeps the kicking leg across his body so the kicking foot doesn't hit the ground or the football as it ricochets upward. This contact forces a quick rotation of the ball into the ground, causing the ball to bounce high into the air as it heads toward its target. Ideally, the football should go at an angle from the tee, gaining distance as it heads toward the sideline to a point 10 yards down-field. The football must come down toward the sideline but not too close. It needs to remain in the field of play to ensure an opportunity for the kicking team to secure possession.

Drive Kick

The drive kick is one of the most common onside kicks. It has been seen often in the last seconds of a football game when everyone in the stadium knows it is coming. A tee especially designed for this particular type of kick includes a notch that supports the football with its tip on the ground (figure 2.9). (This tee also can be used for squib kicks.)

Figure 2.9 The tip of the football is on the ground for an onside kick.

The placekicker positions the football with the tip on the ground and leans it back on the tee considerably more, presetting the ball in the exact position he wants the ball to travel—angling toward the sideline on a low line and continually touching the ground, causing an erratic skip effect as it travels 10 yards. This kick must be hit with some force to generate the unpredictable motion needed to get results. The objective is for the tip of the ball to hit the ground as it skips, causing the ball to jump up in a split-second, making it extremely difficult to predict or handle. This gives the kicking team time to get in position to recover a mishandled ball or to obtain possession before the return team does.

The placekicker aligns the same as he did for the high-bounce kick. The difference is that he strikes the football just below the tip, closer to the center, in order to drive it across the top of the ground. Remember that the tip of the football is touching the ground as the ball leans back and rests on the front of the tee.

Is He Offside?

It might appear that the placekicker is offside when he executes the high-bounce or drive kick because his plant foot is ahead of the football at impact. However, it's understood that a placekicker who's performing a kickoff cannot be offside prior to making contact with the football.

Drag Kick

The drag, or dribble, kick is a tremendously effective onside kick that can be used any time. It's especially useful when the kicking team sees that the front line of the return team is vacating their area prematurely in preparation to block.

The placekicker positions the football and aligns as he would if he were kicking a regular deep kick downfield. This is one of the main reasons the drag kick can be so effective. Another reason is that the kicker is designated to recover his own onside kick.

To be effective, the kicker must appear to be building up speed to drive the kickoff downfield as he approaches the football. At the last moment, as he prepares to swing his leg through to perform the kick, he quickly lifts his leg and simply drags his kicking foot across the top tip of the football. This causes the football to bounce alongside him, traveling at the same speed and just slightly ahead of him as he continues downfield. As he approaches 10 yards downfield, the football is practically waiting for him. All he has to do is recover and down it.

The key to this onside kick is for the placekicker to be a great actor and make the kick look like a regular kickoff. This causes the front line of the return team to anticipate a deep kick and quickly vacate the area, allowing the kicker to recover the onside kick untouched.

All the onside kicks discussed in this section can take advantage of the element of surprise. The kicker simply aligns as he would if performing a normal kickoff. He then adjusts his steps at the last second and catches the return team off guard.

Specialty Kicks

It's wise for teams to have in their arsenal of kicks ways to position the football on the field that will disrupt the strategy of the return team. Specialty kicks can confuse the return team and possibly disrupt the overall timing of the return. The kicking team kicks the football so that it eludes

Watch for Laterals

If the game is in the last few seconds or time has run out, the kicking team must be prepared for the blockers to lateral the kickoff back to their favorite return man. If they're in desperation mode, they might even consider a throwback pass. The return team might have just such a play up their sleeve (think Boise State), so be ready.

the expected return man. Specialty kicks also offer a safe and unexpected way to kick the football to another player on the return team who might lack experience in catching or returning the kick. This combination is the recipe for a turnover and possibly a dramatic change in field position.

Squib Kick

A squib kick usually refers to a type of onside kick. However, a true onside kick is designed to go at least 10 yards and provide the kicking team an opportunity to recover and secure possession. The squib kick is actually what we call a specialty kick because it's meant to go downfield and provide the coverage team a greater opportunity to contain and control the return. Because of its low, line-drive trajectory, rarely will the squib kick travel in the air much more than 10 yards before it erratically starts skipping off of the ground as it heads downfield.

The strategy of the squib kick is simple. The coverage team is willing to give up a few yards of field position in exchange for preventing a long return. The squib kick is also a good way to ensure the football doesn't get into the hands of a talented returner, preventing a big play. The squib kick bounces unpredictably down the field and is usually picked up before it reaches the return man who's the big-play threat. Squib kicks are most often used late in the ball game or with only a few seconds remaining in the first half.

Squib kicks are kicked with power. The placekicker makes impact on the football just above the center mass to create a knuckleball effect, kicking the ball with power on a line drive through a gap in the front wall of blockers. This kick is hard to field. Even if the ball is secured by a blocker or up back, an uncoordinated return usually results.

Another effective way to execute a squib kick is to direct it to a corner, similar to a directional kickoff. The ball travels at more of an angle this way, making it difficult for the return team to decide how to best handle it.

Sky Kick

The sky kick, also known as the bloop kick, is ideal when facing an opponent that has a great kick-return team. Sky kicks are generally directed to a point on the field toward the sideline outside the numbers, between the 35- and 25-yard lines. These kicks are approached like punts—the placekicker is sacrificing distance for hang time. This approach maximizes the time the coverage team has to travel a shorter distance, making it difficult for the opponent to break a big return.

The placekicker needs to be extremely accurate when placing a kick toward the sideline. The ball needs to be kept in play to avoid the out-of-bounds penalty. This being the case, the sky kick is extremely useful for the kicker who lacks the strength to kick the ball deep but has accuracy and can get good hang time by kicking the football at an angle and a shorter distance.

This kick is also effective when the kicking team is facing a strong wind. Because the football won't travel as far into the wind anyway, the kicker might as well take advantage of the effect the wind will have on a high kick. The kicker can kick the football at a lower trajectory into the wind, allowing the wind to hold it up long enough for the coverage team to make the play. Meanwhile, the returner faces a challenge trying to handle a kick that doesn't drop at the normal angle but drifts away as he tries to make the catch.

Many of the kicks discussed in this chapter can be directed toward the corner of the playing field. A placekicker with an arsenal of kicks that resemble other kickoffs, such as directional corner and directional squib kicks, can give his coverage team a tremendous advantage because his kicks are unpredictable and tough to handle.

3

Field Goals and Extra Points

One of the great benefits of being a placekicker is the accountability factor regarding performance. The most obvious factor of accountability is whether or not he makes the kick. Most of his work is done beforehand, in preparation. Many, many hours of practice time go into honing his skills until they become automatic. After that, his role is really quite simple: He must get an accurate kick off without it being blocked. He has a job to do, and he needs to perform to the best of his ability every time.

During a game, many factors affect the success of extra points and field goals. The placekicker might have to attempt several field goals from various distances and from either hashmark. The defense might anticipate a fake field goal and minimize the rush or might decide to send an all-out rush. Regardless of what happens, the kicker must perform the same kick the same way every time.

He must be prepared to perform optimally, which means he can perform every facet of the kick that he controls to the highest level. If he accomplishes this objective, the team can ask nothing more of him.

Every kick within the placekicker's range, both extra points and field goals, is kicked the same way, no matter what adjustments the defense makes or which hashmark he kicks from. Kickers must develop optimal timing when getting the ball off as well as optimal trajectory to clear the oncoming rush. These skills are acquired through repetition during practice.

For the placekicker to compete effectively, he must continually develop his skills through gamelike experiences. In this chapter you'll gain more than insight to the conditions and situations that occur over the course of a football game. If you're a kicker, you'll learn to develop and prepare your skills until they become highly successful habits. Then, as you jog onto the field to kick an extra point or field goal, you'll have nothing else to think about except making the kick. Everything else is beyond your control.

Determining Point of Placement

The moment a placekicker jogs onto the field to kick a field goal, he should already know approximately where he's going to spot the football for the kick. He determines this spot based on where the officials have spotted the football for the snap on the line of scrimmage. As he arrives at the general area of the point of placement, he determines his target zone and then narrows his focus within that area to locate a specific target (figure 3.1).

Once he has established a visual reference of his target, he determines the exact flight path the ball will need to travel by positioning himself at the point of placement, generally 7 to 8 yards behind the snapper. (Usually high school and college kickers determine point of placement at 7 yards; professional kickers align at 8 yards. On the professional level, the extra yard allows the football to clear the oncoming rush at a higher trajectory. This is important since professional athletes tend to be taller, faster, and more skilled). At this point, he marks the exact spot that he wants his holder to set the football. He directly faces his target and aligns his kicking block (for high school) or the toe of his kicking foot (for college and pro) toward his target, allowing the holder time to place the fingers of his holding hand on the exact spot the kicker has determined.

Remember that each kick is performed with the exact same alignment from any position on the field, which is crucial for developing consistency and confidence. This also gives kicker a

Figure 3.1 Target zone and visual target reference.

mental advantage because although field position will change, he'll execute every kick in the same basic way.

The kicker approaches every kick by aligning as if there are no marks on the field whatsoever. All he has to do is identify his target, determine his point of placement, mark off his steps, and then execute the kick with the same timing and same trajectory as every other kick he has previously executed. Because the kicker uses the same kicking motion and trajectory on extra points as he uses on field goals, the football consistently travels the same path and distance.

For the sake of consistency, the kicker must understand that the optimal trajectory for extra points and field goals is the same. If the trajectory is too low, the risk that the kick will be blocked is significantly increased. If it's too high, the distance of the kick will be affected. Although a kicker can sometimes succeed even if he doesn't obtain this optimal level (whether due to poor field conditions, a bad hold, or other factors), he still needs to strive for optimal trajectory in order to be consistent with his kicking motion. Not only will he gain more confidence in his ability to perform the kick successfully, he'll also gain a valuable understanding of his ability to kick a football a specific distance.

The goalposts gradually become narrower as the angle of the kick increases toward either of the hashmarks and when the ball is nearer the goal line. In other words, the angle of the kick is more dramatic the nearer the point of placement is to the goal line and less dramatic when it's farther away (figure 3.2). (See the side angle drill in chapter 5, page 93.) Even so, the kicker still directs the flight of the football toward a precise target that's within the target zone. Although the target zone becomes more narrow, the precise target determined by the placekicker remains the same.

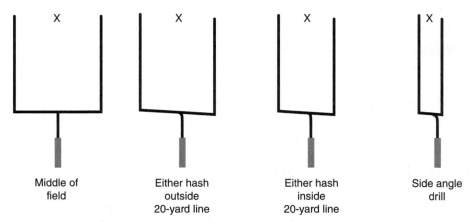

Figure 3.2 The angle of the kick is more dramatic near the goal line and less dramatic farther from the goal line.

The kicker focuses precisely on a target that enables him to send the football directly between the uprights. Although the goalposts are wider in high school football (23 feet, 4 inches, compared to 18 feet, 6 inches for college and professional football; figure 3.3), it's always best for kickers to aim dead center of the target. Aim small, miss small.

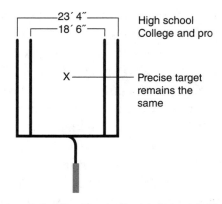

Figure 3.3 Goalpost dimensions of high school, college, and professional football.

Knowing the Snap-to-Kick Time

Timing is one of the most important aspects to kicking the football. You'll need a stopwatch. Kickers should be timed frequently to help them learn to get the ball off quickly, to develop a proper rhythm, and to improve consistency.

When determining a kicker's get-off time, focus on the optimal time to perform, not simply the fastest time. The mentality that faster is always better dramatically hurts the effectiveness of a kicker. A kicker needs to strive continually for the optimal time to perform his skill. He should be timed and charted frequently until his motion becomes a habit and his internal clock takes over.

Time the entire kicking sequence, from snap to kick, when determining optimal times. High school kickers should strive for a 1.3- to 1.4-second snap-to-kick time; college and professional kickers should strive for a 1.25- to 1.3-second snap-to-kick time.

One of the most important benefits of timing the placekicker is that it creates accountability for the kicker and other members of the kicking team. Timing and charting during practice and games will convince everyone that blocked kicks are not the fault of the kicker only. If the kicker does his job at the optimal level but the kick is blocked, the problem lies with the protection. The more quickly the real problem is identified, the more quickly game-altering mistakes can be eliminated.

Achieving Optimal Height

On an extra point or field goal, the football must quickly gain the necessary height to ensure continued flight downfield at a 25- to 26-degree angle (figure 3.4). This responsibility rests completely on the kicker.

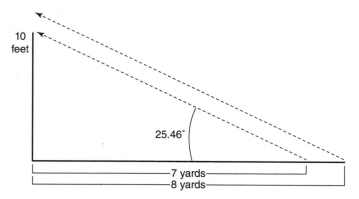

Figure 3.4 Optimal angle.

He must be able to produce the proper trajectory every time for the football to consistently clear the oncoming rush.

On the high school and college levels, the normal point of placement is 7 yards from the line of scrimmage. In order to clear the rush, the football must be 10 feet in the air by the time it travels forward 7 yards. Because professional players often are bigger, faster, and more skillful, usually the point of placement is 8 yards from the line of scrimmage to ensure the kick's altitude is higher when it clears the line of scrimmage.

Extra point and field goal kicks are the same. The kicker must develop that mentality. The alignment is the same, the kicking motion is the same, the optimal get-off time is the same, and the required trajectory is the same. The difference between extra points and field goals is that field goals are sometimes kicked from different angles because of field positioning near one of the hashmarks.

The best ways for a kicker to develop optimal height are to practice drills that naturally develop quick elevation, to work with his snapper and holder, to be timed at every practice, and to kick against a live rush during team practices that simulate the pace and pressure of a game.

Evaluating Optimal Field Goal Range

Optimal field goal range is the distance on the field from which a kicker can kick field goals the most advantageous way. Optimal range goes hand in hand with optimal trajectory. Remember the kick must reach a certain height to clear the oncoming rush and allow the ball to reach a maximum distance. This is where a kicker really needs to know his natural ability and the limits of his performance. This is not to say he can't do more. But he needs an honest assessment of what he's capable of doing at any given moment.

Remember to think "optimal" when performing the kicking motion. Kickers don't need to have the fastest get-off times, the highest elevation, or the farthest distance. They do need to combine every aspect of kicking the ball to get the most ideal result. If they try to be dominant in one area of kicking, they'll affect other areas. Kickers must have everything working together to perform at their best.

For the kicker to determine his optimal field goal range, he needs to press his limits. After he kicks enough footballs to develop his best timing and motion, he needs to gradually work back, kicking from longer distances. Start by working back at 5-yard intervals after every successful kick. Note that he needs to gradually move back—not quickly. He needs time to focus on the accuracy and the flight of the football in regards to where it lands.

As he moves back, he remains disciplined and continues to use the exact same kicking motion he uses for extra points or shorter field goals. He focuses on mechanics and the motion of his body—the things he can control—and visually sees the end result before making the kick.

If he continues to focus on using the exact same kicking motion and remains true to his abilities, he'll gradually see his kicks getting closer to the back of the crossbar as he backs up. The challenge he'll face is kicking with more power. As this occurs, it means he's getting close to the outer edge of his range. The key now is to determine his exact range based on the crossbar. When he reaches the point at which his kicks are barely making it over or barely coming up short, he has found his maximal field goal range. Some kickers are so in tune with their abilities and confident in knowing their exact range that they can actually hit the crossbar quite regularly.

Initially, the kicker will want to determine his optimal field goal range under favorable conditions. Once he determines his range, he can experiment with changing conditions, such as weather. On game day, when he's determining his range in light of current conditions during pregame warm-up, he'll already have a good idea of what to expect. Also, if he has the opportunity, he will want to kick at both ends of the stadium to determine his exact range in both directions, especially if there is any type of wind on game day.

Kicking Longer Range Field Goals

Outside-range field goal kicks are attempts beyond the kicker's optimal range. While determining his limits, the kicker will identify a point at which he just barely comes up short of the crossbar. That exact point is his threshold; beyond that point he must attempt longer range field goals outside his normal range. This is the distance from which he will no longer be able to perform optimally because he'll have to generate more leg speed and power to increase the flight and distance of the kick. Because he's focusing more of his energy on a separate aspect of the kick than usual, in this case more power, he'll have to adjust his mechanics. He won't be as consistent with his motion, and this will challenge his accuracy. The goalposts also appear to be narrower from a longer distance, requiring more precision.

During practice, the kicker should minimize practicing field goals outside his normal range. Longer distance field goals are not often attempted during games. When they are attempted, it's usually toward the end of the half or during the last seconds of a game. Shorter range kicks, those well within the kicker's range, are the kicks that need the most attention because they'll be attempted much more often in games. The kicker needs to execute just a few kicks, perhaps three to five, that are outside his normal range during one practice a week and the same amount during warm-ups on game day. Of course the exact number of practice kicks is entirely up to the kicker, but he needs to be disciplined in how much he works on kicking outside his range. He doesn't want to develop bad habits that cause him to adjust his mechanics to kick the football farther than normal. He also doesn't want to wear out his leg by practicing longer distance field goals when a very high percentage of his kicks will be from a much shorter range.

For the kicker to generate more power when kicking the football, he must be more aggressive on his approach and simply go after the football more. However, this more aggressive approach still needs to be done under control. He must maintain his technique by keeping his focus on his mechanics. Although it's inevitable for the kicker's kicking mechanics to adjust naturally when kicking outside his normal range, whatever adjustment does occur should be subtle. Periodically practicing outside-range field goals helps him understand what he needs to do in such situations, which improves confidence.

Running a Fake

The only time a kicker needs to be concerned about recognizing the oncoming defensive rush is when a possible fake field goal play has been called and the play call is predicated on whether certain defensive positions exist before the ball is snapped. In the vast majority of cases, the kicker does not need to read the defense. Usually that responsibility belongs to the holder, or an interior lineman will alert the holder of a particular alignment. But the kicker must be aware of any fake call so he knows who makes the call and what his role is—does he fake the kick? Does he receive the snap? Does he end up actually kicking the football if the fake is called off?

The kicker always needs to focus on performing the kick. If he does anything other than his normal routine, it will distract him or tip off the defense to be alert for a fake. By approaching every kick the exact same way, he's prepared to carry out a great fake or make a successful kick, regardless of the play call.

Consider the situation in which an overload of players is aligned to one side of the formation. This type of defensive positioning might reveal a weakness in the defense that might grant an offensive advantage. In such a case, it's likely that the holder will identify the overload, or an interior lineman might alert him, and decide whether to make the play-fake call. The kicker simply needs to know the call to determine whether he's kicking or appearing to kick. Remember that the kicker has no responsibility in reading defenses. His job is to kick the football.

4

Compensating for Conditions

Who can forget Adam Vinatieri's 45-yard last-second field goal through a blizzard during the 2001 NFL Divisional Playoffs against the Oakland Raiders, sending the game into overtime? Late in the overtime, when Vinatieri had another opportunity, he booted a 23-yarder, sealing the victory for the New England Patriots.

The great placekickers are mentally strong and don't fret over things that are out of their control. They focus on what they're going to accomplish and allow the habits they've developed through proper preparation take over. Like Vinatieri, all placekickers strive for consistency despite unfavorable conditions. The truly great placekickers come through rain or shine, regardless of the circumstances or environment.

The best way to prepare for kicking under poor field and weather conditions is to practice kicking under such conditions. Every time the kicker steps onto the practice field, he has an opportunity to prepare under a set of circumstances that's ever-changing. Unless you play in a dome, the weather affects field conditions, so whatever mix of elements you encounter on a given day—driving rain with 50-mph gusts of wind, soupy fog, icy snow—gives you a unique opportunity to perform in an environment that you might see again in a game.

Along with weather conditions, the surface of the field also significantly influences the considerations of the placekicker. Regardless of the playing surface, the kicker needs to execute his technique the same way every time. Although he should not make adjustments in technique based on the type of field, he must know how field surface affects his kicking decisions.

Placekickers must learn to adjust to their environment so they can still get the job done.

Theodore A. Wagner/Icon SMI

Executing on Different Field Surfaces

The three types of field surface—natural grass, artificial turf, and field turf—each has its own set of attributes and requires separate considerations for the kicker, especially in the ways each surface is altered by various weather conditions.

Natural Grass

When conditions are favorable, natural grass is still considered the optimal playing surface for kickers. Its natural shock-absorbing properties provide ultimate traction. It's no wonder that artificial turf manufacturers refer to their surfaces as duplicating the feel and playing conditions of real grass.

The main challenge of playing on natural grass is when wet weather conditions cause the turf and soil to loosen, creating poor footing. The kicker in these situations should wear detachable cleats, which are the most versatile (because the cleat length can be changed) and perform the best in normal to wet conditions when the grass is not too firm. (See page 74 for more information on which cleats to wear in rain and snow.)

Artificial Turf

Traditional artificial turf is made of a dense, abrasive rug-type surface (sometimes referred to as carpet) that relies on an underlying shock pad with a cushioning effect for safety. This turf is rapidly being replaced with newer versions of synthetic surfaces.

When kicking on artificial turf, the kicker should wear turf shoes, particularly on the plant foot. This shoe has rubber nubs on the soles and is designed specifically for artificial surfaces. These shoes resemble tennis shoes and generally have multiple cleats molded into the sole. The cleats are usually shorter because there is not much give on the surface because of the safety pad underneath. The multiple cleats on the sole allow the shoe to grip much better on the firm, flat, and consistent surface. This provides the kicker more support and traction, especially when making his plant.

Often a kicker will need to wear a turf shoe for more support and traction on his plant foot but wear his normal kicking shoe, which may have molded or detachable cleats, on his kicking foot. This is because the turf shoe better maintains support when planting, whereas the normal kicking shoe is more lightweight and flexible, making it ideal for kicking.

Field Turf

Field turf is the newest artificial surface on the market. It looks like grass, feels like grass, and plays like grass. The advantage the kicker has when kicking on this type of surface is that in wet weather conditions, the field surface stays constant. The turf and underlying area do not loosen in wet conditions, so traction and footing remain firm.

The kicker has several options on what shoe to wear on field turf. Because the surface is more like natural grass than artificial turf, he may even wear the same shoe on field turf that he would wear on grass. He should experiment to see what works best for him.

Adjusting to a Poorly Maintained Field

The need to adjust to a field that's poorly maintained is rarely a concern anymore at the college and professional levels. Most teams at this level of play have full-time supervisors and staff employed to maintain athletic fields. It's rare to see a football field at a college or pro game that's not immaculately manicured.

On the other hand, high schools often don't share that same commitment, or don't have the financial resources, to ensure football fields are consistently maintained. Most schools with natural grass fields are at the mercy of Mother Nature when it comes to field conditions.

As for the high school kicking game, placekickers have an advantage over kickers at other levels: the use of a kicking tee. On the high school level, the kicker is allowed to use up to a 2-inch placement tee or kicking block when kicking extra points and field goals.

> ## Practicing Indoors
>
> If your team has an indoor practice facility that provides a controlled, comfortable environment, practices need to be planned wisely. If you're the placekicker, you'll sometimes need to leave your near-perfect environment to face adverse conditions in order to prepare for games.
>
> This doesn't mean going outside every time it rains. But you'll need to take advantage of the off-season and early preseason to experience unfavorable conditions so you can hone your skills under challenging circumstances. Once the official season starts, you'll be primed and ready to go, having maximized quality repetitions with your team.

It has long been assumed that the primary reason to use a placement tee is to give young kickers a chance to enhance elevation on the football, which is true. However, another good reason to let high school kickers use a placement tee and a higher elevated kickoff tee is because the field surfaces on which they play lack the consistency you see in the college and professional ranks. A kicker who uses a tee, regardless of where he's playing, has a much better opportunity to kick the football successfully, even if the grass on the football field is high.

Another benefit to using a tee is that it gives the holder a visual place to spot the football in preparation for the kick. At the high school level, it is common to find less emphasis placed on the kicking game than at the college and professional levels. Thus, the holder and kicker don't always get as many quality reps with the snapper. By using a placement tee, the holder benefits by having a much easier spot to locate, enhancing the consistency and success of the kick.

Adjusting the Approach and Plant Step

If field conditions become dramatically challenging, kickers might need to adjust their approach and plant step at any given moment in a game. If the game is being played during a torrential downpour that covers the natural turf field with water, the kicker faces the challenge of dealing with turf that has turned into a quagmire. Snow and ice may worsen as temperatures drop over the game.

The kicker has a chance to determine field conditions during pregame warm-ups, but things change quickly, so he must be able to adjust to conditions at any time. It's crucial that he practice under adverse conditions periodically, especially if these conditions are anticipated in an upcoming game.

Any adjustments to the approach and plant step will be subtle. Essentially, all the kicker wants to do is be more cautious and deliberate with his steps during the approach and plant during the kick. Nothing else changes. Simply being aware of conditions allows the kicker to make subtle adjustments naturally. He's kicking on a surface that responds differently to starts and stops. And though it doesn't change anything, it can be comforting to know that everyone else on the field is facing the same challenges.

Because conditions can change significantly over the course of a game, the kicker might need to modify his approach and plant at any time. He might consider changing shoes if the ground is extremely muddy. He might need a longer cleated, natural grass type of shoe or, if the ground is frozen and hard, more of a gripping type of shoe used for artificial surfaces. The whole premise of kicking the football is based on sound fundamental principles that center on balance and control of the body. If outside factors influence his balance and control, the kicker must adjust accordingly.

A kicker may need to adjust his approach and plant step when

- early in his career, he aligns too close or too far away from the football and it's affecting his consistency;
- weather conditions such as rain or snow affect the field; or,
- field conditions are less than ideal because of poor maintenance, multipurpose design of the facilities, or poor drainage.

Adjustments to the approach and plant step are common among young kickers who are having problems with consistency. But the more he develops and advances in his kicking motion, the less he'll need to adjust.

Most of the challenges kickers face in terms of alignment issues can be taken care of through trial, error, and repetition. The key is to develop a basic understanding of proper kicking mechanics. Once he understands the proper motion, he can apply self-coaching strategies to get results. This lets him figure things out in a gradual, more natural way.

Inconsistency might require the kicker to adjust the distance of his approach or the placement of his plant step. Sometimes he might align too close to the point of placement, making him feel crowded to the football during his approach. This might make him unconsciously position his plant foot too close. Inconsistencies when marking off alignment could be the cause. He might be taking incorrect or long strides when stepping back vertically from the football during the alignment phase. He might be moving forward when he adjusts his footwork just prior to positioning in his stance. Whatever the cause, the kicker needs to review and experiment with the fundamentals of the kick so he can find the problem and correct it.

Inconsistency can be caused by gradual changes in the approach or movements in the alignment that the kicker might not even be aware of. Inconsistency could also be a sign that the kicker's natural kicking mechanics have somehow created a need for a change.

Whatever the reason, the kicker must adjust his alignment to accommodate the need and then adjust his steps to the new alignment so he can mark off his new spot consistently. First, he needs to identify the problem; then he needs to experiment with the fundamentals, remembering to approach everything as if it's a simple tune-up. He reviews how he marks off his steps and aligns. From this approach he can determine if he can simply adjust his stride when stepping back or position his feet slightly differently when setting his stance. Whatever adjustment is needed, more often than not it can be easily identified and corrected. Once the alignment is correct, the kicker will enhance the positioning of the plant step, thus enabling an optimal kicking motion through the football. An optimal kick is one in which the kicker imparts the entire energy of his body, through proper mechanics, to a concentrated area of the football to optimize elevation, distance, and direction.

When facing any challenge, success depends on the kicker performing optimally. He must focus specifically on his target and the range of the kick. Remember that every kick, even in adverse conditions, is performed essentially the same way.

Dealing With Adverse Weather Conditions

When faced with conditions such as wind, rain, snow, and, extreme temperatures, kickers should think in positive terms, realizing what they control and what they do not. This thought process can be very empowering and help alleviate stress.

Simply understanding adverse weather conditions and the effects they have on the football can provide a tremendous confidence boost. Such understanding allows the kicker to develop a strategy to succeed even when the forces of weather he faces are the most challenging. Not only will the kicker learn to kick in these conditions, he will even learn to take advantage of them.

Wind

The direction and intensity of the wind can be identified in several ways: by feel, by looking at flags, or by observing footballs in flight. To determine the exact direction of the wind, the kicker needs to consider all indicators, but the most dependable are the brightly colored flags atop the uprights of the goalpost. This is why the flags are there. These flags are at the ideal elevation to provide an accurate reading of the wind because the optimal target of the kick is precisely between the uprights.

Kicking Into the Wind

Whenever it's windy out, a kicker's first concern is whether he'll have to kick directly into the wind. This direct wind is called a headwind. The most obvious challenge when facing a headwind relates to distance because, clearly, the ball won't travel as far when kicked into the wind. When facing this challenge, kickers (and their teammates) must know their range when kicking into headwinds. This range is determined during practice and pregame warm-ups.

Through practice, kickers discover that the wind not only reduces the distance of the kick but also tends to keep the football up in the air longer. The vertical position of the football combined with its backward rotation increases the time the football stays aloft.

It's interesting to note that as the football climbs it doesn't appear to be affected by the wind as much until it reaches the top of its climb. At this point, as the football's momentum quickly decreases, a more dramatic downward drop is seen (figure 4.1).

The key to kicking directly into the wind is to study the effects of the wind on the football during practice and pregame warm-ups, understand those effects, and determine how the headwind affects the kicker's range on the football field.

When extra points and field goals are kicked into the wind, the trajectory of the kick should remain at the optimal angle (described in chapter 1) to clear the oncoming rush. Because there's no oncoming rush for a kickoff, the football can be driven at a lower trajectory to minimize the effect of the headwind on the distance of the kick. Because the headwind tends to hold the football aloft longer, a good hang time can usually be achieved.

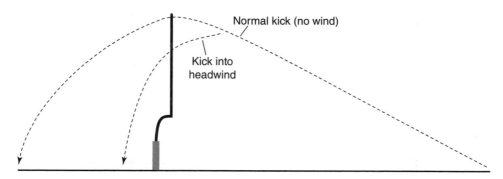

Figure 4.1 Effect of a headwind on the football.

On kickoffs, when kicking into a tremendous headwind, the kicking team prepares for the football traveling less distance. Typically, the kick distance will be reduced considerably, allowing the returner to make possession further upfield. The sky (bloop) kick discussed in chapter 2 is ideal when facing these types of conditions.

If the wind is intense, the kicking team might choose a more driving type of kick that squibs downfield, skipping along the ground. The kick might not travel as far but is more difficult to handle, making it tougher to return.

Kicking With a Crosswind

A crosswind (figure 4.2) blows across the flight path of the ball, causing it to veer to the side of the intended target. Strong crosswinds, especially with sudden gusts, can present significant challenges for placekickers. Again, the flight path of the ball is most vulnerable at the apex of its climb, when momentum decreases and the ball begins to descend at a steeper angle. To deal with a crosswind, the kicker needs to set his alignment toward a *precise target* that will offset the effect of the wind on the football as it travels toward the *intended target.*

To offset the effect of the wind on the football, the kicker aims at a target that represents the approximate distance the wind will move the kicked football. The kicker compensates for the effect of the wind on the football, allowing the wind to guide the football directly to the intended target.

Because the shortest distance between two points is a straight line, the effect of the crosswind on the football slightly increases the amount of time and distance it takes the football to pass between the uprights or

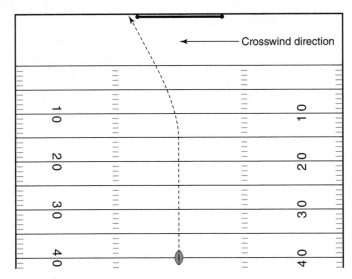

Figure 4.2 Effect of a crosswind on the football.

Precise Target Versus Intended Target

Kickers must understand that the precise target and intended target are not always the same. The precise target refers to the area that is the basis for the kicker's alignment and the target he aims at when kicking the football. The intended target is the ultimate goal, the final destination to which the football needs to travel for the kick to be successful. In ideal conditions, the precise target and intended target are the same. When conditions are unfavorable, such as under a crosswind, the kicker establishes a precise target that enables him to reach his intended target successfully through the wind. The difference in the precise target and intended target might be 1 yard or 10 yards, depending on the intensity of the wind, but the precise target will very rarely be outside of the target zone (the area above the crossbar and beyond and between the uprights).

get down the field on a kickoff. However, the actual distance the football travels downfield in relation to the point of placement decreases slightly.

When a strong crosswind is present, pregame warm-up kicks allow the kicker to get a feel for how much the wind will affect the flight of the ball. He initially sets his alignment as he always does, aiming right down the middle of the uprights. Then, after viewing the effect of the crosswind, he adjusts the distance of the precise target by moving it to the upwind side (the direction the wind is coming from) of his intended target (figure 4.3). Instead of fighting the wind, he tries to take advantage of it, using the

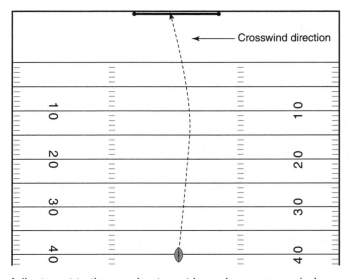

Figure 4.3 Adjustment to the precise target based on a crosswind.

wind to adjust the flight of the football to his benefit. However he should not adjust his target to outside the uprights.

For example, when attempting a 40-yard field goal, the kicker aims at a point that aligns with the right upright. This distance represents a long field goal that will definitely be affected by the wind. Through practice, the kicker knows that when he kicks the football with a strong crosswind coming from the right side, the wind naturally pushes the football to the left, bringing it toward the middle of the uprights as it passes the crossbar.

For kickoffs, the kicker begins by kicking to the same location he would normally kick to and observing the effect of the wind on the kick. Now he can establish an aiming point, a precise target, based on the necessary adjustment that enables him to set his alignment. On the kickoff, the kicker kicks directly toward the precise target, using the wind to direct the ball to its intended target. For example, the kicker might aim his kick directly down the left hashmark, allowing the wind, crossing the field from right to left, to push the football into its intended path between the left hashmark and the left sideline.

Of course kickoffs can be kicked to any area of the field, but field goals are always kicked toward the goalposts. With training, placekickers create a natural habit of kicking the football toward a precise target between the uprights and above the crossbar. Identifying a precise target to aim at is the first step in aligning. Remember that the target zone is the area above the crossbar, beyond and between the uprights. Within the target zone, the kicker locates his precise target. Once he establishes exactly where he's going to kick the football, he must be disciplined and kick the football toward this new precise target as if it were the same as the intended target. He must believe in his alignment, focus on his mechanics, and kick the football. The wind takes care of the rest.

Note that the placekicker very rarely establishes a target outside of the goalposts, that is, outside of the target zone. If he feels the need to do so, he's probably out of his range. The only way to justify a kick in this situation is out of desperation.

Kicking With the Wind

A tailwind is wind blowing in the same direction in which the football is traveling. This type of wind would seem to be the kicker's favorite, but he needs to fully understand both the advantages and the challenges.

The main advantage of having your back to the wind is that the wind adds slight yardage to the kick with no adjustment made to the optimal kicking motion. The wind moves with the football, so there's less resistance (figure 4.4), allowing the football to fly with increased speed and added distance.

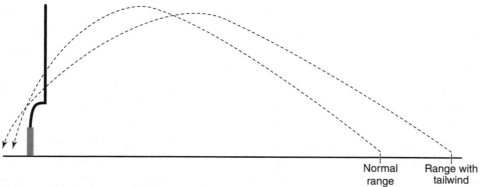

Normal range

Range with tailwind

Figure 4.4 Effect of a tailwind on the football.

Another effect of tailwind on a kicked football (that's generally not mentioned) is that it tends to minimize the elevation of the football in flight—because the wind that's moving in the same direction as the football is also moving above the football. This causes resistance as the football climbs in altitude. But as the football reaches its apex, the top of its climb, the upward resistance subsides and the wind seems to push the football downfield as it begins its descent. The push effect created by the tailwind increases the arc of descent, enhancing speed and distance as the football travels in flight.

The key to kicking with a tailwind is to kick the football normally, in the optimal way. This ensures the ball will travel with optimal elevation, distance, and direction. No adjustments should be needed. The kicker approaches his kick in the exact way he approaches every other kick and takes advantage of the natural elements that work in his favor.

The biggest challenge involves the wind moving above the football. Because the wind is moving in the same direction as the ball, it might cause noticeable resistance as the ball climbs, which might affect the elevation of the ball and slightly reduce hang time. This isn't a concern for extra points and field goals because hang time isn't important.

For kickoffs, the kicker needs to consider the effects of the wind on hang time. The wind tends to resist the football climbing yet assists the football in traveling downfield. This effect is beneficial as long as the football goes deep or out of the endzone, ensuring there will be no return. But if the football doesn't travel a great distance, it might get to the return man more quickly, giving him more time to get upfield before the coverage team reaches him. It's wise for the kicker to consider taking advantage of the tailwind by kicking the football slightly higher to increase hang time and then allowing the wind to push the football downfield. This gives the coverage team more time to cover while optimizing distance and hang time by taking advantage of the wind.

On field goals and extra points, the kicker obviously needs to get enough height on the ball to clear the oncoming rush. As long as the kick clears the rush, the kicker is okay because the effects of the wind are minimal. That's why it's so important for the kicker to kick the ball in the same way he normally does. Kicking the ball normally provides the optimal elevation every time, allowing the kicker to take advantage of the conditions.

On kickoffs, the football can be driven at a higher trajectory, increasing hang time to maximize the effects of the tailwind on distance. By slightly increasing hang time, the kicker allows the wind to carry the football farther down the field. Of course the wind is barely a concern on shorter kickoffs, such as onside kickoffs or other balls meant to squib along the ground.

Usually the kicker emphasizes driving kickoffs downfield for distance. This is accomplished by driving the football at a lower trajectory with just enough hang time to maximize the distance of the kick. If the kicking team's philosophy is to pin the return team deep in its own territory, emphasis needs to be on hang time as well as distance.

To increase hang time, the kicker drives his kicking foot slightly up more through the football than he normally would when driving it downfield. This slight adjustment can be made easily, especially if the kicker is accustomed to emphasizing hang time on kickoffs.

Kicking Against Swirls and Gusts

Kickers might face a real challenge in unpredictable wind conditions because the adjustments they would normally make might not be needed at any given moment. In such situations, the kicker must simply stay well within his range and attempt kicks that have a high chance of success. This will help minimize the effects that unpredictable winds can have on the flight of the football.

Kickoffs are affected by swirls and gusts as well. Because the kickoff is usually driven downfield at a lower trajectory, the wind is not as much of a concern unless it's coming head on. Then it might be wise either to drive the kick more to maximize distance and minimize the effect of the wind or simply to squib kick the ball to get it downfield and make it hard for the return team to handle.

The football is most affected by wind when the momentum of the kick decreases as the football reaches the apex of flight (figure 4.5). By attempting much shorter field goals, the kicker can exercise more control of the football through the momentum of the ball as it climbs toward the apex. The football will clear the goalpost with much more authority.

The most dependable indicators of wind, especially when the wind is extremely unpredictable, are the flags atop the goalposts. These flags tell

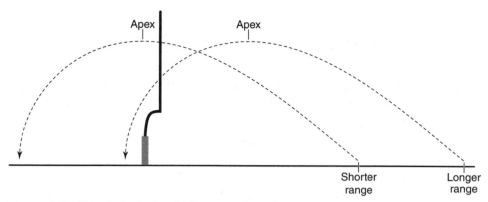

Figure 4.5 Effect of wind as kick momentum decreases near the apex of flight.

you the effects of wind in precisely the area into which you'll be kicking. In times of unpredictable winds, you'll need to check these flags moments before contacting the ball.

Sometimes the wind blows in a combination of ways. For instance, a headwind comes toward the kicker at an angle, which creates a combination headwind and crosswind effect. A tailwind coming from behind the kicker at an angle creates a tailwind and crosswind effect. When the wind is blowing in various directions, the kicker should be prepared to employ any one or a combination of modifications to his normal kick. In any case, he must establish a precise target within the target zone that enables him to reach his intended target.

Rain

Kicking in the rain presents a variety of challenges for the kicker, the most common being slippery or loose surfaces. When kicking in the rain, the kicker who has best developed his skills has a tremendous advantage. Balance and body control, particularly, are crucial on wet, slippery, and loose surfaces. The kicker must rely on his developed skills when dealing with these conditions. He should also focus more on technique when approaching the football. He should not change his approach but rather be all the more sure to stick to basics. Most experienced kickers don't slow their approach at all under slippery conditions.

The soccer-style kicker initially lands on the outside edge of his foot in a heel-to-toe transition as he prepares to pivot during his plant step. This is the point at which he's most vulnerable to wet conditions. By focusing on technique, he can plant his foot firmly and assuredly. Kicking in slippery conditions is all about focus and being prepared. As mentioned earlier, the best way to prepare is to practice kicking in poor conditions with your entire kicking unit. The snapper and holder face their own challenges in handling and positioning the football in rainy conditions.

Choice of Cleats in Rain and Snow

When kicking in the rain, be sure to wear the proper type of cleats. On natural grass, choose a detachable cleat (the most versatile and most popular cleat on the market), which performs best in normal to wet conditions when the grass is not too firm. The best feature of the detachable cleat is that cleat length can be changed to accommodate the terrain.

When kicking in the rain on firm artificial grass surfaces, consider turf type shoes. They resemble sneakers and have very low cleats similar to rubber nubs on the soles. These nubs generally cover the entire bottom of the shoe and provide a better gripping effect when surfaces tend to be harder and less penetrable. They are designed to grip older artificial surfaces that tend to be more firm due to the underlying design.

However, the newer artificial surface known as field turf is much softer, similar to real grass, and is designed to maintain support even in the rain. On this type of surface, you may want to go to a molded bottom shoe that has cleats or small bar-like projections. Molded bottom shoes may not have as many cleats or bars as turf shoes but they are very effective. Since the surface these shoes are designed for is not as firm, the cleats can dig in and grip more. Even detachable cleats can be considered on the newer field turf. A kicker or punter may find that he likes a molded bottom shoe for the plant foot and a different type of shoe for the kicking foot. It is up to the kicker or punter to experiment and find what works best.

When kicking in snow, other considerations arise. If the snow is soft and the footing underneath is loose, consider using the longest cleat available and allowed, especially for your plant foot. Longer cleats dig in more and provide more traction. If the snow is soft and the ground underneath is frozen, longer cleats won't penetrate effectively, so consider using shorter cleats.

If both the snow and the ground are frozen, turf shoes might be the best choice. Again, turf shoes have very low cleats similar to rubber nubs on the soles. When the ground is frozen and regular cleats can't penetrate the surface, turf football shoes might be an effective alternative.

In adverse conditions, you'll want to experiment during your pre-game warm-up to find out what cleat is most effective. Always be prepared by having multiple pairs of shoes available for any condition you may face. Don't rely on someone else to do this for you. Make it your responsibility to be ready for any situation.

Snow

Fortunately, most college and pro football programs have full-time grounds crew and maintenance specializing in game-day preparation of the field. They have preliminary measures to minimize the effects of snow through the protection of field tarps and mobile equipment designed for snow removal. This might ensure the playing surface is ready for kickoff, but after kickoff everything is in the hands of Mother Nature.

Under snowy conditions, initial considerations include the amount and type of snow and the field condition underneath. If it's a very light dusting of fresh snow and the ground is moist but not frozen, approach your kicking as you would under rainy conditions. If a considerable amount of snow has fallen or is still falling, other factors come into play. Is the ground frozen or loose? Has the snow stopped falling, or is visibility poor? Is the snow powdery or hard?

Although these kinds of concerns must be considered, there are unfortunately very limited options under extreme conditions such as blizzard-like snow and wind. Other than wearing the proper cleats and sticking to basics in his technique, the kicker can do little by way of adjustment in the face of extreme weather.

One way for kickers to maintain confidence in snowy conditions is to focus on the control and balance they have developed during their training. They should also remember that everyone on the field is dealing with the same set of circumstances other than the wind may be blowing in the face of the kicker and not the rushers. Even in this rare situation, the kicker and punter have been trained to focus their eyes and head slightly downward, which should minimize the snow's effect on their vision. In fact, because the kicker's normal approach to the football is more of a gradual build-up instead of a burst of speed, he might have an advantage over oncoming rushers. The kicker's normal approach allows for controlled movement that helps him maintain traction. His biggest challenge will be with his plant step, but if he focuses on his technique he can be more deliberate in his steps and maintain total control of his body throughout the kick.

Temperature

When it comes to temperature, only extremely cold weather much affects kickers, mainly because the football becomes harder in cold temperatures. When the football becomes harder, it becomes less pliable, challenging the kicker's ability to compress the ball when he makes contact with his foot. Less compression means less force and speed coming off the foot, resulting in a considerable difference in distance and hang time.

(In moderate to hot temperatures, the ball becomes more pliable, allowing greater compression and thus increasing hang time and distance because of the speed at which the football leaves the foot.) As always, the kicker must determine his range based on the present conditions.

Another challenge kickers face in extremely cold temperatures is staying loose on the sidelines. Even if using a portable heater, the kicker must make valuable use of his time by adequately stretching and performing practice kicks into a sideline kicking net. It's wise to do this primarily when his team has possession of the football and is approaching field goal range. Even if there are not many opportunities to kick or punt during the game, the kicker and punter must make wise use of their time, periodically stretching and staying loose on the sideline. They can take advantage of kicking into a net from time to time as long as they are careful not to overkick and focus more on quality reps.

5

Placekicking Practice Drills

In this chapter the kicker learns the fundamental parts of the kicking process. The drills are designed to develop kicking skills through practice as he transitions to game-day readiness. The drills begin with individual technique warm-up and progress to isolate precise parts of the kicking mechanics. This progression enables the kicker to develop and master each movement before combining skills to complete the kicking motion.

These drills are designed for the kicker to focus on warm-up, development, and performance in the off-season and preseason. An important aspect of each drill is the simulation of gamelike experiences that develop fundamental skills. Because the drills can be used for either warm-up or technique development, they can be done any time before the season starts. As the season begins, the kicker focuses primarily on warm-up drills and drills that simulate gamelike situations.

The kicker practices with a snapper and holder whenever possible, especially at times when gamelike experiences can be created. Also, the entire kicking process should be timed during practice sessions, to develop consistency and confidence.

After progressing through the drills in this chapter, the kicker will be ready to become more self-reliant through self-teaching strategies that give him the ability to coach himself.

Placekicking Drills Without a Football

Placekickers perform these warm-up drills in a progression without using a football. The progression promotes total focus during the setup and alignment, as well as during the mechanics of the kick. Warm-up drills should be done before practice and before games.

Alignment Drill

Objective
The placekicker focuses on every detail of setting up his alignment, ensuring he does it the same way every time.

Equipment
Beginning kickers might want to use a small marker, such as a coin.

Progression
1. Beginning at the point of placement, the kicker marks off his steps to achieve proper depth and alignment.
2. He completes the drill by forming the 90-degree angle from his target line as he's in his stance, facing the point of placement.

Tips From the Coach
- The kicker practices his alignment particularly for kicks on or near the hashmarks. This is where the angles of alignment do not coincide with the yard lines of a football field.
- Beginning kickers benefit by placing some kind of marker, such as a coin, behind their foot. They can then compare their alignment the next time for accuracy and consistency.

Variations
Perform this drill from various positions on the field to simulate alignments that might be needed during a game.

Stance and Start

Objective

The kicker focuses on developing an effective stance that best positions his body for a time-sensitive transition toward the point of placement.

Progression

1. The kicker aligns in his stance. He leans forward to the point that any additional forward lean will initiate movement.

2. Once he's in position, he momentarily pauses to simulate the amount of time he would need to pause in a game before the snap.

3. As he faces the point of placement, he visualizes the holder's hand rising from the point of placement to receive the snapped football.

4. He leans his entire body forward to initiate movement toward the point of placement. This movement, leading with his chest, creates an immediate need for the steps to begin. He takes his initial steps (either two steps or a jab step followed by two steps) and then stops.

Tips From the Coach

- The kicker must lean forward with his entire body to create a natural need for the steps to begin. This is the key to timing and to developing a fluid and rhythmic approach to kicking the football.

- Whether the kicker uses a two-step approach or a two-and-a-half-step approach, leading with a jab step, he still will need to lean immediately when he visualizes the holder raising his hand from the ground in anticipation of receiving the snap.

Visualize the Kick

Objective

The placekicker develops visualization skills that he can use for every kick. He forms a vivid, positive, mental picture of the way he intends to kick the football. He needs to visualize this image in the exact way he would see it from his own eyes while actually performing the kick.

Progression

1. The placekicker stands in the general area of the point of placement. He identifies his target so he can set the exact location where he wants the holder to spot the football.

2. Once he determines both the target and the point of placement, he visualizes the football clearing the goalposts, sailing right down the middle between the uprights and in a direct line with the two points of reference (the target and the point of placement).

3. He steps backward, marking off his steps to determine his depth of alignment. This is where he toes the line and confirms that his kicking foot, point of placement, and target are all in a direct line. He again visualizes the football clearing the goal in direct line with his reference points.

4. He takes two comfortable and controlled lateral steps to the side, pivoting to face the point of placement as he aligns in his stance. He again visualizes the football clearing the goalposts.

5. He begins his approach to kick the football, imagining the time and action of the football being snapped.

6. As he approaches the point of placement, he continues to visualize everything that would happen as if he were actually kicking the football in a game.

7. When he simulates kicking the football, he visualizes the mechanics of his kick coordinated with the direction of the plant foot and the direction of the target.

8. After he simulates kicking through the football and finishing on his plant foot, he reaches the confirmation point at which all of his mechanics come together to accomplish the goal of kicking the football. Here he develops the understanding of how his mechanics align with the flight of the football as it clears the uprights.

Tips From the Coach

- The kicker simulates gamelike conditions throughout the process.
- He needs to develop this technique until it's a habit.
- He visualizes each kick going precisely toward the target and sees and feels his body in the exact position it needs to be in to execute a successful kick.
- This drill improves technique, develops consistency, and increases confidence.

Variations

- Perform this drill from various positions on the football field to simulate different locations of kicks during a game.
- When performing a last-second kick, the placekicker sometimes won't have time to mark off his steps and will have to quickly align and kick the football. To practice this situation, the kicker simulates just the last phase of the drill (the approach and kick) and focuses on the position of his body at the finish.

Arm Position Drill

Objective

The placekicker learns proper arm positioning as his body momentum transitions from an angled approach toward the point of placement to a forward motion that enhances balance and power toward the target. He also learns how his arms serve as a counterbalance to the torque effect of the body as it rotates and enhances leg speed through the football.

Equipment

A kicking block may be used to designate the point of placement.

Progression

1. The placekicker determines the point of placement on the yard line or sideline of a football field and marks off his steps for a normal kick.

2. He slowly begins his approach toward the point of placement in a methodical way by taking his initial jab or drive step and then freezing in that position. As he takes the drive step, his left arm simultaneously extends up and out in front of his body until parallel to the ground and in the same direction as his approach before it opens slightly toward the target. At the same time, his opposite arm moves naturally from his side to slightly behind his body. From this position he can see exactly where his arms need to be when taking his drive step.

3. He takes his plant step and again freezes in position. As he steps, his left arm, still extended, simultaneously moves directly to his side in a lateral position while maintaining its parallel position to the ground. At the same time, his right arm moves from down his side to forward. From this position he can see exactly where his arms need to be when taking his plant step.

4. From the plant step position he executes a no-step kick. To do this he'll need to torque his body while bringing his kicking foot forward. At the same time, his left arm moves toward the front of his body in a slightly upward motion and begins to bend as it crosses just below his face. His other arm moves from a slightly forward position to just behind his right hip.

Tips From the Coach

- The kicker should visualize his foot kicking through the football and, at the same time, focus on the movement of his body downfield toward the target.

- The forward motion of the body should drift slightly away to the left because of the body torque and follow-through of the leg swing.

- At the end of the drill, he should face downfield in the same direction as his target.

Variations

The kicker can perform this drill by focusing on one segment—the drive step, plant step, or follow-through—at a time or by doing each in a slow, methodical succession, hesitating after each position and arm movement.

Bag Drill

Objective

The placekicker develops proper ankle and leg lock through the simulation of the kicking foot compressing the ball at impact.

Equipment

A partner; a round cylinder bag that's normally used as a stand-up dummy for blocking drills.

Progression

1. A partner holds the bag vertically while the placekicker places his plant foot alongside the bag as he would the football on a normal kick (figure 5.1a). He associates the back of the bag with the back of the football.

2. He maintains stability by holding the top of the bag with his right hand. He positions his body, particularly his front shoulder, over the bag the way it would be if he were impacting and compressing the football during a normal kick.

Figure 5.1 Bag drill: *(a)* initial position: plant foot beside bag; *(b)* foot is drawn back; *(c)* impact of foot on bag.

3. The kicking foot is positioned on the ground slightly back behind the body. It is aligned in the same direction it will be drawn back prior to the kick.

4. By lifting the lower leg, he strikes the bag with his kicking foot (figure 5.1*b* and *c*), compressing the bag while locking his ankle and leg.

Tips From the Coach

- This warm-up drill emphasizes technique, so not much power needs to be used.
- The kicker positions his plant foot exactly as if he were kicking a football.
- He relates the back of the bag with the back of the football and aligns accordingly.
- He performs this kick in a deliberate motion that emphasizes leg and ankle lock while demonstrating proper body positioning during a normal kick.
- He focuses on quality repetitions to ensure proper form.

Variations

A safety pad (cylinder shaped), the kind used to encase the base of a goalpost, is ideal for this drill if a partner isn't available to hold the bag.

Although this is a no-football kicking drill, if the kicker doesn't have a round bag, he can do this drill with a slightly deflated football to enable more emphasis on compression. The partner gets on both knees on the ground, with the laces of the football pressed against the knee and thigh of one leg as he firmly braces the football in anticipation of it being kicked. The kicker performs the exact same motion, striking the ball in a controlled and deliberate manner.

Line Drill

Objective

The placekicker works on coordinating the entire mechanics of the kicking motion to come together in one direction, focusing all energy down the line and directly toward the target. He'll be able to determine the proper movement of his body in relation to the initial target line of the kick.

Progression

1. The placekicker determines the point of placement on the yard line or sideline of a football field and marks off his steps for a normal kick.

2. He approaches the point of placement and simulates a kick using about 80 percent effort while focusing on proper mechanics. (Remember that this is a warm-up drill.)

3. As his kicking motion is nearly complete, the skip step of his plant foot moves forward and returns to the ground slightly out and away from the initial target line because of the impetus of the follow-through of the simulated kick.

4. He maintains balance on his plant foot and slowly and with control brings his kicking leg down, repositioning his kicking foot on the ground about a half to a full stride ahead of the plant foot.

5. At the end of the drill, the toes of the kicking foot point straight ahead on a line parallel to and slightly to the left of the initial target line (for a right-footed kicker).

Tips From the Coach

- At the end of his approach, the kicker positions his plant foot alongside the point of placement in a near parallel position to the left side of the yard line.

- As he simulates his kick, he visualizes his foot kicking through the football and, at the same time, focuses on the movement of his body downfield as it relates to the yard line.

- He should visualize a forward motion of his body, drifting slightly away from the line because of the body torque and follow-through of the kick.

- At the end of the drill, he should be facing downfield in the direction of the target line.

Variations

The kicker can do this drill by positioning alongside the yard line, visualizing the point of placement, and then going through the kicking motion down the yard line. As he finishes, he quickly repositions and repeats the drill as he continues across the field.

Placekicking Drills With a Football

These warm-up and technique drills help placekickers develop isolated segments of the kicking motion in a progression while using a football.

Lift Drill

Objective

The placekicker emphasizes follow-through and develops the placement of the plant foot and the impact position of the kicking foot—all while lifting the football to an exaggerated height.

Equipment

A sidekick portable football holder; a placement block, if appropriate; a football.

Progression

1. The placekicker sets his point of placement beginning 5 yards from the goalpost; he then positions his plant foot in its normal location and his kicking foot on the sweet spot of the football.
2. With the kicking foot already in contact with the ball, he begins lifting the football up and over the crossbar.
3. As he lifts his kicking leg, he brings the arm on his plant leg side from outside his body across his chest, keeping it parallel to the ground or moving slightly upward.
4. This entire movement should be done in a natural, smooth motion while maximizing follow-through with the kicking leg. This enables proper balance while controlling torque as he generates power up and toward his target.
5. Once he can do this drill from 5 yards from the crossbar of the goalpost, he gradually works his way toward the goalpost as close as he can.

Tips From the Coach

This drill is more suited for soccer-style kickers because a much wider area of the foot makes contact with the ball, enabling better stability when lifting the ball from the preset position.

Variations

Initially the kicker can perform this drill while keeping his plant foot in contact with the ground to emphasize follow-through. As he gets more proficient, he should add the skip step to emphasize follow-through and balance simultaneously.

No-Step Drill

Objective

The placekicker focuses on developing the proper impact point to optimize compression of the football. This drill develops leg speed as the kicking leg draws back behind the body in preparation for the kick. It also enhances correct follow-through as the kicker's body maintains proper position and balance toward the target.

This is a great drill for developing the kicker's kinesthetic sense when kicking the football. Kinesthetic sense is a sensory skill used by the kicker to understand where his body is in space during movement.

To improve this sense, he must first improve the kinesthetic awareness of his body's position during the kicking motion. He can accomplish this by performing the no-step drill with his eyes closed. This allows him to feel his body perform the kicking motion while also feeling the change in his body's center of gravity. He'll develop a tremendous sense of balance along with awareness of his body's movements in regard to specific joint positioning. When he closes his eyes, he'll need to rely on his sense of feel, improving his kinesthetic sense.

Once he begins improving his kinesthetic sense, he'll be able to feel how his body needs to be in position to perform successful kicks. More important, he'll be able to identify any challenges and, through self-coaching, quickly make any necessary adjustments.

Equipment

A sidekick portable football holder; a placement block, if appropriate; a football.

Progression

1. The placekicker, using a portable football holder, sets the football a short distance from the goalpost. He places his plant foot slightly back and wider than normal. This will allow him to compensate for the body lean normally created by momentum when stepping to the ball.

2. He draws his kicking leg back, positioning the foot directly behind him as high as he can, and at the same time extends the arm opposite his kicking leg out and away from his body (figure 5.2a). At this point, he's preset to perform the drill.

3. As he kicks through the football, he simultaneously brings the arm opposite his kicking leg across his chest parallel to the ground and upward in a sweeping motion.

4. As he makes impact, his hips square up in the general direction of the target (figure 5.2b).

5. As his foot goes through the ball and his kicking leg reaches maximum follow-through (figure 5.2c), his hips continue forward in a thrusting motion, transferring optimal power through the ball.

Tips From the Coach

- Because of the angle of approach and torque of the body, soccer-style kickers generally skip to an area ahead and outside from where the plant was made, with toes pointed slightly in the same direction as the skip. Straight-on kickers simply skip straight ahead toward the target.

- The kicker maintains proper body position with chest over knees throughout the kick. His eyes remain down and focused on the football as he kicks through it.

- There should be no jerking or crunching of the body downward with the head as the kicker kicks the football. His head should remain on a smooth, steady plane as he approaches the football and should remain in this same attitude throughout the kick.

Figure 5.2 No-step drill: *(a)* preset position; *(b)* impact with the ball; *(c)* follow-through.

- The higher the kicker can draw his leg back, the more he can enhance the whipping effect and leg speed of the kick. It's not how strong his leg is that determines power but how fast it's moving when the kicking foot contacts the ball.

Variations

The kicker can simulate kicking extra points or field goals, can kick down a yard line across the field, or can aim at an upright while kicking from the endline. Whatever the case, he needs to focus toward a very specific target line.

As energy is transferred during the kick, the kicker can compensate for his body's forward movement by allowing the plant foot to lift very slightly off the ground and skip forward and out in the direction of his leg swing.

One-Step Drill

Objective

This drill emphasizes and develops proper positioning of the plant foot in order for the place-kicker to make optimal impact with the football. Once the plant step is made, he duplicates the exact techniques used to perform the no-step drill.

Equipment

A sidekick portable football holder; a placement block, if appropriate; a football.

Progression

1. The placekicker positions at the point of placement (the tee or the spot the ball will be held) and locates his target zone. From this position he marks his steps by taking two full comfortable strides back, taking the first step with his kicking foot.

2. At the completion of the second step, he should be facing the target with feet alongside each other. The kicking foot should be in direct line with the football and the precise target.

3. He takes one comfortable and controlled lateral step to the side opposite of the kicking leg then slightly pivots toward the point of placement.

4. He places his kicking foot forward with toes pointed toward the football and the toes of his nonkicking foot pointed at the spot where his plant foot will be placed. In doing this, he simulates the first step (drive step) that he would normally take as he approaches the football.

5. He is aligned in the exact position he would be in just prior to the last step (the plant step) he would take before kicking the ball. He leans forward, chest over knees, to get in preset position (figure 5.3).

6. Focusing on the point of placement, he takes a deliberate step to place his plant foot in the exact alignment needed for optimal body position when making contact with the football.

7. He now executes the same techniques as described for the no-step drill. He draws his kicking leg back, extends his arm, and kicks through the football, reaching maximum follow-through and skipping forward.

Figure 5.3 Preset position for the one-step drill.

Tips From the Coach
To align for this drill, the kicker shortens his depth and width to get in the best position for the plant step. Instead of his normal three-steps-back-and-two-steps-over alignment, he'll need to use two steps back and one step over. This puts him in the most precise distance from the point of placement, allowing him to best simulate the last step of his approach.

Variations
Same as for the no-step drill (see page 86).

Trajectory Drill

Objective

This drill ensures the trajectory path of the football clears the oncoming rush during extra points and field goals. This is done by simulating conditions on the field so the placekicker naturally develops elevation on the flight of the ball.

Equipment

A kicking zone trajectory pad (a self-coaching tool that guides extra point and field goal kicks to the height necessary to clear the oncoming rush); a sidekick portable football holder; a placement block, if permitted; a football.

Progression

1. The placekicker determines the point of placement on the football field for an extra point, or he can prepare to kick a short field goal anywhere on or between the hashmarks.

2. Once he determines the point of placement, he uses the sidekick holder to position the football in preparation for the kick.

3. Once the football is in position, he places a kicking zone trajectory pad directly in front of the football, making sure the football and kicking zone are directly aligned with the target.

4. Once the kicking zone is in place, he pulls the attached measuring strap from underneath and extends it all the way toward the point of placement. This strap accurately determines the proper distance the kicking zone pad needs to be from the football. This distance reflects the minimum height the football needs to clear the top of the pad, thus emphasizing the proper trajectory of the kick.

5. Once the measuring strap is extended, he ensures the very end of the strap is on the ground in front of the football, directly below its widest segment. If the strap doesn't reach, he needs to pull it, sliding the kicking zone pad until it reaches. He might need to move the kicking zone the opposite way if it's too close.

6. He marks off his steps and sets his alignment for a normal kick.

7. He kicks the ball with the goal of clearing the top of the pad (figure 5.4). When he clears the top of the pad, he's kicking the ball at the proper elevation to clear the oncoming rush.

Tips From the Coach

On the high school and college levels, the general point of placement for an extra point or field goal is 7 yards from the line of scrimmage. On the professional level, the distance from the line of scrimmage generally is 8 yards. (The extra yard enables the kick to be considerably higher when traveling over rushers.) When the ball's snapped, the line blockers are to minimize any type of penetration. Defenders will jump as high as they can to try to block the kick, so a minimum height to practice getting the ball above the blockers is 10 feet.

Figure 5.4 Football clears the kicking zone trajectory pad during the trajectory drill.

Variations

Position the kicking zone trajectory pad in the path of any drill to encourage the kicker to work on getting the proper trajectory on every kick. The goal is to practice until this becomes second nature. All kicks, regardless of distance, should be performed with a consistent angle of trajectory.

Line Kicks

Objective

The placekicker focuses his entire kicking motion down a precise target line. By guiding the entire mechanics of the kicking motion precisely in one direction, the kicker maximizes the transfer of energy through the football, ensuring accuracy and optimal power.

Equipment

A sidekick portable football holder; a placement block, if appropriate; a football.

Progression

1. The placekicker positions the football on a sideline or yard line in preparation to kick to a spot (or a partner) down the line.
2. When he approaches the football, the kicker has the advantage of using the yard line as a guide and reference to direct him toward the target.
3. As he plants his foot in preparation for the kick, his eyes remain focused on the ball. He uses his peripheral vision to see the line as a reference, positioning his foot alongside the ball and in a position essentially parallel to the line.
4. At the moment the kicking foot makes impact and the football begins compressing, the entire body—including the plant foot, hips, and leg swing—comes together to maximize the transfer of energy through the football directly down the line and toward the target.
5. As he kicks through the football, the kicker focuses on the movement of his body downfield in relation to the yard line. In doing this, he'll see the forward motion of his body as it slightly drifts away from the line caused by the body torque and follow-through of the kick.
6. When he finishes the drill, he's facing downfield in the direction of the target line.

Tips From the Coach

- The kicker's plant foot should land alongside the football in a position essentially parallel to the line.
- At the moment the football is kicked and compressed, the entire mechanics of the kick should coordinate with the direction of the plant foot, which has transitioned to a firm and flat position, and come together to focus all energy directly down the line and toward the target.
- By using the line as a guide, the kicker can easily tell if he's positioned properly after every kick.
- When the kicker focuses his entire kicking motion toward a target, he ensures accuracy and maximum power.

Variations

This is a great drill for the kicker to use to perform kick passes. Kick passes are done with a fellow kicker, giving both kickers an opportunity to use the same line to kick back and forth to each other. The kickers start out at a shorter distance and gradually adjust the depth as they warm up. Distance depends on ability, but 15 to 20 yards is a good starting point. This drill creates high-quality reps because of the kickers' focus on kicking accurately to each other.

Side Angle Drill

Objective

The placekicker's overall accuracy improves by dramatically increasing the angle of the kick and narrowing the target zone.

Equipment

A sidekick portable football holder; a placement block, if appropriate; a football.

Progression

1. The placekicker, using a sidekick portable football holder, places the football at the point where the 5-yard line and the sideline intersect (figure 5.5). This dramatic increase of angle causes the uprights of the goalpost to seem narrower, creating the need for the kicker to narrow his focus.

2. The kicker aligns and kicks the football as if it were an extra point or field goal. The narrower angle to the goalposts makes the kick more challenging, enhancing focus and accuracy.

3. The more the kicker improves, the closer he needs to move toward the goal line and beyond.

Tips From the Coach

- As the kicker increases the angle, the uprights seem to get closer and closer together, which conditions the kicker to aim more precisely at his target, enhancing his confidence when he's kicking between the hashmarks and the target is much wider.

- The increased angle of the kick creates more of a vertical target line. This encourages the kicker to place more emphasis on the follow-through, ensuring the kicking motion is moving precisely toward the target.

Variations

The placekicker performs this drill from both sides of the field to simulate field goals from either hashmark. This allows him to determine the true flight path of the football and promotes proper rotation. It also reinforces the idea that all kicks are performed in basically the same way.

Figure 5.5 The ball is on the 5-yard line and sideline during the side angle drill. Note the narrower angle to the uprights.

Skip Step

Objective

The placekicker works on the transfer of energy through the football by naturally developing the skip step. This maximizes power and control by allowing the body to maintain optimal balance as it becomes momentarily airborne and returns to the ground.

Equipment

A sidekick portable football holder; a placement block, if appropriate; a football.

Progression

1. The placekicker aligns and performs a normal kick, focusing on the natural lift of his plant foot off the ground, which is created by the forward motion and follow-through.

2. He then performs an identical kick but focuses on his body position and the direction of the leg swing.

3. Next he focuses on how and where the skip step returns to the ground. It should reposition on the ground in the direction determined by the swing of the kicking leg, with the toes of the plant foot pointed in the same direction that the skip traveled, which is slightly outward in relation to the target line.

4. Once he becomes proficient in each of these phases, he performs the same kick while putting it all together and accomplishing each phase systematically.

Tips From the Coach

- The placekicker focuses on each position of the plant—the liftoff, direction, repositioning to the ground. This helps remind him not to become a spectator and prematurely follow the flight of the football. Once he's proficient with the skip step and finishes in complete control of his body, then he can follow the direction of the football and reference his body position to determine if he's using proper mechanics.

- Although the skip step drill can be done without a football, it's best to use a ball because the kicker needs to focus on and feel this particular movement through actual contact with the ball.

Variations

The skip step drill can be combined with the one-step drill (see page 88). Because the focus of the one-step drill is the plant step, it's a natural progression for the placekicker to incorporate the skip step drill.

Plant Foot Balance

Objective

The placekicker strives to maintain balance and body control at the completion of the skip step, enhancing optimal power and accuracy throughout the kicking motion.

Equipment

A sidekick portable football holder; a placement block, if appropriate; a football.

Progression

1. The placekicker aligns in position to perform a normal kick with the intent to focus entirely on his mechanics as relating to the finish of his kicking motion.

2. After he makes contact with the football, follows through toward his target, and performs his skip step, he returns to the ground at the end of the skip step and maintains balance entirely on his plant leg.

3. For this drill to be effective, he must hold this balanced position on the plant leg while slowly bringing the foot of his kicking leg down to about knee level of his plant leg.

4. After counting "one-thousand-one, one-thousand-two," he slowly brings his kicking leg all the way down to the ground out in front of his body in the general direction of his target. The kicking leg should be out in front on the ground, with the inside edge of the kicking foot aligned near or with the inside edge of the plant foot. The kicking leg should not be directly in front of or on the other side of the plant foot.

Tips From the Coach

- This drill focuses on the postkick position, at which all the mechanics performed by the placekicker come together to accomplish the goal of kicking the football optimally.

- If the kicker is balanced and in complete control of his body during the finish of his kick, this shows that his focus is on his body mechanics to perform the kick successfully. If he's out of balance at the completion of the kick, his body needs to compensate in some way for being out of balance, so the kick won't be optimal. For instance, if he's out of control with too much forward momentum at the end of his kick, his kicking leg will need to come down very quickly for him to regain balance. This minimizes his follow-through, which affects his leg speed, which is generally enhanced by optimal follow-through.

Variations

This is a great drill for performing the postkick check (see page 27). The placekicker can determine the flight path of the football by viewing his mechanics and identifying his body position on completion of the kicking motion.

Upright Drill

Objective

The placekicker naturally develops accuracy, height, and vertical rotation on the football as he kicks toward a very narrow and vertical target.

Equipment

A sidekick portable football holder; a placement block, if appropriate; a football.

Progression

1. The placekicker positions the football at the point where the endline (the back line of the endzone) and the sideline intersect. This is the exact point where the uprights are positioned on the football field. If the field has no markings, the kicker needs to be in the general area of the sideline and the endline of the football field.

2. From this side point of view, he looks at the uprights and aligns himself until he sees both uprights coming together to form one (figure 5.6). Once he sees only one upright (because the other is blocked), he's in proper alignment to perform the drill correctly.

3. He marks off his steps and tries to hit the upright or kick directly over it.

Figure 5.6 In the upright drill, the placekicker stands in such a way that there appears to be only one upright.

Tips From the Coach

It's best to perform this drill from the endline at the back of the endzone. The kicker shouldn't practice this drill on a normal playing field because it might encourage him to perform the kick incorrectly by aiming at an upright. Remember that the kicker is drilling to create good habits that will translate to game-day performances. At no time during a game will a kicker be on the playing field attempting to hit an upright. Every time he kicks on the playing field, he kicks toward a specific target that allows him to narrow his focus to make a successful kick through the uprights.

Variations

The more the kicker improves the height of his kicks, the closer he needs to move toward the upright. By kicking toward this very narrow and vertical target, the kicker will enhance the vertical rotation on the football and his follow-through. More importantly, he will challenge his accuracy by aiming at such a precise target.

Game-Ready Placekicking Drills

These game-ready kicking drills simulate gamelike situations and prepare the placekicker mentally and physically to perform successfully in a game. The kicker will need a sidekick portable football holder and a placement block (if allowed) for these drills.

Spot Drill

Objective

This drill simulates gamelike situations in which kicking angles and distances might be dramatically different with every kick.

Equipment

A sidekick portable football holder; a placement block, if appropriate; a football.

Progression

1. The placekicker scatters footballs across the field from hashmark to hashmark to simulate kicks that might be required in actual games.

2. The idea is for the kicker to kick the football and then move to the football that's the farthest away. For instance, if the first football kicked is on the right hashmark at the 40-yard line, the next kick needs to be made from nearer the goal line on the left hashmark. Each succeeding kick should be executed from farther away than the previous kick.

3. This is a great way for kickers to work on various angles and distances while kicking.

4. The kicker should incorporate this drill into his routine every time he goes out to practice.

Tips From the Coach

This is a great drill to use as the kicker develops his kicking mechanics. When he becomes more proficient and confident, he is ready for more gamelike situations with the snapper, holder, and entire kicking team.

Variations

The zigzag drill is a more methodical way to work on various angles and distances and is similar to placekicker assessment at the professional level. The kicker begins the drill by positioning the football on the left hashmark at the 10-yard line. After one to three kicks, he moves back 5 yards and to the opposite hashmark and repeats this sequence, moving back 5 yards each time and continuing as far as he can (figure 5.7). Once at his maximum range, he begins to work forward from the opposite hashes as he returns to his starting distance. The placekicker should focus on short- and intermediate-range kicks because long-range kicks are not as common in games.

The around-the-world drill begins with an emphasis on shorter field goals and gradually progresses to longer field goals. Once the kicker reaches the longest kick, he begins to work back down to shorter field goals. He places 10 or more footballs up and down both hashmarks, ranging from the 5-yard line back to the 40-yard line, depending on his range (figure 5.8). He starts by kicking the shortest kick from one hashmark, and then works his way back to the longest. Once he kicks the longest from one hashmark, he proceeds to the next hashmark and kicks the longest kick from that hashmark. He gradually works his way down the hashmarks until he kicks the shortest distance.

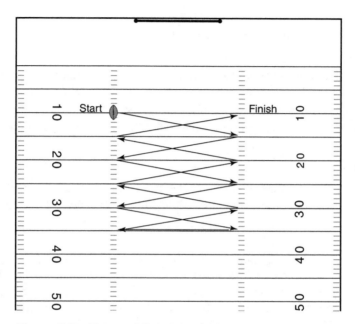

Figure 5.7   Zigzag drill.

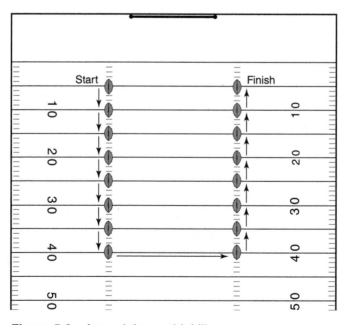

Figure 5.8   Around-the-world drill.

Bad Hold and Mishandled Snap

Objective

The placekicker works on dealing with unforeseen situations such as bad holds or mishandled snaps.

Equipment

A sidekick portable football holder; a placement block, if appropriate; a football.

Progression

1. The placekicker sets the football in various positions that simulate a bad hold, such as angled too far back, angled too far forward, or angled too far to one side.

2. He positions the football with the laces facing him. This makes it difficult for him to strike and compress the football consistently, but he can still perform the kick successfully.

Tips From the Coach

Proper preparation begins during practice. The best way to handle a challenging situation is to practice it. Practice is the most opportune time to develop and perform game-day strategies.

Variations

The placekicker can practice with a coach or a teammate (but not the actual holder or snapper) to simulate a variety of bad snaps and bad holds. This increases the placekicker's confidence as he learns to adjust his approach with hesitation steps, if needed. Through repetition, he develops a repertoire of natural adjustments. The normal holder and snapper should not participate in this drill because it might introduce bad habits.

Last-Second Kick

Objective

This drill prepares the kicker to perform last-second, game-winning kicks when no time-outs are left.

Equipment

A sidekick portable football holder; a placement block, if appropriate; a football; a stopwatch.

Progression

1. A portable football holder holds the ball. The placekicker practices running from the sideline to a predetermined point of placement, getting quickly aligned, and performing the kick.

2. Once he feels comfortable, he does the same drill with an actual snapper and holder.

3. As he becomes more proficient, he repeats the drill while being timed by a coach. He should complete the entire process in 25 seconds or less.

4. Once he can do the drill in 25 seconds or less, he executes it as if he has no time to mark off his steps, forcing him to quickly position and get set in a manner that feels most natural for him to execute the kick.

Tips From the Coach

- This is another type of kick that's needed when it's least expected. It could come right before the half or at the end of a game.

- The placekicker must be in his stance and completely set before the center snaps the football.

- The kicker always needs to keep his head in the game and know what's going on. He needs to simulate being on the sideline in his designated area during a game or near the yard line where the football will be spotted for the kick. This gives him the straightest approach path to quickly get set up.

- Practicing a few of these kicks during a weekly routine can make a big difference in the kicker's total preparation. Knowing he has practiced last-second kicks will give him a confidence boost.

Variations

To promote performing these kicks most effectively, the kicker should be timed frequently and work with his complete kicking unit.

Range Finder

Objective
The placekicker works on determining his field goal range when performing at his peak.

Equipment
A sidekick portable football holder (if the snapper and holder aren't available); a placement block, if appropriate; a football.

Progression
1. The placekicker warms up by kicking footballs until he's performing at his best. Warm-up distances vary by individual. Usually kickers start on the 20-yard line or closer when warming up. Many begin at extra-point range (10-yard line).
2. He then works his way back, though not too quickly, kicking from longer distances.
3. As he moves back, he must remain disciplined and continue to kick with the exact same motion as he would use for an extra point or a shorter field goal.
4. If he can continue to focus on the exact same kicking motion and remain true to his abilities, he'll gradually see his kicks getting closer to the back of the crossbar as he continues to back up.
5. When he reaches the point from which his kicks barely make it over the crossbar or barely come up short, he has reached his optimal field goal range.

Tips From the Coach
- To perform this drill correctly, the placekicker must kick the way he feels is optimal—the same way he would kick extra points or shorter field goals.
- The kicker must move back gradually, not too quickly. This gives him time to focus on his accuracy and the flight of the football.
- It's best for the kicker to perform this drill from both ends of the field, especially if there is any wind. He can determine his exact range with a head- or tailwind.

Variations
Initially the placekicker should determine his maximal field goal range in favorable weather and field conditions. Then he can experiment and determine his range when conditions change. Then when game day arrives and he's determining his range during pregame warm-up, he'll already be confident in his expectations.

Snap to Kick

Objective

The placekicker develops optimal timing while working with the snapper and the holder as a unit or with the entire team.

Equipment

A placement block, if appropriate; a football.

Progression

1. Timing the snap to the kick should begin immediately after the placekicker, snapper, and holder warm up.
2. The kicker should be timed frequently, not only to determine how quickly he gets the ball away but also to help him develop proper rhythm and improve consistency.
3. The total time from the snap to the kick should be 1.3 to 1.4 seconds for high school players and 1.25 to 1.3 seconds for college and professional players.

Tips From the Coach

- The best way to develop consistent timing is to have the snapper, holder, and placekicker work together as much as possible. This is critical for determining optimal timing as well as developing tempo with the kicking unit.
- Make time to chart snap-to-kick times. Being timed will make the snapper, holder, and placekicker focus better.

Variations

These repetitions should include kicking situations that might arise in a game. To improve consistency and accountability, everything should be timed.

Varying Conditions

Objective

The placekicker works on being prepared to kick in all directions and from all positions on the field, regardless of field or weather conditions.

Equipment

A sidekick portable football holder (if snapper and holder aren't available); a placement block, if appropriate; a football.

Progression

1. The kicker warms up in a field location that's favorable for warm-up drills (usually this is the 20-yard line or closer).

2. Once he's warmed up, he executes kicks from the most favorable and least favorable positions on the field. If possible, he should kick with and against the wind. He also seeks areas of the field where footing might be questionable. He kicks from any potential position on the field, preparing as well as he can.

3. It's best to kick from the most favorable position initially and progress to the least favorable. He sets up and goes through the entire kicking motion.

Tips From the Coach

- The placekicker needs to practice kicking in all directions and from multiple positions on the field.

- The more proficient he becomes in dealing with adverse weather, especially wind, the more confident he'll become when inclement weather occurs in a game.

- He needs to be the one to come through in the clutch when all odds seem to be against him.

Variations

The placekicker performs in varying conditions with the entire kicking team. This will help everyone involved understand the effects of adverse conditions and increase their confidence when facing these challenges.

II

The Punting Game

6

Punting Fundamentals

Every time the punter prepares to punt the football, during practice or in a game, he should have a target area in mind and a purpose for punting to that location. There is much more to punting than how far the football travels. Punting is all about placement. For the punter to be most effective, he must first communicate his objectives to his punt-coverage team and then carry out these objectives by being precise in where he punts the football.

As the punter jogs onto the football field, he should already know the game situation and the opponent's tendencies so he can quickly determine exactly where he wants to punt the ball. By combining precision placement with maximum hang time and optimal distance, he can perform at his optimal level, allowing his coverage team to cover anywhere on the football field.

Depth and Alignment

College and professional punters set up at a depth of 15 yards from the line of scrimmage. High school punters usually set up 12 or 13 yards back. Exact depth should be determined by the coach and might vary with the ability of the snapper. Every punter should place his punting foot in a direct line with the ball or in a line that splits the snapper's crotch (figure 6.1).

Although the distance of the punter behind the snapper varies depending on skill level, the required snap time remains the same. As the snapper becomes more proficient as he advances to the next level of play, he should offset the added distance by increasing his snap speed to maintain the overall snap time.

Figure 6.1 Punter setup behind the line of scrimmage with punting foot in line with the ball.

Every play in the kicking game except the kickoff starts with the snapper. No matter the level of play, the snap time needs to be near 0.8 seconds or slightly faster. This is the optimal time for both speed and accuracy.

Stance and Body Position

The punter stands in a comfortable, relaxed, and balanced position that enables him to quickly adjust to and meet the snapped football (figure 6.2). His position allows him to move left, right, up, or down quickly and effectively, if necessary.

His feet are slightly less than shoulder-width apart, approximately under the armpits, with the toes of the nonpunting foot about 6 inches ahead of the toes of the punting foot. This is a toe-to-instep position. The punter may choose to position his feet almost parallel when his steps and approach need to be more abbreviated in regard to space and time, such as when he's punting from deep in his own end zone. This adjustment allows him to take quicker steps in a minimal distance, especially if there is an intense rush on.

Shoulders and hips are square (parallel) to the line of scrimmage with body weight evenly distributed on both feet. His body is in a vertical position with hips and shoulders perpendicular to the ground. This same perpendicular body position is needed not only during the initial stance but throughout the approach, the punt of the football, and the follow-through.

Knees are slightly flexed so the punter can move efficiently in any direction. His trunk is bent slightly forward at the waist to abet the forward motion. Leaning very slightly forward, chest over toes, puts him in the most efficient position to meet the football after the snap, again minimizing wasted motion. Pre-positioning the body enhances the effectiveness of the forward motion required for the punt.

His arms hang relaxed at his sides, nearly motionless. This prevents tension in the shoulders and arms, which can happen if the arms are extended

Figure 6.2 Punter ready for the snap: *(a)* front view; *(b)* side view.

forward and out from the body. He can loosen up even more by moving his fingers quickly as his arms hang relaxed and perpendicular to the ground.

His eyes are focused on the ball in strict concentration, especially as the snapper places his hands on the football in preparation for the snap. Once the snapper's hands are on the football, the punter anticipates the snap and is ready to execute.

Stay Loose

The punter keeps his arms relaxed and down by his sides. Some believe he should extend his arms to let the snapper know he's ready to receive the snap and to create a target for the football. This is not the case. The moment the snapper places his hands on the football, the punter should be ready to receive the snap. The snapper is trained to deliver the snap in the region of the punter's hip and thigh. Thus the snapper doesn't need the punter to create a target for him. A punter who stands with his arms extended tends to become more tense in the shoulders and arms and thus might not catch the football effectively. A receiver doesn't run downfield with his arms outstretched in anticipation of catching a pass, so why should a punter outstretch his arms to catch a snap?

Approach

The punter's approach begins the moment the center snaps the football and ends when the foot and ball make contact. In less than 2.1 seconds, the punter must execute all the components of the approach in order to successfully punt the football. The components of the punter's approach include the following:

- Stepping pattern (two and a half or two steps)
- Leaning to meet the snap
- Receiving the snap
- Positioning the hands and gripping the ball
- Aligning the football
- Releasing the football
- Swinging the leg
- Making contact with the football
- Following through

By following these principles, including moving to meet the snap with a two-and-a-half-step approach, coauthor Ray Guy was able to maximize his leg speed and power on every punt and get away 619 punts without ever having one blocked or returned for a touchdown.

Stepping Pattern

The two-step and two-and-a-half-step approaches are by far the most popular stepping patterns for punters. Each begins as the punter leans to meet the snap.

Although the two-and-a-half-step approach is the most common, the two-step approach can be just as effective. Through proper training and repetition, the punter naturally develops the stepping pattern that's best for him. Once the punter develops his foundational approach, he can build on it until he can accomplish the goals set by his team.

The punter can use either a two-step or a two-and-a-half-step approach, provided he punts the football a reasonable distance and on time. After taking the proper steps, he should be no more than 4 yards (ideally about 3 ½ yards) from his starting point. Variations within these two stepping patterns can be used when faced with adverse conditions, an intense rush, or the need to punt out of the end zone. These situations are discussed in chapter 7.

Two-Step Approach

The two-step approach begins when the punter receives the snap. The two-step is identical to the two-and-a-half-step approach except it doesn't have the short, quick half-step. The first step is a full directional step with the punting foot, and the second step is a longer plant step with the nonpunting foot. (Both the directional step and the plant step will be discussed in more detail in the section on the two-and-a-half-step approach.)

Many believe the two-step approach is better than the two-and-a-half-step approach because the punter needs less time to get the punt off. This is not necessarily true. Although the two-step approach eliminates the quick half-step, the distance traveled by the punter is about the same. The half-step included in the two-and-a-half-step approach is a natural movement by the punter that enhances the quickness of the subsequent steps.

The key to both approaches is the length and quickness of the steps, not the number of steps. A properly trained punter executes the two-and-a-half-step approach over the same distance and in the same amount of time as a punter who uses a two-step approach. The punter using the two-and-a-half-step approach simply shortens his steps. He might need to do this if punting out of his own end zone because the depth of the punter from the line of scrimmage is less than ideal.

A true two-step punter, one who takes the first step with his punting foot, tends to take this first directional step with a more deliberate motion because the step comes directly from the stance. The lack of a half-step means the punter won't be able to make as smooth a transition from stance to approach. This is why the two-and-a-half-step approach can be just as effective as the two-step approach—the punter makes up the difference in timing through a more natural, fluid motion that's enhanced by the initial half-step.

Two-and-a-Half-Step Approach

The two-and-a-half-step approach can begin as the punter moves to meet the snap or at the moment the punter catches the football. The punter might want to take the initial short, quick half-step as he catches the football, or he might feel more comfortable taking the initial quick half-step the moment after he receives the football. His preferred approach will develop naturally through timing and repetition.

The initial step is a short and quick half-step with the nonpunting foot (figure 6.3*a*). (Some punters use an even shorter jab step.) The half-step begins the approach toward the general target area, enhancing the steps that follow.

Figure 6.3 Two-and-a-half-step approach: *(a)* half-step; *(b)* directional step; *(c)* plant step; *(d)* follow-through; *(e)* postpunt check.

The half-step naturally progresses from the punter's body lean. Some punters take the half-step as they catch the snap, and some take it the moment after. The punter's body, from the ankles up, leans to meet the football. The punter doesn't bend at the waist. His back remains flat.

Once forward motion is initiated and the body lean is established, the punter's upper body remains motionless during the approach. The upper body maintains a perpendicular orientation to the ground throughout the entire approach and the punting motion. His head is slightly down because of the forward body lean.

The moment the punter begins his lean, his arms extend out to receive the snap, ideally in the hip and thigh area. His eyes watch the football all the way into his hands. The moment he catches the football, he begins to mold it in preparation for alignment with the target, his arms still outstretched.

The two steps that follow the quick half-step are the directional step toward the target with the punting foot and the plant step with the non-punting foot, which stabilizes the body during the punt. The full directional step with the punting foot (figure 6.3b) is positioned precisely in the same line as the football, near the right edge of the center line of the body, and in direct alignment with the target. This step enhances the momentum of the approach as the punter prepares for the final plant step.

During the directional step, the punter's body continues its forward lean, and the back remains flat. The upper body is motionless. Hips and shoulders are square and directly face the target. Arms are extended. He quickly aligns the ball with the target and elevates it near the base of the rib cage. This level plane position, often called "setting it on the table," represents proper alignment.

As body motion continues forward, the weight shifts to and directly over the directional step on the ground. The punter slowly opens the arm on the guide hand side from the shoulder, similar to opening a gate, and releases the guide hand from the side of the football. Only the drop hand now holds the ball. The arm on the guide hand side remains extended and gradually moves out and up, away from the football, toward a point out from the shoulder opposite the punting leg in preparation for the release of the ball. The guide hand release needs to be so smooth that the football remains motionless on its level plane as it's held forward by the drop hand.

The head remains down slightly (caused by the forward body lean). Eyes stay focused on the football to ensure proper alignment. The head stays on the same plane and level as body motion continues forward.

The final step is the extended plant step with the nonpunting foot (figure 6.3c). This step is longer than the directional step. The foot reaches out and lands heel first with toes up ahead of the punter as his body transitions from a forward lean to a backward lean. This transition shifts his forward momentum upward as he prepares to punt the ball.

The guide hand remains extended and even with the shoulder, parallel to the ground.

As the punter's body transitions from a forward lean to a backward lean, the drop hand smoothly releases the football at the very moment the toes of the plant foot align slightly ahead of the punter's body. The plant foot continues forward, aligning directly ahead of the knee, positioning on the ground heel first. The drop hand remains extended as it moves down and out away from the body. The head remains slightly down and on the same level plane, with eyes focused on the football, as body motion continues forward. The punter follows through (figure 6.3d) and checks his punt (figure 6.3e).

Leaning to Meet the Snap

At the moment the football is snapped, the punter, with eyes focused on the football, allows his entire body to lean forward, keeping his back flat, as he anticipates receiving the snap. This lean will develop naturally through repetition and timing. Its purpose is to initiate the need for the punter's first step and to enhance the timeliness of the approach and the get-off.

When the punter leans to meet the football, he places his body in position for a step to be needed or taken as he catches the football. Thus, the moment the football arrives and touches his hands, the punter has shifted his body weight ahead, and is already into his forward motion.

At this point, the trained punter gains a tremendous advantage by executing his mechanics in the most effective and efficient way. By simply leaning to meet the football, the punter maximizes the use of his time, allowing his performance to be more fluid throughout the punting motion. The lean also enables him to quickly and smoothly build forward momentum, giving him a split-second edge over the rushers. More important, he develops a natural rhythm that produces confidence, consistency, and success.

Receiving the Snap

Once the punter is in his stance and completely relaxed, he focuses entirely on the football. He checks the center's hands on the ball, waits for the up back's ready call, and then totally blocks out the crowd noise and any distractions out front. His top priority is to catch the snap and get the punt off effectively.

The snapper delivers the football to the hip and thigh area of the punter's punting leg. This is the ideal location for the punter to receive the snap because it allows the punter to catch the football in a position that's most natural for his hands as he leans to meet the football. This snap placement enhances the transition from reception to alignment because it helps the punter maintain his slight body lean as he continues his forward motion to punt the football.

The punter looks the football into his hands. He catches the ball in front of his body with arms outstretched and hands open (figure 6.4). He doesn't want to bring the football into his body and then extend it out for the punt. This extra movement increases handling time and risks a block.

Figure 6.4 Catching the football in front of the body with arms outstretched and hands open while leaning to meet the snap.

Positioning the Hands and Gripping the Ball

As soon as the punter catches the football and begins his initial steps, he adjusts the football quickly and molds it with his hands. With his fingers spread, he quickly and naturally positions the football where the laces can be viewed on the top half of the football. This ensures that he can make contact with the bottom-center area of the football opposite the laces, which is more pliable, thus allowing more compression when the football impacts the punting foot.

Through proper training and repetition, the punter can naturally develop the skill of positioning the laces of the football consistently on top to the point at which doing so becomes a habit.

Although the punter can effectively punt the football on the laces, it's believed the extra tightness and leather lacing doesn't allow for optimal ball compression. Having the laces on top enhances the impact point and provides a natural reference for the punter as he aligns and positions the football during his approach and drop.

There are three basic ways to grip the football with the control, or release, hand (the hand on the side of the punting leg): hand underneath, hand on top, or hand on the side (figure 6.5).

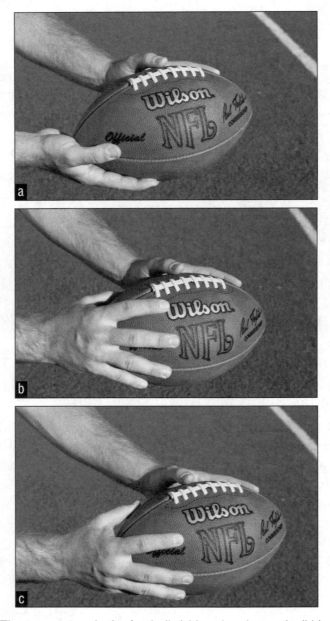

Figure 6.5   Three ways to grip the football: *(a)* hand underneath; *(b)* hand on top; *(c)* hand on the side.

Whichever position the punter chooses, he must develop a soft touch with his fingers. He must learn to hold the football with very light pressure, ensuring a smooth and consistent release and drop.

The recommended grip is the hand-on-the-side grip. The hand is positioned with the fingers slightly spread as if the punter is preparing to greet someone by shaking hands. This is the most natural way for him to hold the football for several reasons. For instance, when a person stands with his arms relaxed and down to the sides, the palms of both hands naturally face inward. This is the same position when greeting someone to shake hands. The hand-on-the-side grip also places the fingers in the most natural position to grip the football. When the punter opens his drop hand to grip the back third of the football, his fingers naturally spread open to fit ideally from the end point of the football all the way up to the wider segment. The hand and fingers conform to the football in a conelike manner in which the fingertips spread wide to accommodate the wider circular area toward the middle of the football and then the narrow effect as the football tapers to a point at the bottom. The fingers need to remain spread with the middle finger on the outside seam of the football (laces up).

The guide, or cradle, hand is the hand opposite the punting leg. The punter places this hand toward the front half of the football on the opposite side. This hand provides support for the release hand until it's removed from the side just before the football drop.

It's extremely important for the punter to keep some air between the football and the palms of his hands. This helps prevent palming of the football and allows the fingers and fingertips to provide primary support. A punter who palms the football tends to grip the ball too tight. This won't prevent the fingertips from developing a soft touch, but the release of the football during the drop won't be as smooth or consistent.

Aligning the Football

One of the most important aspects of the approach is based on the punter's alignment of the football. This teaching principle is one of the most overlooked when coaching punters. Often the punter's wayward steps during the approach are mistakenly assumed to be caused by the punter needing to step more toward his target. Actually, the punter needs to correctly align the football with the target first, and then his steps should follow directly toward the football. Proper alignment of the football determines the punter's exact stepping approach and is the key to directing his entire punting motion toward his target.

By positioning the center mass of the football in a direct line with the target, the punter prepares for a direct step approach toward his target.

In other words, if the football is placed directly on the correct target line, the punter will step exactly where the football is, which is directly on the correct target line.

When the punter does step outside his target line, his steps aren't necessarily incorrect; rather, his placement of the football is incorrect. The alignment of the football determines the direction of the punter's steps during the approach. A punter who has improperly positioned the football to the outside of the correct target line will have to cross over with his leg swing, bringing the punting leg across his body, because his steps will follow the football. When the punter does make contact with the football, he will have stepped outside the target line and must pull his leg across his body to get the football back on target.

The punter is simply trying to punt the football. Wherever he aligns the football, he'll step directly to that area during his approach. You'll not see a successful punter's stepping approach head toward an area where the football is not positioned.

There are two main reasons why punters step outside their target line during the approach:

1. When he receives the snap, the punter tends to position the football directly ahead of the punting foot based on the alignment of the stance. What he really needs to do is anticipate the placement of his directional step (his punting foot) and align the football where the directional step will be placed during the approach, which is more toward the center line of the punter's body.

2. Sometimes angling the football, turning the nose inside, is a psychological challenge for the punter. Based on the proper alignment of the football, he's trying to make contact with an object that's angled to the left (for a right-footed punter), while he's supposed to step straight ahead at a target, which is also straight ahead. This is like driving a car straight ahead while the hood of the car is angled to the left. Though it can be done, it messes with the mind a little and takes some getting used to.

Correct football alignment is the key. Correct alignment guides the punter down a precise path, improving get-off times and maximizing the result of the punt. Proper alignment also guides the forward motion of the body in a direct line, ensuring maximum power. This focuses the energy of the body in a precise direction, enabling optimal hang time, distance, and control of the punted football.

Before aligning the football for the approach, the punter needs to understand that as he leaves his stance, in which his feet are underneath his armpits, his feet naturally draw closer together to better support the body's center of gravity as he steps forward. (When we walk or stride, our feet are much closer together than in a stationary stance, which requires a wider base.) This means the punter needs to align the football to the right of the very center of his body, just inside his right breast, in anticipation of his feet coming closer together during the approach. By doing this, he can better align the football directly to his target.

Throughout the punting motion, the punter keeps his hips and shoulders facing directly toward his target and perpendicular to the ground. This straightness of form enhances the punting motion by directing all the body's energy toward a particular target.

Proper football alignment determines the punter's exact stepping approach and is the key to directing his entire punting motion toward his target. Proper alignment is also the key to determining how the football is dropped and is ultimately a guide of how the football will maintain the same position as it contacts the punting foot. The alignment of the football remains the same during the initial approach, the drop, and the contact with the punting foot.

The blueprint for aligning the football during the approach is designed to produce a drop that places the football in the most precise position, enabling the punter to obtain maximum compression and a spiral. This aerodynamic rotation of the football creates optimal control as well as accuracy, hang time, and distance.

It has long been believed that the drop is the single most important aspect of punting, but before the drop can be executed correctly, the football must be aligned correctly.

While holding the football in the drop hand, the punter comfortably extends the arm forward as if preparing to shake hands (figure 6.6). This naturally flexes his elbow

Figure 6.6 Punter holding the football in alignment, just before the drop.

slightly, putting the football and forearm in a parallel alignment to the ground.

With the arm extended out, the slightly flexed elbow should naturally be in direct line with the bottom of the rib cage while the inside of the elbow is tight to the body and aligned directly over the outer edge of the hip of the punting leg.

Once the elbow is aligned, the punter puts the back tip of the football, which is held by the drop hand, in a direct line with the outer edge of the thigh of the punting leg. The front tip of the football needs to be in direct line with the inside of the knee. This places the football directly over the punting leg, parallel to the ground, with laces in line with the outer edge of the shoulder on the punting-leg side.

The left arm (for a right-footed punter) extends to move the guide hand toward the front half of the football opposite the drop hand. Because the arm needs to extend further out and across the center of the body, there will be less flex in the elbow.

The punter angles the front point of the football slightly inward, with the laces aligned toward the outer edge of the near shoulder (the right shoulder for a right-footed punter). He keeps the football parallel to the ground and aligned with the base of his rib cage.

Some punters initially position the football at chest level as they begin their approach. As they continue their forward motion, they gradually lower the football to the drop point, which is near the base of the rib cage. Although this works for some punters, it's not the most common method. It's much more consistent to position the football on a level plane and allow the ball to move steadily across the same plane until the drop. Imagine the football on a table; it moves steadily across the table, the level plane, until it falls off. This makes it much easier for the punter to make contact with the football with as little movement as possible.

Another benefit to releasing the football from rib-cage level is that it allows the punter to maximize control of the football by minimizing float time—the time it takes the football to drop from the release hand to making contact with the punting foot. By holding the football lower, the punter needs to hold onto the football longer or the drop will begin too soon. The lower drop is closer to the ground and thus closer to the punting foot. If the football is released too soon, it will drop prematurely to the punting foot before optimal power can be generated.

If the football is held at rib-cage level, and thus held longer, not only will the ball fall a minimal distance, it won't even come close to building the momentum caused by gravity that would be developed from falling from a higher level. A football that drops at a slower, steadier rate falls more consistently with less potential movement. Also, the foot makes contact with the football at a more consistent spot.

Releasing the Football

The main factor when determining how the football is to be released and dropped and ultimately how it maintains the same position as it makes contact with the punting foot is the alignment. Once the punter receives the snap and aligns the football properly, he has created a blueprint that will guide him throughout the entire punting process.

The punter follows this natural guide by keeping the football in the exact same alignment as it was during the approach—parallel to the ground with the front point angled slightly inward, the laces pointed toward the outside edge of the near shoulder. This same positioning must be maintained throughout the approach, release, and drop, even to the exact moment contact is made with the punting foot.

The football is angled inward and parallel to the ground to enable optimal compression of the football as well as produce a punt that has the aerodynamic benefits of a spiral.

The drop of the football consists of two phases: the release of the guide hand and the actual drop of the football (figure 6.7). As the weight shifts over the directional step, the punter slowly opens the arm on the guide hand side from the shoulder and releases the guide hand from the side of the football so only the drop hand holds the ball. The arm on the guide hand side remains extended, gradually moving away from the football

Figure 6.7 Football drop: *(a)* release of guide hand; *(b)* drop of football.

and out from the shoulder opposite the punting leg. The guide hand release is smooth, so the football remains on a level plane.

The drop hand smoothly releases the football when the toes of the plant foot align slightly ahead of the punter's body.

The football is held with the fingertips during the approach, so it should be released with the fingertips. All fingers, including the thumb, simultaneously open. Once the hand opens completely, the arm moves the drop hand away from the football and outside the body. This technique is the most effective way to develop a smooth and consistent drop. By using the fingertips, the punter develops such a soft touch that the release leaves the football motionless. The drop hand remains extended as it moves down and out. The head remains slightly down and on the same level plane, with the eyes focused on the football as the body motion continues forward. A one-handed drop enables the punter to hold on to the football a little longer and to extend it farther forward, allowing for better control and a better transfer of energy. The football should be dropped, not tossed or pushed, and should descend to the foot in exactly the position in which it was released. As the football descends, the forward momentum of its descent remains constant with the forward momentum of the punter. As the football drops from the base of the rib cage to the level of the support knee, it descends down the front of the punter in a position parallel to the backward lean of his body (figure 6.8).

By making the drop from a point near the lower rib-cage level, the punter can minimize the amount of float time from release point to foot impact. This is extremely important, especially when dealing with

Figure 6.8 Descent of the ball is parallel to the punter's backward lean.

adverse conditions such as wind. A shorter float time is always effective in relation to timing and getting the ball off quickly.

Swinging the Leg

As the punter completes his directional step, his body begins the transition from forward lean to backward lean in anticipation of the plant step. During this transition, his body from the neck down moves like a pendulum as his head maintains the exact same position and level plane it was in during the approach.

The punter initiates the leg swing just prior to the plant of the non-punting foot. The instant before the plant step, the punting leg completely extends out in the opposite direction, directly behind the punter. For a brief instance, both of the punter's feet are barely off the ground. This happens simultaneously when the toe of the punting leg behind the punter lifts off, and the heel of the plant leg in front touches down. At this moment, the punting leg is behind the punter, directly in line with his right buttock, with the leg completely extended out and the toe pointed downward and near the ground (figure 6.9).

As the heel of the plant foot touches the ground, the upper part of the punting leg begins to move in a pendulum motion from the hip, generating momentum by quickly pulling the punting leg forward. This motion aligns the lower part of the punting leg and the punting foot directly behind the right buttocks of a right-footed punter in a parallel position to the ground. This movement elevates the lower part of the punting leg into a precocked position that will dramatically enhance the leg snap as the punting foot ascends to the football.

Figure 6.9 Initiating the leg swing; punting leg is behind punter.

As the heel of the plant foot transitions to a firm planted position on the ground, stabilizing the punter, it creates a rolling effect with the foot. This movement enhances the forward motion of the body and the movement of the hip and thigh as it dramatically pulls and accelerates the lower part of the punting leg forward and upward. This entire motion creates a whiplike effect with the punting leg that produces the power known as *leg speed*.

The plant step stabilizes the forward momentum of the body and dramatically enhances the pull of the punting leg, which swings forward from the hip at the very moment the plant step is made. As the upper part of the punting leg swings forward and then upward, knee first, it generates tremendous momentum as the lower part of the punting leg snaps up through the football with tremendous speed and power.

The punter brings his leg from directly behind his buttocks forward as his swing takes the punting leg near his plant leg, passing under and toward the front of his body (figure 6.10). By bringing the punting leg to close proximity with the plant leg, the punter has concentrated the power of his motion down a very narrow path called the target line.

By combining the momentum of the body, the forward thrust of the hip, and the forward pull of the thigh of the punting leg, the punter creates a lever effect with his lower leg that dramatically accelerates the speed of the punting foot as the leg nears lock-out.

As the punting leg moves forward and upward, the left arm—which is even with the shoulder, directly to the side of the punter, and parallel to the ground—moves forward and upward or outward, offsetting the move-

Figure 6.10 Leg swings from *(a)* behind the buttocks to the *(b)* front of the body.

ment of the punting leg. More important, the motion of this arm serves as a counterbalance to the punting leg, enabling the punter to concentrate the motion of his body toward his target as he punts the football.

As he takes his plant step with the heel first and toes up, his plant foot rolls forward in a heel-to-plant action, stabilizing his forward movement and shifting his body momentum from forward to upward. This upward shift of the body's momentum enhances the speed of the leg as the punter pulls the punting leg, which is extended directly behind the buttocks, forward, up, and through the football.

From the very beginning of the approach, the football has been aligned on the target line and the steps have been taken down the target line. Now the punting leg needs to pull forward, up, and through the target line. This entire process guides the momentum of the body down a direct path that enhances optimal power in the punting motion.

Swinging Through

A common way for the punter to ensure he swings his punting leg straight through and toward the target is to make sure the leg swings up through the football and aligns with his right eye as it peaks at the height of its upward motion. This is a great follow-through technique that can guide the entire mechanics of the punt.

Making Contact With the Football

The culmination of the approach is the precise moment the punting foot makes contact with the football. At this point, every aspect of the punter's alignment, mechanics, momentum, and timing come together as one force to compress the football and propel it toward its target.

The football should be flat and in the exact same alignment it was in during the approach, release, and drop: parallel to the ground with the front point angled slightly inward and the laces pointed toward the outside edge of the near shoulder (figure 6.11).

Figure 6.11 Contact with football results from good alignment, mechanics, momentum, and timing by the punter.

The punter strives to match the slight angle of his foot with the center mass of the football. This is the most favorable way to contact the football to achieve optimal compression, enabling the punter to get maximum distance and hang time.

By positioning the football at an angle, across the foot, the punter prevents the front and back points of the football from making contact with the toe or ankle of the kicking leg, which allows the punting foot to create a cradling effect with the football. This positioning enables optimal compression of the football and produces a punt that has the aerodynamic benefits of a spiral.

In general, the foot contacts the football at about the level of the support knee, though the contact point might vary slightly with the individual, weather, and other factors.

At the moment of impact, the knee of the support leg generates power from the ground up at the same time as the lower leg snaps the punting foot up through the ball with tremendous speed and power. The punter drives his punting foot squarely through the sweet spot of the football (the center and bottom of the ball) as the leg begins to straighten out naturally. At this point, the toes of the punting foot should be fully extended, depressed, and pointing in the direction of the target area. This foot positioning keeps the top of the foot flat and enables the hard bone area on top of the foot, directly under the shoelaces, to make contact with the football.

The punting foot impacts and compresses the football before the punting leg locks out. Although many think the punter makes contact with the football at leg lock, leg lock actually occurs a millisecond after the football leaves the foot. This is understandable because once the leg locks leg speed begins to diminish. Thus, optimal leg speed is obtained a split-second before leg lock.

During the exact moment of impact, the force created by the controlled momentum of the approach, the proper mechanics, and the speed of the punting leg drive the foot into the football, causing it to compress. At the very moment maximum leg speed and compression of the football are reached, as the punter continues to punt through the ball, the football begins to decompress in the area of impact. These two combined forces—leg speed and compression—cause the speed of the football to dramatically accelerate as it separates and rises from the punting foot. At this point, the punting leg locks and the follow-through of the punt begins.

When the punting foot makes contact with the football, the plant foot is facing in the general direction of the target to complement the straightness of form. The plant foot is firm and flat and serves as a guide and anchor to the punter as he transitions his mechanics and body motion up and forward through the ball.

The support leg stabilizes the punter's body as it begins to transition from a backward lean to a more vertical alignment. This resolute support of the leg enables the forward motion of the body and the upswing of the punting leg to work together to generate power through the football. This allows the punter to produce additional power from the ground up. Although the plant leg is nearly locked, a slight flex in the knee facilitates the up-and-forward movement of the punting motion.

The punter's body is in a vertical position, his hips and shoulders perpendicular to the ground (figure 6.12). The hips and shoulders also directly face the target. This precise positioning of the body concentrates the power generated through the forward motion and proper mechanics of the punt to a more direct and specific area.

Figure 6.12 Punter's vertical position at impact: *(a)* front view; *(b)* back view.

Ensure Proper Arm Position

Figure 6.12*a* shows a technique Ray Guy used to ensure he had proper arm positioning. He would make sure the inside of the arm on his drop-hand side grazed across the outside edge of his thigh.

Following Through

An optimal punt occurs when the punter imparts the entire energy of his body, through proper mechanics, to a concentrated area of the football in a way that optimizes elevation, distance, and direction of the punt. In order for this to be accomplished consistently, there must be correct follow-through.

The follow-through is the culmination of the entire punting motion, aligning the mechanics of the body with the direction of the football as it travels toward the target. The follow-through begins the moment the punting leg locks as the football accelerates and rises from the punting foot.

As the football leaves the punting foot in the direction of the target, the punting foot continues to ascend as if uninterrupted by the impact with the football. By punting through the football, the punter imparts maximum power, allowing the leg to momentarily maintain the same speed through contact with the football before deceleration begins.

As the football leaves the foot and the punting leg begins to follow through, the support foot comes up on its toes, and the momentum of the leg swing lifts the punter off the ground (figure 6.13).

Figure 6.13 As the punter follows through, his momentum lifts him off the ground.

The punter should never force the follow-through; he should let it happen naturally. He keeps his shoulders and hips parallel to the ground throughout the motion.

After the follow-through, the plant foot returns to the ground slightly ahead of where it lifted off, with the punter balanced and in complete control of his body. He should still face the same direction as during the approach—square to and facing his target—as his punting foot slowly returns to the ground in a deliberate motion. As his punting foot touches the ground, it needs to be in a direct line with his target.

Once the punter has completed his postpunt check, he becomes a safety, positioning downfield about 20 to 25 yards ahead of the return man. From this vantage point he mirrors every move the returner makes and serve as his team's last line of defense in case the return breaks through.

Optimal Timing

As we've mentioned elsewhere, punters should be timed frequently to help train them to get the ball away quickly and to aid them in developing rhythm and consistency. The optimal total time from snap to punt should be 2.0 to 2.1 seconds for college and professional players. This is an attainable time for high school players as well because they tend to align closer to the line of scrimmage, so the snap doesn't travel as far. When you break down the timing of the entire punt, it looks like this:

Center snap to punter's hands: 0.75 to 0.8 seconds

Handling time and punter's approach: 1.25 to 1.3 seconds

Total get-off time: 2.0 to 2.1 seconds

Snap-to-touch time begins on the long snapper's first movement. The timer must be precise and start the stopwatch the instant he sees the football move. At this precise moment, the rushers begin their immediate burst toward the punter to attempt to block the kick.

The next phase of timing is called either hand-to-foot time or touch-to-toe. The optimal hand-to-foot time is 1.25 to 1.3 seconds. This time begins the instant the snapped football touches the punter's hands and continues until his foot contacts the football.

The third phase of timing the punt is the total get-off time, commonly referred to as snap-to-kick or, in this case, snap-to-punt time. The optimal time for snap to punt is 2.1 seconds. Ultimately, it's up to the punter to ensure this time is met regardless of what else happens. If there's a bad or mishandled snap, the punter must make up for lost time by speeding up his normal approach. The punter does whatever it takes to get the punt off. It's his responsibility.

The fourth phase of timing the punt includes hang time, which is simply the duration of time the football stays in the air.

To motivate the punting unit, you might record the entire play, including the snap, get-off, hang time, and how long it takes for the coverage team to end the play. If all goes well, the total get-off time will be 2 seconds, hang time 4 to 5 seconds, and punt-coverage 7 seconds or less.

On game day, a stopwatch comes in handy. By timing every punt during the game, the coach can confirm consistent get-off times and identify protection problems. For instance, if a punt was close to being blocked, but the punter's get-off time was ideal, the problem was with the protection.

Postpunt Check

The postpunt check is the confirmation that all the punter's mechanics came together to accomplish the goal of punting the football optimally.

This confirmation point provides a self-coaching method that every punter can use to ensure the football is traveling its intended course based on the exact position of his body. The dedicated and focused punter develops this technique until it becomes habit. When he punts the football, he knows exactly where it goes simply by evaluating his mechanics and identifying his body position on completion of the punting motion. He need not even look at the flight of the ball.

If a punter starts his punting motion correctly and finishes his punting motion correctly, his entire punting motion will be correct. The postpunt check is a form of teaching backward. By teaching the finish, the punter can focus on what he wants as the end result, thus providing a mental and physical advantage that allows the body to execute the skill automatically.

Beginning with the initial step, everything—steps, hips, shoulders, leg swing, punting foot, and follow-through—should be done in a direct line with and square to the target. The forward motion of the body moving in a direct line ensures maximum power.

The spiral is achieved by the positioning of the ball and the straightness of the form, not by swinging the foot across the football.

A punter wants to develop a rhythm throughout the punting action. He keeps his head down throughout the punt and watches his foot compress the football. He uses his arms and hands to provide stability and balance. He allows his arms to extend naturally. He starts and completes the punt in balance and in total control of his body. He knows the game situation, the alignment of the opponent, and the direction in which he wants to punt the football. After launching an effective punt toward his target area, he becomes a safety and monitors the punt return, ready to do whatever it takes to help his team.

7

Situational Punting

There is much more to punting a football than power and distance. Direction, hang time, and placement all are extremely important and must be considered for every punt. For the punter to perform at optimal level, he must identify each punt's objective and adapt his kick to the game situation. Ultimately, his goal is to win the battle of field position for his team. Thus, every time the football is punted, he must have a purpose.

Determining and Communicating Objectives

By knowing the objectives of each punt, the coverage team will be prepared and markedly more effective. This being the case, the purpose of every punt needs to be communicated, usually via the coach to the punter and then via the punter to the rest of the team.

Through practice and preparation, the entire punting unit can anticipate the objective of each situation. Sometimes the punter has the option to change the direction of the punt based on the rush. He might change the punt from the line through communication calls just prior to the snap.

Some type of rush toward the punter should be expected at all times. For the punt-blocking unit, the rush is not only an attempt to block the punt. This unit is also anticipating a mishandled snap, trying to identify any attempt at a fake by the punting team, and ensuring the punter doesn't intentionally delay getting the punt off. If the punter is allowed to take more time getting the punt off, the coverage, the outside gunners, will have more time to get downfield and cover.

The closer the punter punts from his own end zone, the more he can expect to experience an intense rush. The proximity to the end zone magnifies the rushing team's objectives and adds the incentive to hurry the punter's get-off time and rhythm in hopes of forcing a bad punt so they gain an advantage in field position. Even worse, the rushing team might score a quick touchdown after a blocked punt or mishandled snap.

The closer the punter is to the 50-yard line, the less likely the opponents will aggressively rush, in part because they are leery of a possible fake by the punting team.

Punting for Hang Time

Situation

Any time the punter is punting in the open field of play and the threat of a return exists (figure 7.1).

Objective

To optimize distance and maximize hang time to give the punt coverage team ample time to cover downfield, minimizing or eliminating a return.

Essentially, every punt is performed in the same way. The punting mechanics are the same. The difference is in the hang time and placement and, even then, the differences are subtle. For instance, if the punter is trying to maximize hang time, he'll need to optimize distance. He'll sacrifice distance to increase the height of the punt. To accomplish this, he might slightly raise his drop, hold on to the football a little longer before he drops it, or try for a combination of these techniques. Most important is that he does all of this automatically.

If the punter prepares in practice by creating situations that arise in games and responding to them, he'll naturally, or automatically, make the necessary subtle adjustments to accomplish his intentions. It's better to learn through experience by placing punters in situations with the end result in mind. It's a form of learning backward. Instead of telling the punter to raise his drop to get more hang time, it's best for him to get on the practice field and focus on the purpose and placement of the punt, letting his body mechanics naturally adjust to execute the kick.

A common practice by truly great punters is to sacrifice distance for hang time. It's not about how far you can punt—it's how effective each punt is. A high gross punting average is not the goal. You punt to best benefit the team.

To truly enhance hang time, the secret is to optimize the distance the ball travels in the air. Consider that a ball punted 45 yards with a 4-second hang time is likely to be caught and returned, let's say, for 5 yards. Another ball punted for 40 yards with a 4.5-second hang time is likely to be caught but not returned because the coverage team has more time

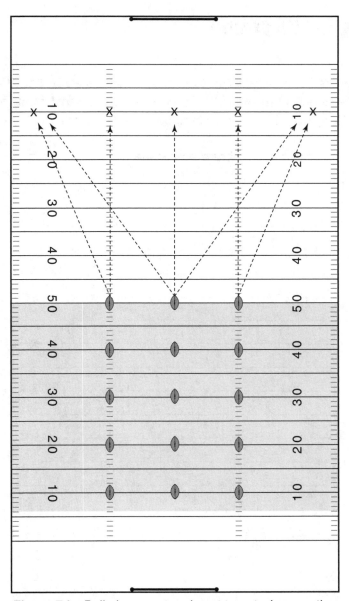

Figure 7.1 Ball placement and punt target when punting for hang time.

and less distance to travel. Both punts finish with the same net distance (40 yards), but the second punt was more effective because there was no return. No return means no chance for the opponent to return the punt all the way. To have the most effective punt-coverage team, you'll want to lead in two main statistical categories: net punting and percentage of punts not returned. In meeting these two objectives, you'll see a dramatic change in your coverage.

Punting for Direction

Situation

The football is in the open-field area, usually between the 20-yard line and the 50-yard line (figure 7.2). In general, the return team focuses on returning the punt. The punter can expect a moderate to heavy rush.

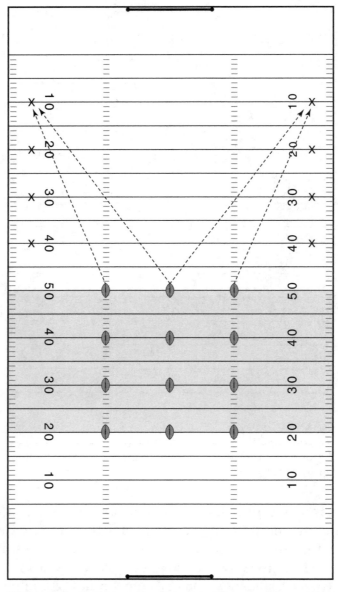

Figure 7.2 Ball placement and punt target when punting for direction.

Distance and Hang Time

The optimal hang time for a punt can be calculated based on the distance of the punt by adding a decimal point to the distance. For example, a punt of 40 yards would optimally have a hang time of 4.0 seconds or better. (An optimal hang time for a high school punter is 4.0 or better; for a college or professional punter, it's 4.5 or better. A 42-yard punt with a 4.2-second hang time or better is considered an optimal punt; pro players strive for a 50-yard punt with a 5.0-second hang time.

Objective

To optimize hang time and distance while placing the football in a position on the field that minimizes the coverage area.

Always be prepared to direct the flight of the ball to a particular spot to minimize the coverage area and allow the cover team to quickly blanket the return man. Take advantage of the closest sideline when the ball is placed on or near the hashmark. Remember that when you combine precision placement with maximum hang time and optimal distance, your coverage team can cover the entire field effectively.

If the ball is in the middle of the field, or any time there's an overload or the punter feels there's too much pressure coming from the outside (the direction he intends to punt), then he needs to immediately consider changing the strategy by punting the ball straight downfield with maximum hang time and optimal distance. By punting straight downfield, the punter can stay well within the center of his protection. This places him in the safest position to get the punt off successfully.

Every time a punter punts the football, he performs a directional punt, directing the football to its destination. When referring to the strategy of directional punting, it's most important that the punt accomplishes a purpose that minimizes or virtually eliminates any return and gives the punting team an advantage in field position. In general, directional punts are performed in the open field all the way to or just across the 50-yard line. In this area, it's crucial for the punter to obtain optimal hang time and distance, enhancing the success of the coverage team and maximizing the distance the opponent must go to score.

By selecting an exact target, the punter can focus his entire punting motion in that direction, thus optimizing hang time and distance. Beginning with the initial step, everything—steps, hips, shoulders, leg swing, punting foot, and follow-through—should be done in a direct line with and square to the target. The forward motion of the body moving in a direct line ensures the generation of maximum power and control. Proper mechanics can also be achieved when the punter aligns with his target from start to finish.

Some punters, particularly at the professional level, occasionally adjust their alignment in a slightly offset position to compensate for the direction they'll be stepping in their approach. This offset pre-positions them, so by the time they complete their approach and kick the football, they're better aligned within their punt protection.

For instance, if the punter is attempting a punt toward the right, he might adjust his stance slightly offset to the left outside of the stance of the long snapper (figure 7.3). This adjustment is so subtle the snapper has no problem snapping the football slightly to the left. This simple adjustment allows the punter to receive the snap, complete his approach, and successfully punt the football to the right while maintaining a safe position well within the center of protection.

Figure 7.3 Punter offsets slightly left of the long snapper's stance to punt right.

Punting to the Corner

Situation

The football is near the 50-yard line (figure 7.4). Because the football is near midfield, an intense punt rush by the return team is less likely because of the increased probability of a fake punt by the punting team.

Objective

The punter wants to angle his punting approach toward either sideline at a point between the 10- and 5-yard line markers to place the football inside the opponent's 20-yard line at a position nearest the goal line.

The coffin corner is either corner of the playing field formed by the sideline and just in front of the end zone. A punter might try to place the ball so that it lands and goes out of bounds or is downed near the corner, thus forcing the receiving team to play very close to its goal line and maximizing the distance the receiving team must travel to score.

The coffin corner punt is a controlled drive punt normally driven at a lower trajectory out of bounds with the intent to pin the opponent deep in its own territory. The punter tends to hold the football on his approach slightly lower and longer before the drop. This natural adjustment produces more of a drive punt that's more proficient in accuracy and distance. Because the objective is to have the football land completely out of bounds and off the field of play, minimal hang time is needed (because there's no threat of a return).

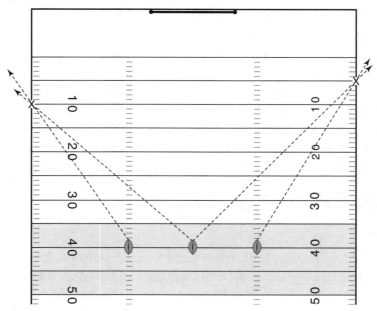

Figure 7.4   Ball placement and punt target for corner punts.

Sometimes a punter attempts to punt for the corner when he's outside of his range; in this case, the ball might simply roll dead deep in the opponent's territory before going out of bounds. This might prove effective, but the coverage team must be alert in case of an attempt to return the football.

Punting to the Right Corner

When punting to the right corner, the right-footed punter needs to consider aiming at a particular point out of bounds that's closer to the goal line, preferably the 5-yard line. When punted correctly by a right-footed punter, the ball will spin clockwise and tend to fade to the right as it noses over. By aiming tighter to the goal line, the punter plays the natural fade and allows room for the punt to be effective. For example, if the punter truly aims at a point directly over the 5-yard line, as the football turns over and begins to fade, it should go out of bounds within the 10-yard line, well within the 20-yard line objective.

By aiming over the 5-yard line, the punter gives himself a 5-yard cushion to either side. This allows him to play it safe and keep the football out of the end zone, avoiding a touchback. This strategy enables him to place the football well within the 20-yard line and actually closer to the 10-yard line.

Punting to the Left Corner

When punting to the left, the right-footed punter considers aiming at a particular point out of bounds that's more away from the goal line, preferably the 10-yard line. Again this allows him to play the fade. As it noses over, the punt will fade naturally toward the right and go out of bounds, ideally near the 5-yard line mark or even closer.

A left-footed punter will need to reverse these instructions. The football will spin counterclockwise, tending to fade to the left as it noses over. This means a left-footed punter will need to aim closer to the goal line over the 5-yard line when going for the left corner and aim more toward the 10-yard line when going for the right corner.

Punting Out of the End Zone

Situation

The football is generally within the punt team's 5-yard line (figure 7.5), creating a tight punting situation in which the normal depth of the punter's alignment is minimized. The likeliness of an all-out rush increases the closer the punting team is to its own goal line. In this case, a hard rush is expected because the punter is standing deep in his team's own end zone.

Objective

Because a heavy rush is expected and the normal stepping pattern distance is decreased, the punter adjusts his approach to quickly get the punt off. Punt distance is desperately needed to regain some field position and get the punting team out of the hole. More important, hang time is crucial to minimize a return.

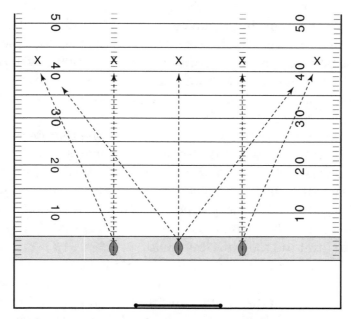

Figure 7.5 Ball placement and punt target for punting out of the end zone.

Obviously, punting out of the end zone tends to bring the most intense rush. Because the punt team has a limited distance to protect, the punt-return team has a greater opportunity to block the punt and a chance to speed up the punter's rhythm and force a bad punt. The punt-return team also would anticipate a mishandled snap allowing them a quick opportunity to score.

In this situation it's challenging for the punter to punt the football toward the numbers outside the hashmark in order to use the sideline to minimize the coverage area, especially because an intense rush will likely come from outside the protection and up the middle. Thus the punt team must first protect the punter and second release and cover effectively.

Because of the likely rush pressure from outside, the punter should punt straight ahead to maximize protection. By maximizing hang time and distance, he provides a greater opportunity for the coverage team to protect and be more effective getting downfield to minimize the return.

Even if the return team is unable to block the punt, it can cause the punt team to do a poor job of covering downfield by forcing them to focus more on protection of the punter.

When punting out of the end zone, the punter focuses on his alignment and stance. He's deep in the back of the end zone and close to the endline. He needs to position his feet well ahead of this line and not right up against it while in his stance. If a punter inadvertently moves his foot back as he receives the snap and steps on the back line, he would be ruled out of bounds. This is a technique that the punter develops through practice. By aligning at least a foot ahead of the back line, he minimizes the risk of stepping out of bounds, especially if he uses proper technique by moving forward to meet the snap.

Another aspect of punting out of the end zone that needs to be considered regarding alignment is the distance from the line of scrimmage. If the football is inside the 5-yard line, the distance separating the punter from the oncoming rush is reduced as well. (This is commonly called a tight punt situation.) The more inside the 5-yard line the football is spotted, the less room the punter has to take his normal steps during his approach to punt the football downfield.

The best way to approach this type of punt is for the punter to shorten his steps to cover less distance. By practicing this technique and allowing it to develop naturally, the punter can still maintain a quick, rhythmic get-off time. This technique allows him to use his normal stepping approach (two or two and a half), which keeps the approach consistent with his normal stepping pattern.

An advantage of punting from a tight punt formation inside the 5-yard line is that the snapped football has less distance to travel and thus will be received by the punter quicker than usual. This faster snap assists the punter, along with his shorter and quicker steps, allowing him to offset the closer distance between the block point of the punt and the oncoming rush.

Executing Pooch Punts

Situation

Field position is generally across the 50-yard line or closer (figure 7.6). This is an area too far for a field goal and too close for an optimal punt, in which 40 yards or more is needed.

Objectives

Punt the football with maximum hang time to a position just across the 10-yard line in order to eliminate chance of a return and challenge the returner by placing the football in a position that makes it difficult to catch, thus creating an opportunity to recover a mishandled ball, or to simply down an uncaught football as it rolls as close to the goal line as possible.

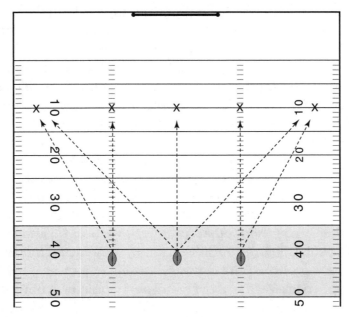

Figure 7.6 Ball placement and punt target for a pooch punt.

The pooch punt is an alternative to kicking the ball out of bounds. This type of punt is usually executed when the punting team is too far from the end zone to attempt a field goal but too close to punt the football normally and keep it out of the end zone.

The pooch punt is usually a high towering kick that lands, ideally, on the field of play near the 10-yard line. This positioning is most effective because returners are usually coached not to catch any punt that will land inside the 10-yard line. Once the punt lands inside the 10-yard line, it has a good chance of rolling into the end zone, resulting in a touchback.

The pooch punt forces the returner to make a decision: catch the punt and attempt a return; make a fair catch and put his team in poor field position; fake the fair catch but let the ball land, hoping it will roll into the end zone for a touchback; or attempt to catch the football but risk fumbling it.

All of these factors have made the pooch punt one of the most effective ways for the punting team to gain the advantage of field position.

A pooch punt can also be punted lower than normal in order to place the football in an area where the return man can't receive it or gain control. This gives the coverage team ample time to down the football as it rolls close to the goal line.

The American football pooch punt is executed by the punter naturally shortening his steps and slightly raising his drop. This allows him to maximize his hang time without worrying much about distance because he's extremely close to the end zone. By placing the punt at a position just across the 10-yard line, the punter forces the returner to make a decision to fair catch the football or let it go. If the returner attempts to catch the ball, there's always the chance he'll mishandle it, creating a turnover opportunity. If he lets the football drop, there's an opportunity for the punt team to down the football even closer to the goal line.

In American football, the Australian end-over-end drop punt has gained popularity in recent years because of Australian players coming to the United States and punting at the professional level. This Aussie-style punt is performed similar to an American football drop kick. The difference is the ball is punted, not kicked, before it touches the ground.

The punter holds the football in a near vertical position. The ball is dropped and then, before it hits the ground, is contacted toward the lower end with the top of the punting foot, similar to a punt. This causes the football to spin backward end over end, as it would on a normal field goal kick except with much more height. This backward-spin rotation creates an accurately placed punt that seems to stay in the air longer than normal, making it harder to catch. If the ball hits the ground instead of being caught, the backward, vertical rotation gives it control. The ball tends to grip the field immediately and more predictably, quickly stopping and giving the coverage team a chance to down the ball near the goal line.

Craig Hentrich, the punter for the Tennessee Titans, is credited with inventing another version of the pooch punt called the *knuckleball*. The punter holds the football sideways during the drop to create a knuckleball effect as the ball falls from the sky. The unpredictable rotation makes a knuckleball pooch punt extremely difficult to catch.

Another good punt for a punter to have in his arsenal is the rugby punt. The rugby punt is punted at a low trajectory so it will bounce and roll forward, pinning the return team deep in their territory. The right-footed punter rolls out to the right sideline, takes several steps, and kicks a low line drive punt that goes end over end to get a favorable roll. The rugby punt has gained popularity because of the effective rolls created, leading to an advantage in field position for the kicking team. The rugby punt is an effective surprise punt. The punter's closer alignment even permits various and effective fake plays. However if the rugby punt becomes predictable, the return team will become more aggressive and dramatically reduce its effectiveness.

Compensating for Conditions

The punter should practice punting in all directions and from all positions on the field. The more proficient he becomes when dealing with adverse weather conditions, especially wind, the more confident he'll be when it occurs in a game (see page 66).

Punting with the wind can be just as challenging as punting into it. Crosswinds present their own challenges. The key to punting into the wind is to hold the ball a little longer and slightly lower to minimize the drop time and maximize control by reducing the effect of the wind on the drop. Essentially, when punting in extreme conditions, the punter tries to punt the ball as soon as he drops it, driving the football into the wind at a slightly lower trajectory. This is the same technique used when punting for distance, punting to the coffin corners, or punting out of bounds or away from a returner. The purpose is to maximize distance and use the wind resistance to hold the punt in the air. Punting with too much hang time into the wind will allow the wind to dramatically affect the distance. By punting at a lower trajectory into the wind, the punter retains more control of the drop and is more likely to produce a punt that maximizes distance and hang time.

When punting with the wind at his back, the punter should take advantage of the wind as much as he can. He should try to contact the ball as he would for a pooch punt that he's trying to nose over. At the same time, he's trying to keep the ball out of the end zone. Kicking the ball like a pooch punt keeps the punter from overpowering the ball, enhances the nose-over effect, allows the wind to carry the ball, and maximizes hang time.

When the wind is at the punter's back but blowing at an angle, the punter should consider punting with the angle of the wind. For example, if the wind is blowing from behind and angling toward the far right corner of the field, the punter can enhance the flight of the ball by directing the punt toward the far right corner. For a right-footed punter in this situation, the wind will complement the ball's clockwise rotation and propel it even farther as it noses over in flight.

In situations like these, the punter must always be alert to what the punt-return team is doing. An opponent with a good special teams coach will be paying close attention to the direction of the wind. The special-teams coach will anticipate the direction of the punt and prepare his punt-return and block teams accordingly. He may even bring a heavy rush from the side he anticipates the punter will direct the football. This does not mean the punter has to change direction, especially if he offsets his stance to the opposite side. It does mean that he must pay attention and be alert for anything.

Driving for Distance

The distance of the punt determines the potential for hang time. If a punter is trying to drive the punt for distance, he'll sacrifice some hang time in order to get the football farther downfield. In this case, he'll need to lower the football prior to the drop, hold on to it longer, or both. The punter should practice this situation so his body can make these adjustments naturally.

A drive punt is an effective way to punt out of the end zone when the coaching strategy is to maximize distance. More importantly, it is an effective way to punt when facing a challenging headwind. By driving the punt into the wind at a lower trajectory, the punter maximizes distance and takes advantage of the natural effects of the wind, which holds the ball in the air longer and gives the coverage team time to make the play.

8

Coverage Recognition and Pickup

The greatest advantage in field position in football is most often created by the punting and punt-return teams. That's why it's so important for the punter and punting team to always be prepared.

Through effective practice habits, meticulous film breakdown, and responsive game-day adjustments, everyone on the punting team has the opportunity to contribute. Every player involved in protecting the punter must know the overall objective of the punt and be decisive about whom he's going to block. Once the ball is snapped, the transition from protection of the punter to coverage must be quick, rhythmic, and flawless. The objective of the punter is to quickly recognize where the greatest pressure is coming from so he can adjust his approach, if necessary, to get the ball off successfully.

Adjusting the Punter's Approach

Before we talk about punter adjustments, there is one thing the punter should never change, and that's the way he receives the snap. Any time the punter is on the field in his stance and ready to receive the snap, he should stand with his arms relaxed and down at his sides. Some punters, especially in high school football, are taught to stand with their arms outstretched in anticipation to receive the snap to cue the snapper they are ready and provide a target for the snapper to aim at. Although this seems to make sense, it is unnecessary and could cause the punter to tense his shoulders and arms. Extending the arms also could tip off the defense when to rush. The snapper needs to be coached to snap the football to the punter's hip and thigh area. If the snapper is coached correctly, he does not need the punter to extend his arms to provide a target. The punter always must be ready the moment the snapper puts his hands on the football in preparation to snap it.

The punter should be ready to adjust as necessary to the unfolding series of events as they occur on any given play. Through repetition and timing, he and the punting team can develop an inner clock that allows them to work together in unison, knowing at the moment of the snap they have no more than 2.1 seconds (college and pro) before the ball begins its flight toward its target. If the snap is on its mark, the punter can execute the punt using the natural rhythm he has perfected through repetition. If the snap is off the mark—too high, too low, or to either side—he'll need to use his athleticism to receive the snap and make up for the lost time caused by the snap's inaccuracy.

Prior to the snap, the punter should note the alignment of the rushers and the number of rushers on either side of the center. If he sees an overload or unbalanced look with more men to one side of the center than the other (figure 8.1), he'll need to react immediately in order to get off

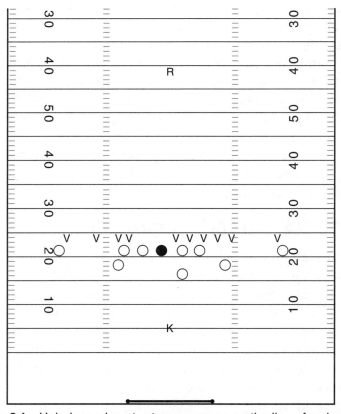

Figure 8.1 Unbalanced punt-return coverage on the line of scrimmage.

an effective punt. He may punt into or away from the rush, based on his team's philosophy, or he may simply punt straight away, staying within the center of his blockers to ensure maximum protection.

For example, if the punter intends to place a punt between the numbers and the sideline and he sees an overload to that same side, he must quickly consider adjusting his approach to avoid punting directly into the rush. His options are to quicken his steps and execute the same punt, punt to the opposite side of the field, or simply punt straight ahead while centered behind his blockers to ensure he obtains maximum protection. The decision is based on the preparation and strategy determined by his coaches.

Decreasing Distance From the Snapper

The most common situation in which the punter must adjust the distance of his alignment in relation to the snapper is when he's punting from deep in his own end zone. In this area of the field he has no choice because of the limited distance allowed him. Otherwise he would position himself outside of the field of play. He may shorten his normal alignment as much as 3 to 5 yards, depending on the position of the football within the 5-yard line.

Rarely will the punter adjust the depth of his alignment unless he has to. He may slightly offset to the right or left of the snapper to stay more centered behind his protection when directing a punt to one side of the field or the other.

Unless the punter is punting deep from his own end zone, he won't adjust his depth. For example, if the ball is on the 6-yard line, a college or professional punter can still align at his normal 15-yard depth. However, if the ball is on the 5-yard line, he'll have to adjust his depth to 14 yards to stay in bounds and far enough from the endline. If the football is on the 3-yard line, he can be only 12 to 12 ½ yards deep from the snapper.

Changing Steps During the Approach

Situations arise in games in which the punter must change his steps during his approach. To develop natural responses to such situations, he should practice every scenario imaginable. Ideally, his athleticism will help him respond in a way that's natural for him.

One of the more common game situations that might create the need for the punter to change his steps is when it's obvious an all-out rush is coming in an attempt to block the punt. He might be punting from near or deep within his own end zone or when the game is on the line. In this situation, he may abbreviate his normal stepping approach by taking shorter and quicker steps. He may simply take just one step. Either way, he can dramatically minimize the distance and time taken during his approach and reduce the chance of a blocked punt. Scouting reports, game tendencies based on previous plays, personnel substitutions, and knowledge of the situation are all sources the punter draws on as he anticipates the intensity of the oncoming rush.

Regardless of what happens on a particular play, the punter and punt team are trained to get the punt off successfully. Frequent timing of punts during practice and games helps develop a can-do mentality. The punter consistently aligns at a set depth, and the entire punt team is timed to ensure that the total get-off time is 2.0 to 2.1 seconds, regardless of the rush or situation. As long as everyone does his job, the risk of a blocked punt is low. Optimal depth plus ideal timing and protection generally equals a successful punt.

To help prepare for an all-out rush, the punter considers several factors. First, he must understand that an all-out rush could happen at any time. Some teams like to surprise the punting team by rushing when the game situation doesn't dictate a rush. At the line of scrimmage, an obvious indication that an all-out rush is likely coming is if everyone on the punt-return team is on the line in a sprinter-type stance. No return man deep to field the punt is a big clue the opponent is not planning a return. This type of rush sometimes is dictated by desperation, when the punt-return team needs more than possession of the football, they need a quick score to have a chance at winning the game. In such situations, the punter can count on tremendous pressure, especially if the opponent is indeed rushing 11 men.

Learning From Previous Punts

Tendencies, field position, and game situations all come into play to determine how the opponent will respond to the punting team and the punter. This information is just as important to the punting team in determining what to expect regarding the opponent's rush, the type of returns they prefer, and the capability of the returner. In other words, it is just as important to scout your own team for tendencies as it is to scout your opponent. Only then can you truly anticipate what your opponent will do on a given situation. The punter's top priority is simple. He is to receive the snap and execute the punt without it being blocked. His next priority is to place the punt in a strategic position on the field using maximum hang time to minimize any chance of a return.

Each time the punter punts the ball he should observe every detail regarding his opponent. He might start by anticipating any tendencies the opponent has shown in previous games and on previous plays in the current game. This accomplishes two things. First, it confirms his expectations. Second, it reveals any new adjustments the opponent might make during the game regarding personnel, alignments, punt blocks, and types of returns. The punter has a tremendous vantage point to view anything new that the punt-return team might unveil.

When the punter identifies an opponent adjustment, such as the returner aligning at a certain depth or favoring one side of the field, he communicates this information to the special teams coach. Instead of punting in the direction favored by the returner, he considers punting to the other side. This simple adjustment might prevent the returner from fielding the punt. If he does field the punt, his timing might be disrupted, affecting his chances for an effective return.

Frequently a punter can identify a subtle adjustment that the coaches on the sideline or in the press box won't pick it up. This is why the punter keeps his head in the game.

Kicking Away From the Return Men

Regardless of the game situation or the ability and speed of the punt returner, the punter should always consider placing the football in a position on the field that gives his team field advantage and minimizes the chance of a return. The most common way to do this is to angle the punt toward the sideline just outside the numbers. This placement eliminates one direction—toward the near sideline—in which the returner can run. This positioning also benefits the punt-coverage unit because they don't have to cover the entire field. The returner has only two directions he can go rather than three. Because the returner is looking to get upfield for positive yards as quickly as possible, he'll more than likely head upfield. The coverage unit knows this and responds accordingly.

By angling his kick to the near sideline, the punter is choosing the least angle of approach, not to mention the shortest distance to the sideline. This can be tremendously effective in obtaining the greatest distance on the punt. Should the return team decide to rush from that same side, the punter can either execute the same punt by abbreviating his steps or he can punt toward the wide side of the field and away from the rush. The punter always has the option to punt straight down field to ensure maximum protection as long as he optimizes distance and maximizes hang time so the coverage team can blanket the returner and make the tackle.

Always remember that the punter's top priority is to receive the snap and execute the punt without it being blocked or tipped. His next priority is to place the punt in a strategic position with optimal distance and maximum hang time to minimize the chance of a return.

Returner's Ability and Speed

It might become obvious during the course of a game that the opposing team has an extremely talented returner. Clearly, you want to avoid putting the ball in this player's hands. In such a case the normal strategy of minimizing any chance of a return through placement of the punt should be modified—you now want to eliminate any return whatsoever. This is accomplished by punting the football to a position on the field where distance is optimized (about 40 yards) before the football goes out of bounds (figure 8.2). By punting the football to an optimal point and then out of bounds, the threat of the return is eliminated.

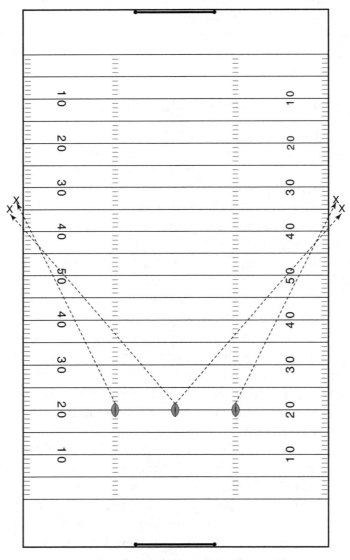

Figure 8.2 Punting away from the returner for optimal distance before the ball goes out of bounds.

Returner's Willingness to Return in Traffic

Any punt returner who wants to earn the opportunity to return punts for his team must display the willingness and ability to return punts in traffic when multiple tacklers are present. Rules cover how much space a punt returner must be given before he can be contacted. In any case, he must be given the opportunity to make the catch before being tackled or to call for a fair catch. In general, punt returners are coached to catch any punt outside the 10-yard line (figure 8.3). This strategy is used to gain a field position advantage and minimize how far the punt travels.

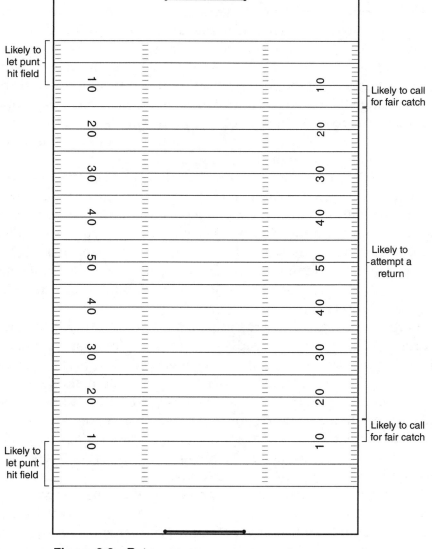

Figure 8.3 Return zones.

Whenever a punt is placed inside the 10-yard line, the returner is coached to leave it alone and not to attempt to catch it because the ball will probably bounce or roll into the end zone, resulting in a touchback.

Challenging the Returner

In some cases a punter might choose to surrender distance in exchange for increased hang time to force the returner to call for a fair catch. Based on strategy, coaching, and the game situation, the returner must determine whether to let the punt bounce and be downed, call for a fair catch to minimize the total distance of the punt, or try to break a punt return for positive yardage and maybe even a score.

The advantage of getting tremendous hang time on a punt is to allow the coverage team to surround the returner, giving him no room for a return. Experienced punt returners often have a feel for when the coverage team is upon him. First, he knows how deep from the football to align, so the moment the ball begins to climb off the punter's foot, he can quickly gauge the range and adjust his position to catch it. Second, as the football climbs to its highest point, he can easily determine the hang time. By watching the football, he can see whether it spirals and jumps off the foot and thereby assess the ball's distance and height.

The aerodynamic effect of the spiraling rotation of the football helps propel the ball smoothly and efficiently through the air. The slower the rotation of the football, the more effective the punt tends to be. If the football is not spiraling, it won't travel as far and will have little hang time. Such a kick usually results in a high, short punt that's not easily fielded. This type of punt often ends up rolling downfield until someone downs it. All of this information is processed by the returner within a matter of seconds.

As the punt returner aligns in position to catch the football, he also figures into the equation his distance from the coverage team. This is where his experience kicks in. His feel enables him to determine if he needs to make a fair catch or try to field the punt and make a return. This feel is influenced by the distance he has moved to position himself to make the catch, the spiraling effect of the football in flight, and the angle of climb that determines the amount of hang time. All of this information combined with his experience enables the returner to choose from among his options within a few seconds.

For example, if the returner aligns directly on the football 50 yards away, he might be anticipating a punt in the 40- to 45-yard range. By aligning deeper than the anticipated punt, he can more easily move forward to catch the football, which is what he wants to do. (It's much more difficult to follow and catch a punt when moving backward.) Focusing on the punter, the returner watches the direction of the punter's steps as he approaches the football to punt, which generally determines the direction the football will travel. This is especially true of a very skilled punter.

If the ball jumps off the punter's foot in a spiral and climbs at an increased angle that optimizes hang time, the returner can anticipate a punt in the 40- to 45-yard range with optimal hang time, which translates into great coverage and likely a short return. The experienced returner considers his options. He'll have to decide to make the fair catch, make the catch and try to return it, or allow the football to hit the ground and roll into the end zone.

To control returns and minimize big plays, you must challenge the return man. It's tough enough to catch a high, towering punt, but adding strategically placed punts to the mix gives the returner a lot to think about. For instance, if the ball is near midfield and on the hashmark, instead of punting out of bounds or into the end zone, aim for a target well outside the numbers near the sideline on the 10-yard line. Try to obtain maximum hang time with an optimal punt of nearly 40 yards and no farther.

When the punt is near the sidelines, the punt returner must choose to catch the ball or let it go. If he lets it go, the punt will hang long enough to be downed by the coverage team, or the flight path might take the ball out of bounds well inside the 20-yard line. If the return man decides to catch it, he won't have much room to work with because of the proximity of the sideline. Plus, there is always a chance that he will mishandle or fumble the football. By combining effective placement and hang time, you can virtually eliminate any return. The goal is a 40-yard punt with no return and pinning your opponent back inside the 20-yard line.

Drawing Defenders Offside

In some cases, the punting team should take advantage of field position and the game situation and attempt to draw the defense offside. For example, if the punting team is facing fourth down and a penalty would give them a first down, they might want to consider a quick shift with an up back or even try to use an abrupt cadence to entice the opponent to jump offside. This is especially effective when the punting team anticipates a heavy rush attempt to block the punt or is facing a team that continually goes after the punter to block the punt or force a bad kick. The benefit of an unpredictable change-up in the cadence or snap might make the rushing team more cautious and less aggressive.

Usually the punting team will attempt to draw the defense offside very early in the cadence before calling for the actual snap. The up back who's calling the signals might abruptly use a different tone in an attempt to cause a defender to jump offside. If this doesn't work, the up back simply finishes the cadence and allows the snapper to snap the ball in time to still be effective. A similar strategy can be attempted late in a game with more than 25 seconds on the clock. The punt team simply lines up and delays the snap of the football until the clock runs down, just prior to the last 25 seconds, snapping just in time to avoid a penalty. Although the objective is to run seconds off the clock to minimize how much time the opponent has to score, the delay in the snap might cause the defensive team to jump offside.

When the punting team is well inside the 50-yard line and punting toward the end zone, calling for a delayed snap might also draw the defense offside. This ploy can be effective because in this area of the field the punting team can take a penalty for delay of game but still be close enough to be effective with the punt. Sometimes the penalty puts them in a better position because the punter has more room to work with.

9

Punting Practice Drills

The drills in this chapter are designed to develop fundamental punting skills through practice as the punter gets ready for game day. The drills begin with individual technique warm-up and progress to isolate parts of the punting mechanics. This way the punter can properly develop each movement as he progresses and combines the segments of his technique to complete the entire punting motion.

An important aspect of each drill is the simulation of gamelike conditions while developing fundamental skills. Each drill can be used for warm-up and technique development and can be done at any time leading up to the regular season. As the season nears, the punter should focus primarily on warm-up drills and drills that simulate gamelike punting situations.

Each drill enables the punter to develop specific punting mechanics. He focuses on warm-up, development, and performance in the off-season and warm-up and performance during the season. Through these drills, the punter can become more self-reliant through self-teaching strategies, giving him the ability to coach himself.

The punter should practice with a snapper as often as he can, especially during team periods so more gamelike conditions can be created. During practice, the entire punting process should be timed to help promote consistency and confidence.

Once the season starts, punts should also be timed in games for assurance and accountability. Regularly timing punts helps coaches quickly identify get-off or protection concerns, as well as the solutions they need to address them.

Punting Drills Without a Football

These warm-up drills provide the punter with a blueprint for achieving proper technique. He should perform the drills progressively to gradually warm up his punting leg. By not using a football, he can focus more on the setup and alignment and on the proper mechanics of the punt.

AP Photo

Ray Guy, punter for the Oakland Raiders, at Super Bowl XV, January 25, 1981.

Visualize Punt

Objective

The punter focuses on the setup of his alignment and stance, his steps in his approach, and the correct direction of his leg swing. By not using a football, he can attend to the mechanics of the punt instead of the flight of the football to help ensure proper technique is performed the same way every time.

Progression

1. Beginning at the correct depth and alignment from the football, the punter simulates an actual punt, directing his punting motion toward a target. The punter's initial target is straight downfield. A simple target is the base of the goalpost, right down the middle of the uprights.

2. He completes one repetition of the drill when he executes the entire punting motion and finishes directly toward and facing his target.

Tips From the Coach

- The punter practices by simulating the direction and type of punt he would like to execute.

- This is a common drill that punters perform on the playing field during games. Just prior to getting in his stance, the punter goes through his punting motion as sort of a practice run prior to the actual punt.

- Simulating an actual punt is a visualization technique that allows the punter to warm up while vividly focusing on his body mechanics. This allows him to place his entire focus on his body's exact position as it relates to his target.

Variations

The punter can perform this warm-up drill by simply standing and swinging his leg toward the target, or he can do a more advanced version from various positions on the field, simulating the alignments he might need to use during a game.

Escape Gravity

Objective

By using a line on the football field as a reference, the punter simulates his entire punting motion, beginning and finishing on the proper course. He makes sure the momentum generated by his approach and leg swing lifts him up and forward toward his target. This up-and-forward movement enhances the transfer of energy and promotes leg speed, producing a more powerful kick.

Progression

1. The punter initially aligns by straddling a yard line between the hashmarks and placing the inside edge of his punting foot flush with the outside edge of the line.

2. The nonpunting foot is placed about 6 to 8 inches from the opposite side of the line (figure 9.1*a*). This puts the punter the proper width from the line and in position to assume his stance.

3. To begin the drill, he leans and extends his hands simultaneously as if receiving the snap and takes a short jab step with his nonpunting foot (figure 9.1*b*).

4. Regardless of whether he uses a two- or two-and-a-half-step approach, the punting foot steps forward directly on the line (figure 9.1*c*), while the nonpunting foot steps forward to a position flush with the outer edge of the line.

5. As he completes his approach, he plants and swings his punting leg up and forward in the precise direction of the line and target.

6. As his punting leg reaches maximum follow-through, the momentum generated by the body and the upward swing of the leg lifts him off the ground (figure 9.1*d*).

7. The plant foot lifts off and moves upward. Because of the momentum of the approach, the plant foot moves forward as well, landing 6 to 12 inches ahead of where it lifted off the ground. The up-and-forward motion promotes leg speed and power to the football and complements the trajectory of the ball's flight (figure 9.1*e*).

8. After the up-and-forward motion, the punter lands firmly in balance on the ground and in complete control of his body. He then brings his punting leg down to the ground and places his punting foot directly on the line, facing his target.

Tips From the Coach

- The punter must lean as he extends his hands to simulate catching the snap. By leaning to meet the snap, he learns the importance of flowing into the snap and making a smooth transition from his stance to his approach. Remember that the lean creates the need for the steps to begin. This movement is crucial in developing proper timing and rhythm.

- By the punter positioning his feet in this manner, he can better step on a more natural path, keeping his punting leg on the line during his approach, because his feet will naturally draw closer together to maintain his center of gravity as he takes his steps forward.

Variations

Focus more on the balance of the body as the punter lands after his up-and-forward motion. He lands and remains momentarily on his plant leg while he very slowly brings his punting foot down to the ground and positions it directly in line to the target. This action creates more control of his body, thus promoting follow-through and ultimately leg speed.

Figure 9.1 Escape gravity drill.

Punting Drills With a Football

These warm-up and technique drills are designed for punters to develop isolated segments of the punting motion in a progression while using a football.

Stance and Reception

Objective

The punter works on effectively transitioning from the stance to the approach. Beginning with a proper stance, he leans to meet and receive the snap, then molds the football and positions it in the proper alignment with his body while taking his initial full step. This best positions him for a time-sensitive transition to meet the snap and begin his approach.

Equipment

A football and a snapper.

Progression

1. The punter gets in a proper stance with his arms down to his sides to anticipate the snap.

2. As the football is snapped, the punter leans to meet it while he extends his arms and makes the catch, all while keeping his arms outstretched.

3. The instant the football is caught, the punter, keeping his arms extended, begins his initial jab or first step and simultaneously molds the laces of the football to the top.

4. As he completes the first full step, the directional step, with the punting leg, he comes to a complete stop. At this point he should have the football in proper alignment with his punting leg and the target (figure 9.2).

Tips From the Coach

- The first full step (not counting the jab step) is taken with the punting leg. This directional step is placed ahead of and inside where it was in the stance, more toward the center line of the body.

- The punter should anticipate the placement of his first directional step and align the football directly in line with this step. Remember that the feet naturally draw closer together as steps are taken to accommodate the center-of-gravity needs of the body.

- Meeting the snap is the key to timing and to developing a fluid and rhythmic approach to punting the football.

Figure 9.2 Stance and reception drill.

Variations

The punter can accomplish more quality repetitions if the snapper is in closer proximity. He can also add to the drill by taking the second plant step and simultaneously removing the guide hand (the hand opposite the drop hand). He finishes the drill with the football extended out with one hand in drop position while maintaining proper alignment with the punting leg and the target.

Ball Drop

Objective
The punter develops consistency in dropping the football in the proper position so that it makes contact with his foot in the exact same position as when it was dropped from his hands. This same positioning of the football must be maintained throughout the approach, the release, and the drop, even to the exact moment contact is made with the punting foot.

Equipment
A football.

Progression

1. The punter stands with his punting foot directly on a yard line between the hashmark and sideline. (He can use only the sideline if space on the field is limited.) His nonpunting foot is staggered ahead of his punting foot in the plant step of his approach. He extends the football in the proper drop position while aligning the ball directly in line with his punting leg (figure 9.3a).

2. While holding the football in the predrop position, he releases the guide hand (the hand opposite the drop hand) while maintaining the exact same positioning of the football with the drop hand (figure 9.3b).

3. He releases the football in the exact position level to the ground. The football should drop all the way to the ground, landing directly on the yard line while maintaining the exact same position (figure 9.3c).

4. By dropping the football cleanly, the punter enables it to drop level. This ensures that the football makes contact with the ground in the exact position in which it was held and dropped. This positioning causes the football to land flat on the ground, making it bounce straight up.

Figure 9.3 Ball drop drill.

Tips From the Coach

- For the punter to develop consistency, he must simulate an actual punt, so he performs this drill by dropping the football with his drop hand.

- This is a versatile drill that can be done almost any time and anywhere—during practice, at home, or during games. The punter can constantly work on his drop to perfect it.

- For a truer bounce off the ground, do the drill on a hard surface, such as a track, gym floor, or sidewalk. Find a line on the track or gym floor. On the sidewalk, the punter might need to visualize a line.

Variations

To increase the volume of repetitions while maintaining quality, the punter can drop down to the knee of his punting leg, placing it directly on the line (figure 9.4). He places the nonpunting foot firmly on the ground ahead of him with the inside of his foot near the line. He can execute the same drill more quickly because of the minimized distance to the ground.

The punter also can incorporate this drill into his approach. He begins by positioning his body at the point in his approach where he has taken his first full step. With the football extended in both hands in its proper alignment in preparation for the drop, he removes the guide hand and simultaneously begins his plant step. As the plant step is about to make contact with the ground, he releases the ball and allows it to hit the ground on the line. Once the plant step is firmly on the ground, the forward motion stops and the focus is on the drop of the football.

Another great way to perform the drop drill is by using minifootballs. This makes performing the drop much more challenging and provides a great change-up to encourage the punter to focus more intently. Because a minifootball is much smaller and lighter than a football, it's more challenging to control the drop without affecting the attitude of the football as it free falls.

Figure 9.4 Ball drop drill: one-knee variation.

Punt Pass

Objective

The punter develops a consistent drop that enables him to properly impact the football and achieve an accurate spiraling punt. This drill brings together the basic mechanics of the punt—including stance, approach, drop, and impact—in one activity.

Equipment

A football and a partner to catch the punt.

Progression

1. The punter stands on a yard line between the hashmarks across from a partner, another punter, or a coach at least 10 yards away.
2. The punter straddles the line and places the inside edge of his punting foot flush with the outside edge of the line.
3. He places his nonpunting foot about 6 to 8 inches from the opposite side of the line.
4. Regardless of whether he uses a two- or a two-and-a-half-step approach, he steps forward with his punting foot directly on the line, while his nonpunting foot steps forward to a position flush with the outer edge of the line.
5. He places the football in the proper drop position, takes his steps, drops the football, and punts a low spiraling punt to his partner, similar to a pass.

Tips From the Coach

The punter needs to take a slower controlled approach in order to focus more on the drop. He is striving for control of the punt as well as achieving an aerodynamic spiral with the football.

Variations

The punter can change his stance so that he begins at an angle to the left or the right of the line. Now he must step to the right or the left in order to punt down the line. This simulates a directional punt. The punter also can increase the distance from his partner as he becomes more proficient with the drill.

Rocker Step

Objective

To develop explosive leg speed and power through a concise method of punting the football. In the early days of American football, the rocker step was a form of quick-kicking close to the line of scrimmage. This surprise type of kick generally was used from a formation similar to an offensive play. The element of surprise usually kept the football from being caught, especially if the kick was performed prior to fourth down, generating additional distance as it rolled and bounced downfield.

Equipment

A football and a snapper.

Progression

1. The punter gets in his stance with his feet either side by side or staggered with his nonpunting foot ahead.
2. As he receives the snap, he simultaneously steps back with his nonpunting foot, creating a rocking motion with his body (figure 9.5).
3. He quickly pushes off his nonpunting foot and steps forward, planting his nonpunting foot directly at his target.
4. As his nonpunting foot moves toward the plant position, he drops the football while naturally drawing his punting leg forward to swing through and punt the ball.

Tips From the Coach

- This drill tends to make the punter exaggerate the leg swing and drive up through the ball.
- The punter must stay balanced and in control when following through directly toward his target.

Variations

Performing this drill along a yard line across a field ensures straightness of form and direction.

Figure 9.5 Rocker step drill.

Line Drill

Objective

The punter works on keeping his entire punting motion on course. Using a line on the football field as a guide, he simulates his punting motion while following a direct path toward his target. By using the line as a reference, he can ensure that the alignment of the football and his complete punting motion begins and finishes on the proper course.

Equipment

A football.

Progression

1. The punter straddles a yard line where it intersects with the sideline and places the inside edge of his punting foot flush with the outside edge of the line. He faces the center of the field to begin the drill.

2. He places his nonpunting foot about 6 to 8 inches from the opposite side of the line. This puts him at the proper width and in position to assume his stance.

3. While remaining in his stance, he positions the football in the proper position in preparation for the drop. In this position the football is aligned directly over the line. This is the precise position where the punting foot will be placed during the approach.

4. The key to a direct approach toward the target is based on the correct positioning of the football in preparation for the drop. Wherever the football is positioned, the punting leg will follow. This drill challenges the punter to be precise, position the football correctly on the line and directly toward the target, and to follow the lead provided by the correct alignment of the ball.

Tips From the Coach

- By positioning his feet in this manner, the punter can better step in a more natural path during his approach. He must remember to step directly on line toward his target.

- Strive to develop consistency, control, and confidence, all while achieving a tight, spiraling punt. This is a great drill that keeps the punter accountable.

- By starting and finishing on the line, the punter knows the result and what he needs to do to accomplish the punt successfully.

- Due to the natural fade effect caused by the rotation of the spiral, the ball should land on the line or slightly to the punting-leg side of it.

Variations

This drill can be done anywhere on the football field that has lines. The punter can use the sideline or even punt across the field on the 50-yard line (when space is limited such as when the team is practicing on both ends of the field).

Balance Drill

Objective

The punter works on developing balance and body control throughout the punting motion to promote leg speed and power. By focusing on balance from start to finish, he can swing his punting leg more fluidly, and thus more quickly, through the football.

Equipment

A football.

Progression

1. The punter performs the line drill (page 166), emphasizing the finish of the punt. As his punting leg reaches maximum follow-through, he's lifted off the ground by the momentum generated by his body and the upward swing of his leg.

2. The plant foot lift offs, moving upward, and moves forward as well because of the momentum of the approach. The plant foot lands 6 to 12 inches ahead of where it lifted off the ground.

3. After the up-and-forward motion, the punter needs to land on his plant foot firmly and in balance. He must stay in complete control of his body.

4. After landing, he holds this position and remains balanced while his punting leg slowly descends and remains held out in front for at least a 2-second count (figure 9.6) before it comes back in contact with the ground. The punting leg slowly descends down from the follow-through during the 2-second count and remains off the ground. This momentary pause controls the forward motion of the punter to ensure the transfer of energy is up and forward but not too much forward.

5. The punter slowly returns his punting foot to the ground directly on the line and toward the target.

Tips From the Coach

- If the punter is off balance and has too much forward momentum, this might inhibit the follow-through because of the need for the punting leg to quickly return to the ground to maintain balance and support the forward motion of the punter's body.

- The up-and-forward motion promotes the leg speed and power transferred to the football and complements the trajectory of the ball's flight.

- The premise is that if the punter starts and finishes correctly, his punting motion is more likely to be correct.

Variations

You can incorporate this drill into any drill in which the punter goes through his entire punting motion.

Figure 9.6 Finish position of the balance drill.

Chute Drill

Objective

The punter works on guiding himself down a precise path during his approach to improve his get-off time, ensure the generation of optimal power, and maximize the result of the punt.

Equipment

The Punter Chute Football Alignment Zone and Stepping Guide feature the exact dimensions that determine the width of the stance and the distance to be traveled throughout the approach to punt the football. The optic color provides a highly visual reference for the punter to determine if the football is properly aligned. If a Punter Chute Football Alignment Zone and Stepping Guide is not available, use cones and dummies. You also need a football. Standup dummies are required for one of the variations of the drill.

Progression

1. Beginning with a comfortable, relaxed, and balanced stance, the punter begins his approach, allowing the specific dimensions of the chute to guide his forward motion, keeping him in a direct line and facing the target (figure 9.7).

2. The border effect of the chute provides the punter a visual reference to ensure he keeps the football within the framework of his body and in line with his target and punting leg throughout his approach.

3. By following the direct path created by the guide, the punter develops a natural stepping pattern. Once he completes his entire punting motion, he can use the chute as a reference to determine his alignment.

Tips From the Coach

It's very important that the punter position the football in a direct line with the target throughout the approach. This enables everything—steps, hips, shoulders, leg swing, punting foot, and follow-through—to be done in a direct line with the target and square to it.

Variations

This drill can be done without a snap by having the punter prealign the football in his approach or by the punter simply tossing the football up and catching it to simulate receiving a snap.

The punter can also position standup dummies on the outside edge of the chute to create a narrow alley effect. This challenges him even more to ensure he positions the football within the framework of his body during his approach.

Figure 9.7 Chute drill.

Optimal Stride, or Block Point, Drill

Objective

The punter works on naturally adjusting the stride of his approach according to the type of punt needed for a certain game situation, such as punting out of the end zone or making up for a bad snap. This enables him to optimize his approach at any given time.

Equipment

A Punter Chute Football Alignment Zone and Stepping Guide, a football, and a cone, dummy, or other marker. If a Punter Chute Football Alignment Zone and Stepping Guide isn't available, cones and dummies can be used.

Progression

1. The punter assumes his proper stance in the chute, completes his approach, and punts the football.

2. After a few repetitions, a partner or coach should determine the block point (the point where the football is vulnerable to being blocked as it is punted). Once the block point is determined, it is marked on the ground with a cone, dummy, or other marker (figure 9.8).

3. Once the natural block point is identified and marked, it is gradually moved back toward the punter. The punter must shorten his steps during his approach to accommodate the distance of the newly established block point.

Figure 9.8 Optimal stride, or block point, drill.

Tips From the Coach

Gradually adjusting the mark toward the punter allows him to adjust his steps naturally. The best way for the punter to adjust to the block point is by simply shortening his steps, which in turn makes them quicker. This enables him to effectively adjust his steps without changing the number of steps in his approach.

Variations

The drill can be set up for a more dramatic adjustment by minimizing the distance for the approach or by positioning a standup dummy in front of the punter to simulate an attempted block.

Fade Punt

Objective

The punter works on punting with precision and accuracy through understanding the rotation effects of a football as it spirals during flight. A right-footed punter creates a spiraling punt with clockwise rotation, which causes the football to fade to the right, especially as it descends. A left-footed punter creates the opposite effect—the ball will spin counterclockwise and fade to the left.

Equipment

A football; field cones to mark reference points.

Progression

1. Position a cone about 40 yards downfield (or a shorter distance, if necessary) measured from where the ball will be snapped directly in front of the punter, ideally on either a hashmark or a yard line. Place a cone about 5 yards to each side.

2. The punter aims for the cone straight ahead to observe the natural fade effect of the football. When a right-footed punter punts directly toward the center cone, the spiraling football should naturally fade toward the right cone. If he aims at the cone to the far left, the ball should naturally fade toward the cone in the center.

Tips From the Coach

The punter needs to be disciplined and truly aim at a particular cone, allowing the natural effects of the ball rotation to do the rest. This will teach him to focus his punting mechanics directly toward a target but understand how to play the natural fade to be more precise in his placement.

Variations

The punter can incorporate this training technique into any type of punt, particularly to punts near the sideline.

Rapid Fire

Objective

The punter works on receiving snaps in rapid succession to develop consistency in executing the punt when seconds matter. By placing immediate emphasis on focusing to receive the next snap, the punter becomes conditioned to finish his punting motion and get quickly aligned for the next. This drill can be used in pregame warm-up to make effective use of limited time.

Equipment

Several footballs and a snapper.

Progression

1. Place several footballs on the field. Predetermine a different game situation for each football. The snapper and punter take the field as if they were hurriedly sent into a game.

2. The snapper and punter quickly align and go through the entire punting sequence. Based on the specified game situation, the punter places the punt to a purposeful position on the field. For example, if the situation is punting out of the end zone, place footballs on the 5-, 4-, 3-, 2-, and 1-yard lines. This will position the punter in a gamelike situation. Each time the football is snapped, the snapper positions at the next football, counting all the way down to one. The punter makes sure he is aligned properly, especially as the distance of each snap decreases.

Tips From the Coach

This is a great drill for simulating gamelike situations. It teaches athletes to perform under pressure in a limited amount of time. The drill helps develop confidence in the punter's skills by placing him in situations in which he must react quickly and not think as much.

Variations

This drill can be done in several ways. For instance, the footballs can be scattered all around the field. Each football has a different purpose for the punt, based on its placement on the field.

Another effective way to perform this drill is by placing footballs down the hashmarks on one side of the football field. Beginning at the 10-yard line, place a football every 5 yards all the way to the opponent's 45-yard line. This gives the punter 10 opportunities to perform a situational punt based on the yard line position of each football. After each snap, the snapper moves to the next football all the way down the field.

The punter can work on punting for hang time and distance until he gets to the 30-yard line. Then he can execute directional punts between the numbers and the sideline. When the snapper and punter reach the 50-yard line, the punter can either pooch punt or punt out of bounds. Other variations will work as well. The key is to incorporate team strategy into each situation presented by the different yard line distances. Once the snapper and punter have punted all 10 footballs, they repeat the sequence on the same side of the field, beginning at the 10-yard line and working their way back. By staying on the same side of the field, the punter creates the opportunity to punt on both hash angles, the left hash going down and the right hash coming back.

Field Goal Punt

Objective

The punter develops his placement skills by punting toward a target. Because the football field features limited objects for the punter to aim at, this 6- to 8-yard window (depending on whether the goalposts are college or high school width) provides an aiming point that includes two vertical references: the uprights.

Equipment

A football and a snapper.

Progression

1. The punter aligns near midfield.
2. He aims and punts the ball through the uprights.
3. If the snapper is unavailable, the punter can perform the drill by holding the football.

Tips From the Coach

The punter steps directly toward his target and maintains proper alignment throughout the punt. The goalposts provide a reference point for the punter, helping him face the target and keep his body square to it.

Variations

The punter can position near midfield and set up at an angle, aligning his body to face the corner of the end zone. As he receives the snap, he quickly adjusts his approach and steps directly toward the goalpost.

Blindfolded Punt

Objective

The punter develops his kinesthetic sense of the punting motion by training while blindfolded to better understand the movements of his body. By developing this sense, he can enhance his performance and learn faster.

Equipment

A blindfold (or a scarf, towel, or head band).

Progression

1. The punter is blindfolded. He begins by holding the football in his hands and tossing it into the air to simulate a snap.
2. As he catches the football, he begins his approach to punt the football toward a predetermined target.
3. Because he can't see what he's doing, he becomes more in tune with his body mechanics and feels what he's doing as he goes through the punting motion.
4. Once he has punted the football, he finishes in proper position.
5. He immediately determines the direction the football traveled and communicates it. Only then can he take off the blindfold and view the result.

Tips From the Coach

- This is a good change-up type of drill that will interest the punter. He focuses on mechanics so he can be more in tune to his body as results improve.
- He needs to know how it feels to execute his skill exceptionally.

Variations

The punter can attempt directional punts. This brings an additional element to the process. He'll feel his body change direction during the approach.

Soccer Ball Punt

Objective

The punter improves his ability to make contact with the center mass of a football, thus improving compression, power, and control. Because a soccer ball is round, it has a truer center mass, making it very unforgiving unless contacted correctly.

Equipment

A soccer ball, basketball, or kick ball; a partner.

Progression

1. The punter assumes his stance on a yard line across from a partner. The initial distance is 10 yards, gradually increasing to 20 yards, about the distance from hashmark to hashmark. He begins the drill by punting the soccer ball to his partner.

2. He tries to achieve a direct flight down the line toward his partner with minimal rotation.

Tips From the Coach

The punter must make contact with the ball directly on the center mass or it won't go straight. This drill impresses on the punter the importance of making contact with the center mass of the football.

Variations

You can use a kick ball, volleyball, or even a basketball (because punts are short distances). The punter can also deflate the ball a little, enabling him to easily compress the ball and develop a better feel for getting the most compression.

Ball Drill

Objective

The punter works on becoming more consistent at catching the football and positioning it for a proper drop. Through repetition, he develops the skill to receive snaps and gains confidence in his ability to perform under pressure. These drills enable the punter to develop his catching ability naturally until it becomes second nature.

Equipment

A football.

Progression

1. The punter practices catching footballs from a snapper, a quarterback, a receivers coach, another punter, or a Jugs machine. (A Jugs machine, which snaps footballs at a predetermined speed to simulate actual snaps, is a great way to increase quality reps.)

2. He positions in his punting stance and faces his partner or coach in preparation to receive snaps or passes that simulate snaps. His arms are relaxed and down at his sides.

3. As the snap is delivered, he leans to meet the football while extending his arms to make the catch in front of his body.

4. As the catch is made, he's still moving forward, keeping his arms outstretched, and he quickly turns the football laces up. All of this is done while simultaneously positioning the football in preparation for the drop and taking his first step: the directional step.

5. The drill ends with the directional step. At this point the punting foot and football, in drop position, are directly in line with the target.

Tips From the Coach

- The punter keeps his arms relaxed and at his sides before the snap. This prevents his shoulders from getting tense.
- Once he catches the ball, he keeps the ball out away from his body as he steps and moves the ball into proper position.
- Emphasize developing soft hands to enhance catching ability.

Variations

For more practice, the punter can participate in the ball drills that receivers do during practice. Even better, he can hold for placement kicks. This is an ideal opportunity for the punter to get involved with his teammates. Make sure to use new footballs for ball drills to prepare for what will be used in games. Practice ball drills when the weather is adverse, especially in wet conditions.

Game-Ready Punting Drills

These game-ready drills simulate gamelike experiences. They prepare the punter mentally and physically to perform successfully in competition.

Punters are timed frequently so they get the ball off quickly, develop rhythm, and improve consistency. The punter who is timed regularly knows his ideal time and can maximize his effectiveness every time he punts. By timing every punt during the game, the coach can confirm consistent get-off times and identify protection problems.

Hang Time

Objective
The punter develops his natural ability to increase hang time effectively during a game.

Equipment
A football and a snapper.

Progression
1. The punter stands at a point on the field where a punt of no longer than 35 to 40 yards would be needed. Set up as a drill by using a line with cones, or simulate a game situation in which the football is on the 50-yard line or slightly closer to the goal line.
2. Emphasize minimal distance. By shortening the length of the punt, the punter can transfer some forward power to more upward power to increase hang time.

Tips From the Coach
Instead of telling the punter how to increase hang time (slightly raise drop), put him in a situation in which doing so is a must. This is more gamelike and challenges him to execute the task at hand. He'll develop the proper technique naturally.

Variations
If there's a safe opportunity to punt over an object, such as a light pole, scoreboard, or video tower, have the punter do so. This gives him a visual of the trajectory needed, and he'll be able to adjust his body naturally to accomplish the objective.

Coffin Corner

Objective

The punter develops the skill of punting out of bounds inside the 20-yard line to eliminate any chance of a return and to gain an advantage in field position.

Equipment

A football and a snapper.

Progression

1. The punter stands near midfield at a point from which he can confidently punt the football out of bounds with authority. If the wind is at his back, he can be even farther back.

2. The aiming point to the right corner is where the sideline and the 5-yard line intersect. To the left corner, the aiming point is where the sideline and the 10-yard line intersect. The aiming point varies from side to side because of the football's fade effect to the right caused by the clockwise spiral rotation. This is switched for left-footed punters.

3. The punter faces forward to receive the snap. As he receives the snap he simultaneously shifts his direction precisely toward his target.

4. Because he's driving the ball out of bounds, hang time is not important. He kicks the football at a lower trajectory to ensure distance, placement, and accuracy.

Tips From the Coach

- This drill is ideal for working on punting fundamentals because it focuses on placing the football in a precise direction, necessitating a focus on proper mechanics.
- To drive the football at a lower trajectory, the punter simply holds the football slightly lower and slightly longer before making the drop. Allow him to develop this skill naturally through repetition.

Variations

If the situation calls for it, the punter can punt the football out of bounds at any time during the game, especially if punting against a great return man. When executing this type of punt, it's important to gain the maximum amount of distance and ensure the punt clears the sideline before it hits the ground. By doing this, the threat of any type of return is eliminated.

Redirect Drill

Objective

The punter develops the ability to adjust his body effectively to receive snaps directed to either side.

Equipment

Two kicking zone trajectory pads, one square standup dummy, a snapper.

Progression

1. The punter stands directly behind a square dummy lying length-wise in front of him. About 1 yard to each side of the square dummy are the kicking zone trajectory pads. This setup creates an alley to either side of the center dummy for the punter's approach.

2. The football is snapped to either side of the punter, making him quickly react to meet the snap and redirect his approach straight ahead, ensuring he's behind maximum protection from the oncoming rush.

3. He must not only redirect but must make up the time lost by the displaced snap.

Tips From the Coach

When meeting the snap to either side, the punter moves at a forward angle to receive the football. This way he gains ground slightly as he moves laterally, which helps him maintain momentum on the approach and make up some time to get the football off.

Variations

This drill can be set up with two snappers positioned to snap while looking back at a coach who's standing behind the punter. When the coach points to the side he wants the snap to come to, the snapper to that side snaps the football. The punter sees the snap coming and reacts accordingly.

The punter also can perform directional punts to either side instead of straight-ahead punts.

Placement

Objective

The punter works on optimizing hang time and distance while placing the football in a position on the field that minimizes the coverage area. He wants to master any type of punt his team needs to improve field position and minimize or eliminate a return.

Equipment

A football and a snapper.

Progression

1. The football is placed in the open field area anywhere from the 20-yard line to or just across the 50-yard line.
2. The punter aims for a point between the sideline and the numbers about 40 yards away. This precise positioning forces a return man to decide to make a fair catch or attempt a return. Because the kick is near the sideline, the return area is minimized.
3. The punter optimizes his distance to maximize hang time—crucial in this situation because the football stays within the field of play.

Tips From the Coach

Initially it's best to use cones or hoops to provide a visual for the punter. Once he becomes proficient and confident, he can aim for the normal field marks, just as he would in a game.

Variations

It's best to practice this drill from various positions on the field, such as close to midfield. This creates some different variables for the punter to consider, such as being closer to the goal line, where he'll want to avoid touchbacks.

Out of the End Zone

Objective

Through proper practice, technique adjustments, and game strategy, the punter develops confidence when punting out of the end zone.

Equipment

A football, a snapper, punting protection unit, and punt-rush unit.

Progression

1. The punter must do this drill by punting out of the end zone against a live rush. This helps him overcome the psychological challenge of punting from this area of the field.
2. He begins the drill in his stance with feet well ahead of the back line, not right up against it.
3. The more inside the 5-yard line the football is spotted, the less room the punter has to take his normal steps. The best approach is to shorten his steps to cover less distance, allowing him to use his normal stepping approach.
4. He should still maintain a quick and rhythmic get-off time.

Tips From the Coach

- Distance is desperately needed to regain some field position and get the punting team out of the hole. Hang time is more important to minimize a return.
- Practicing this type of punt helps the punter develop a quicker adjustment that he's comfortable with, allowing for more consistent and effective punts.

Variations

The punter works on this type of punt whether there's a rush or not. He can work on it by himself when the protection and blocking units are unavailable. He needs to realize that even though this punt is from deep in his own end zone, it's like every other punt. The only difference is that he needs to hurry to beat the rush.

The punter should practice drive punts as well as hang time punts out of the end zone. This will help him prepare strategically to drive the punt when facing a headwind. Use cones to determine the distance of each punt, based on the punter's ability. For instance, for a college punter set a cone 40 yards from the line of scrimmage to represent the distance for a hang time punt and another cone 55 yards away to represent a drive punt. The punter alternates between hang time punts and drive punts by placing the football directly at the designated cones. This will require him to adjust the football each time and make proper technique adjustments for the desired punt. There is no better way to enhance the punter's skills and understanding than by putting him in gamelike situations.

In another variation, the punter starts at the 5-yard line and, after each snap, the snapper sets up 1 yard back. This allows the punter to punt from the 5-, 4-, 3-, 2-, and 1-yard lines, setting up a true gamelike situation. This same drill can be used during pregame warm-ups to effectively prepare in a limited amount of time.

Pooch Punt

Objective

The punter works on punting the football with maximum hang time to just across the 10-yard line to eliminate a return.

Equipment

A football.

Progression

1. The punter takes a position on the field where he can simulate a football being snapped from an area near midfield or closer to the goal line.

2. He punts the football, emphasizing hang time and minimizing distance to make the football land at or near the 10-yard line.

Tips From the Coach

Pooch punts, also known as sky punts, are designed to minimize distance and maximize hang time. This combination provides effective placement and the time needed to improve coverage and field position. Pooch punts also decrease the chance the return man will make a successful catch. There is always a chance the returner will mishandle a catch and provide the punting team the opportunity to recover the football in great field position.

Variations

The pooch punt can also be effective when placed near the sideline. This positioning gives the return man even more to think about when deciding to catch the punt or let it go. If he decides to let it go, there's a greater chance the football will go out of bounds.

An Aussie-style pooch kick is an effective punt to use in this drill.

Punt After a Safety

Objective

The punter prepares to execute a rare type of punt: the kick that puts the football into play after a safety.

Equipment

A football.

Progression

1. With no snap, the punter practices punting from the designated area onfield, just behind the 20-yard line. He practices performing a kick after a safety.

2. The punter strives to optimize distance and maximize hang time to give the punt coverage time to cover downfield, minimizing or eliminating a return.

Tips From the Coach

This is a drill that needs to be incorporated into the practice schedule weekly so the punter is prepared and knows what his coach and team need for him to do in this situation.

Variations

Place punts in various positions on the field to promote effective coverage.

Bad Snap

Objective

The punter works on being prepared for the unexpected bad or mishandled snap.

Equipment

A football and a partner to snap.

Progression

1. The punter does this drill with someone other than his usual snapper. (You don't want your snapper to practice bad habits.)

2. The punter works on low, high, and wide snaps. He must secure each snap and then redirect his approach to make up for time lost by the bad snap.

3. If a ball is thrown over the punter's head, he must retrieve it and turn back toward the line of scrimmage to get off the punt. He needs to get in position to maximize his leg swing. Therefore, right-footed punters turn counterclockwise; left-footed punters turn clockwise.

Tips From the Coach

Bad snaps force punters to quickly redirect body position and speed up the punting process to make up for lost time.

Variations

The punter handles snaps that skip off the ground or roll back to him. He needs to experience this type of snap and adjust toward the ground to receive the football without letting his knee touch the ground, which would immediately down the football.

Tackling Practice

The punter must be prepared in case he's the last player who can make a game-saving tackle. Most importantly he must learn the proper technique to be able to make the tackle safely without risking injury.

There's no better way to learn how to tackle than to spend time with the defensive backs and their coaches. The secondary understands the importance of being the last line of defense. They are experts at making open-field tackles. Understanding the angles of approach and proper tackling techniques equips the punter with confidence and skills that might make the difference in a game. If the punter is not training with the defensive backs to learn to open-field tackle, he must take the initiative to get involved. Not only is this the best way for the punter to learn to tackle successfully, it's the best way for him to learn to tackle safely.

III

Countdown to Game Day

10

Snaps, Holds, and Recovery Plays

Although most long snappers snap for both placement kicks and punts, some teams prefer to have a long snapper for punts and a short snapper for extra points and field goals. The fundamental techniques of long snaps and short snaps are the same, but there are some subtle differences.

For field goals and extra points, the placekicker must be able to rely on the hands of his holder to catch and securely position the football for the kick. In the past, quarterbacks and receivers were often the designated holders because their primary positions require soft, dependable hands. Recently, however, particularly on the college and professional levels, the punter has become the primary holder because of the reliability of his hands from working with the snapper and receiving snaps himself. Also the punter and kicker normally work alone together during practice due to their specialized positions and individual skill needs. They better understand each other's position and the responsibilities and pressures faced. It also is quite common for them to back up one another in the kicking and punting positions when both have experience kicking and punting at the high school level or have acquired skills simply by working with each other.

The most successful football teams place tremendous emphasis on the kicking game. If they didn't, they wouldn't be successful. Every professional football team emphasizes this third phase of football because they must to remain competitive. This is why pro teams hire special teams coaches.

In this chapter, we'll cover the fundamentals of long snapping, holds, and recovery plays. Even for the best kickers and punters, their performance hinges on the success of the snapper. The kicker also must rely on the success of the holder. Extra points, short field goals, and punts often appear to be automatic plays, but breakdowns do occur in the course of a game. When faced with a challenge, the kicking team must be prepared to adjust. Remember, it's not what happens to you but how you respond. In this chapter, you will not only learn the fundamentals of the snapper and holder positions, you also will learn to respond in various situations.

Long Snapping Fundamentals

A placekicker or punter who lacks a dependable long snapper will have continual challenges no matter how well he develops his kicking and punting skills. The long snapper has tremendous impact on the kicking game. His consistent snap of the football initiates the success of every placekick or punt.

The long snapper is one of the least recognized positions on a football team. Often the only time anyone learns the name of the snapper is when he has a bad snap; then everyone knows his name. This lack of recognition is in part because long snapping the football has evolved to being part of a play that's considered to be automatic. So when a bad snap or a missed extra point occurs, the reaction is disbelief.

A big concern is the lack of knowledge in properly coaching the long snapping position. Teams that have coaches and players who place a great deal of emphasis in developing these positions tend to have the most successful kicking games. They also understand the importance of developing the special teams units and the impact these teams have in winning football games.

Approach and Setup

With the football in position on the ground, the snapper's approach should be exactly the same every time—he keeps the ball directly in line with the center of his body. Whether the snapper is practicing snaps by himself by snapping into a net, snapping to a holder or punter, breaking from the huddle, or running onto the field from the sideline, he should approach the football as if the official in an actual game has just spotted the ball on the field. Simulating gamelike situations during practice helps develop consistent habits and is the best way for the snapper to prepare. The snapper shouldn't develop the habit of positioning the football in his hands and then getting into his stance. This is not how it's done. In a game, the official always spots the football.

Feet Positioning

As he prepares to make the snap, the snapper positions about an arm's length behind the football (figure 10.1). His feet are slightly wider than shoulder width and evenly aligned to make it easier to snap the ball between his legs. He shouldn't spread his legs too wide because a very wide stance means he's more straight-legged, dramatically affecting the speed, power, and consistency of the snap.

His feet are even, not staggered. Any type of offset positioning of the feet during the snap can cause the hips to turn slightly and the hands to finish unevenly. Either problem might contribute to an errant snap to either side of the punter or holder.

Figure 10.1 Snapper is an arm's length from the ball, his feet wider than shoulder-width apart and even.

Stance

Keeping his heels in contact with the ground, the snapper sits back similar to a free-weight squat position in which the tops of the thighs are almost parallel to the ground (figure 10.2).

Once in this position, the snapper ensures his knees don't extend past his toes. He needs to familiarize himself with this balanced stance position. The heels touch the ground, and body weight is evenly distributed across the feet. The snapper can check

Figure 10.2 Snapper sits back on heels, thighs nearly parallel to ground.

the width of his stance to ensure he's balanced by simply hanging his arms directly down so that his elbows align just inside his knees. Like all athletes, snappers are not built the exact same way, so there will be some slight variances in the stance relating to the size and body position of the snapper.

Arm Position and Hand Placement

From the sit-back position in the stance, the snapper extends his arms and places his hands on the football. To learn to straighten his arm without making it rigid, he first locks out the arm on the side of his dominant hand and then very slightly relaxes the arm at the elbow. The snapper's arm on the side of the guide hand can bend a little more at the elbow, depending on the placement of the guide hand as it adjusts to complement the dominant hand.

Placement of the Dominant Hand

When the snapper initially reaches out to position his hands on the football, the ball is flat on the ground and points straight downfield. As he grips the ball with the hand on his dominant side, often his right hand, he places his fingers on the laces and lifts the front point of the football so it's at an angle to the ground (figure 10.3). The angle of the football can range from 30 to 45 degrees to the ground. An angle outside this range could keep the snap motion from flowing smoothly. The ball should never be completely flat on the ground or completely on its point. The exact angle is determined by the snapper. Too much or too little angle can cause inadvertent contact with the ground when the snap is initiated.

The snapper grips the football with the dominant hand in the same way a quarterback grips the football when throwing a pass. The palm is off the football; the fingers provide leverage, ensuring a smooth, clean release.

Figure 10.3 Gripping the football with the dominant hand.

Placement of the Guide Hand

The guide hand provides more than just stability and assistance to the dominant hand. The guide hand also adds extra leverage and support, enhancing the rotation of the football and the accuracy of its flight.

A snapper has several options in gripping the football with the guide hand. Commonly, the guide hand is on the back middle to lower half of the football with fingers spread while the middle finger is directly on the vertical seam or in a position parallel to either side (figure 10.4a). The thumb of the dominant hand is in a horizontal position, generally in line with the top of the fingers on the guide hand.

In another position, the index finger of the guide hand is directly on the seam (figure 10.4b). In yet another position, called the C-minus grip, the guide hand is high on the football, typically with little space between the index and middle fingers (figure 10.4c). The index and middle fingers are placed near the top point of the football; the other fingers and thumb are spread wide on the ball.

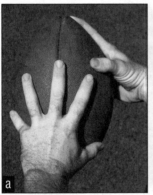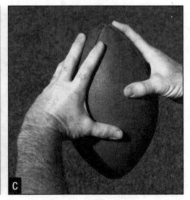

Figure 10.4 Options for the guide hand on the ball: *(a)* fingers spread wide with middle finger on vertical seam; guide hand on back middle to lower half of the ball; *(b)* index finger directly on the seam; *(c)* C-minus grip: fingers have little spacing.

The snap is essentially a pass between the snapper's legs to the punter or holder. Whatever grip the snapper chooses, he must make sure his guide hand accommodates the natural positioning of the dominant throwing hand. This can be done, in part, by ensuring the back seam of the football (opposite the laces) is aligned toward the shoulder on the guide hand side while in the pre-snap position.

Football Placement

Once the snapper has properly gripped the football, he needs to place the ball in position so its front point tilts forward at a 30- to 45-degree angle.

When a longer snap is needed, the football can be tilted downward more, decreasing the angle.

Now that the snapper's arms are properly extended and the football is properly tilted, the snapper is in the most efficient position to deliver a timely and accurate snap (figure 10.5). This placement of the football minimizes any type of wasted motion, such as a hitch.

Figure 10.5 Snapper in position to deliver the snap.

Body Position

Being able to see the target is crucial for the long snapper. He must position in a way that provides him clear visibility and enables him to deliver the most accurate snap in the optimal time (figure 10.6).

Figure 10.6 Snapper's view of the *(a)* punter and *(b)* holder prior to the snap.

The snapper's back remains flat; his tail is in the proper position. Both feet remain flat on the ground, arms are extended with a slight flex, and the snapper's weight is back toward his hips. This positioning maintains balance and body control. The snapper keeps his chin to his chest (double-chin position) to keep his head down and in correct alignment.

Gradually, the snapper lifts his tail until he can see his target. This gradual movement ensures that his back remains flat and that his knees are in good position to provide leg power back toward the target.

Snap to the Punter

Because he's bent over, when the snapper gets into position and looks back through his legs, he'll see an inverted visual. From this perspective, he looks for a target zone from the punter's hip-thigh area down to his knees. The snapper delivers the ball to the area just inside the inner hip or inner thigh of the punter's kicking leg. This location is ideal because it prepositions the football in the area where the football will be aligned as the punter begins his approach.

The snapper lifts his tail just high enough to see the lower half of the punter's body and focuses on his target zone. If he can see the punter from head to toe, he's too high, which means he's more likely to make a high snap. He keeps his eyes on his target throughout the release of the snap, dramatically improving his mechanics and his accuracy.

Snapping Motion

The snapper begins his motion by pulling the football back toward the punter, leading with his elbows. At the same time, he executes an aggressive leg explosion. The power generated moves the snapper's body back several inches. As this occurs, his hips release slightly upward as his legs begin to lock out. The force from this movement causes his heels to come off the ground. His toes, still in contact with the ground, are dragged back.

The entire motion of the snapper's body (figure 10.7) complements the football being drawn back as the elbows cock in preparation for the snap. As

Figure 10.7 Snapping motion.

the snapper moves the ball from the ground, his elbows seem to collapse as they naturally bend in preparation for a whiplike release.

Follow-Through and Finish

The entire motion of the snap finishes directly toward the target. Finishing directly in line with the target ensures proper technique while creating consistency in both speed and accuracy.

The snapper's hands move with equal speed back between his legs. As he releases the football, his arms finish by making contact with his inner knees or inner thighs, with palms facing out and thumbs pointing up (figure 10.8a).

Figure 10.8 Finishing position: *(a)* back view; *(b)* side view.

If he finishes properly, the snapper can momentarily see his target between the backs of his hands. From the side (figure 10.8b), his body position looks like a plus sign, with arms parallel and legs perpendicular to the ground.

In a game, the snapper might not have time to exaggerate his finish because of his blocking responsibilities. Through repetition in practice, he can develop a feel for the correct finish position and be able to deliver accurately placed snaps.

Snap-to-Punt Timing

Snappers, kickers, and punters should be timed frequently and regularly during practice. This helps them get the ball off quickly, develops proper rhythm, and improves consistency. More important, snappers, kickers, and punters must develop optimal times for game-day performance. There is such a thing as getting the ball off too quickly when it's not necessary.

Another reason to time each phase of the kicking game is to create accountability, especially in games. During a game, when a kick or punt is nearly blocked, the first thought that comes to mind in the heat of battle is that the kicker or punter is taking too much time. Often this is not the case. If the entire kicking and punting sequence, including the snap, is timed during practice and in games, it's easy to determine if optimal times are met. If a punt was nearly blocked, but the timing was optimal, the problem lies in the protection. If the get-off time of the punt was slow, the punter created the problem. Frequent timing of the kicking sequence helps everyone understand why a kick was blocked so that the kicker or punter is not automatically (and often incorrectly) blamed.

Some coaches and players aren't aware of the optimal get-off times for kicks and punts but assume that faster times are always better. This mentality can reduce the effectiveness of kickers, punters, and coverage teams. If, for example, a coach tells a punter to speed up the delivery of every punt, the punter's performance will likely be compromised. Plus, he won't be able to establish the rhythm he needs to produce optimal punts. The situation is made even worse when the blame for a rushed and poor punt is put on the punter and protection is not improved. When the punt is rushed, especially unnecessarily rushed, the punting team delivers the football too quickly to the return man. This gives the return team an advantage in field position because the return man has more time to pick up yards before the coverage can reach him.

Optimal punt times are as follows:

0.75-0.8 seconds for the center snap

1.25-1.3 seconds for the punter to handle the ball (hand to foot)

2.0-2.1 seconds total get-off time

Snap Timing

It's important to time both the snap and the punt so that you can easily identify the consistency of the punting sequence. Begin the accountability process by letting the snapper and punter know their individual times. Snappers, punters, and kickers whose times are regularly charted gradually develop a natural rhythm in accordance with the desired time.

The most reliable way to accurately time the snap is with a stopwatch. The best stopwatches on the market are affordable and provide dependable service. A stopwatch with split-timing capabilities allows a coach to record each segment of the punting or kicking procedure in sequential order as well as determine the total time. The coach or teammate holding the watch needs to know how to use it objectively. Most accurate stopwatch times are achieved by starting and stopping the stopwatch with the index finger, not the thumb, because the index finger has a faster, more reliable reaction time.

For the timer, the snap is when timing begins. The timer focuses on any movement of the football. Oncoming rushers key on the very first movement of the snapped football, so the timer must do the same. This is the main reason the snapper shouldn't show any sign of a hitch or false movement. The timing begins at the precise moment there's any sign of movement.

Another technique to ensure the most accurate time is for the timer to be in a position in which he can view the entire snap-to-punt or snap-to-kick sequence. He focuses on the football and uses his peripheral vision to keep the full kicking unit—snapper and punter, or snapper, holder, and kicker—in view. This way he can follow the entire flight of the football and recognize the precise moment to start or stop the watch.

The watch is stopped with the same precision with which it was started. When recording the snap time, the timer stops the watch the instant the ball touches the punter's hands. This is the accurate snap time. Although the distance of the punter behind the snapper varies at different levels of play (12 or 13 yards for high school football; 14 or 15 yards for college and pro), the required snap time remains the same. No matter what level of play, the snap time needs to be 0.8 seconds or slightly faster. This is the optimal time for both speed and accuracy.

Avoid fostering a track meet mentality when it comes to timing snaps or kicks. Kicking is not about being the fastest—it's about achieving the optimal time in regard to speed and accuracy. Although some professional snappers can snap faster than 0.7 seconds, they know they're at their consistent best when snapping near 0.74 seconds.

Because the snapper becomes more proficient as he advances to the next level, he maintains the same snap time and adjusts to the added distance by increasing his snap speed. In high school, a snapper might have the standard snap time of 0.8 seconds when snapping at a distance of 12 yards. To progress to the college level, he'll need to improve his snap speed to maintain this same snap time because the distance in college is 15 yards.

Hand-to-Foot Timing

The instant the snapped football touches the punter's hands, the timer starts the stopwatch for the second phase of the punt—the hand-to-foot time (also known as touch-to-toe time).

The punter receives the snapped football about 1 yard ahead of where he was in his original stance. If he began 15 yards from the point where the snapper will snap the football, he'll receive the snap at about the 14-yard mark.

With arms outstretched and the football in his hands, the punter simultaneously begins his approach and positions the football for the punt. At this point, the timer focuses on the football in anticipation of the moment it's dropped. As the football descends and the foot rises to meet it, the timer stops the watch at the precise moment of foot-to-ball contact.

The punter must use proper mechanics as he leans to meet the snap. This anticipation by the punter, created by the lean, gives him an edge to optimize his time.

The optimal total get-off time is between 2.0 and 2.1 seconds. A time of 2.2 seconds is bordering on too slow; a time of 1.9 seconds is bordering on too fast. Obviously, the punter will need to be quicker than usual if he's in a tight-punt situation with limited distance and a heavy rush. However, when punting from deep in the end zone, the punter will receive the snap somewhat more quickly due to the shorter snap distance.

Holding Fundamentals

The holder must have reliable hands for catching the football. As mentioned earlier, the holder is commonly the punter, which makes sense because the punter is familiar with receiving snaps and usually has soft, dependable hands. He also understands the kicker's responsibilities and pressures. The holder and kicker must have quality time to work together during practice, preferably with the snapper, to get the repetitions necessary for them to be successful.

At the high school level, the punter might also be the placekicker, which means he can't be the holder. In this case, the first-, second-, or third-string quarterback or receiver are usually good candidates for holding. Any play position that depends on regularly handling or receiving the football will train a player to have soft, dependable hands.

Point of Placement

Once the placekicker establishes a visual reference, he determines the exact flight path the ball needs to travel by positioning himself at the point of placement, usually 7 or 8 yards behind the snapper.

This deeper alignment is recommended at the college and professional levels because no placement tee is used. The added distance separates the kick farther from the rush and provides more immediate elevation to the kick. Also, linemen are taller and faster at the higher levels.

At this point, the kicker marks exactly where he wants his holder to set the football. A high school kicker directly faces his target and aligns his kicking block toward his target. A college or pro kicker faces the target and aligns the toe of his kicking foot toward his target as the holder places the fingers of his holding hand on the desired spot.

By establishing two points of reference—the target and point of placement—and creating an imaginary line toward the specific target, the kicker sets a benchmark for proper alignment that serves as a natural guide for the direction of every kick.

Holding Technique

The holder takes a knee on the ground to the right side, very near to where he anticipates the kicker will mark his spot. He places his right knee on the ground while keeping his left leg up and his left foot firmly on the ground and slightly behind the anticipated spot for the kick (figure 10.9). (For a left-footed kicker, the holder would kneel to the left side and put his left knee on the ground.)

Figure 10.9 Holder kneels on the ground.

Once the kicker determines his point of placement, the holder extends his left arm toward the ground, keeping the back of the arm pressed against the inside of his left leg, and places his index finger on the spot marked by the kicker (figure 10.10). His right hand stays on the top of his right thigh.

Figure 10.10 Holder extends left arm and places index finger on point of placement.

The point of placement is now a reference point for the kicker and the holder. The holder keeps his hand in this position without moving it, no matter what.

As the kicker marks off his steps, the holder ensures his left foot is firmly on the ground by distributing his weight in position that places his right buttocks on the back of his right heel.

While seated on his right buttocks, with the back of his left arm pressed against the inside of his leg and his hand on the spot, the holder opens his chest in the direction of the snapper (figure 10.11). He makes sure the snapper and rest of the kicking team are in proper position prior to the snap. His right arm hangs down toward the ground with his hand resting on the inside of his knee.

Figure 10.11 Holder sits back, index finger on point of placement, and opens chest in direction of the snapper.

Figure 10.12 Holder raises right arm toward the snapper and flashes his palm with the thumb down.

As the kicker finishes marking off his steps and gets into his stance, the holder turns his head and focuses on the kicker in anticipation of the acknowledgment that the kicker is ready. The kicker usually communicates that he's ready with a simple nod.

Once the kicker nods that he's ready, the holder immediately turns his head in the direction of the snapper. He raises his right arm, slightly bending it at the elbow, and positions his hand over the point of placement. The hand should also be aligned near the level of the left knee, creating a natural target line for the snapper. As the holder positions his hand, he simultaneously flashes his palm with his thumb down over the target line (figure 10.12). This thumb position eliminates wasted motion by prepositioning the hand in the exact position it will be when the snap arrives. He gives a ready–set call or some form of cadence. This acknowledges to the snapper and the rest of the kicking team that the kicker is in position and ready for the snap.

Empower the Snapper

The center controls the moment when the football is snapped. The snapper shouldn't be forced to deliver the snap on cadence. This helps to ensure a consistent snap that's both timely and accurate.

Snap to the Holder

The snapper addresses the ball just as he does when snapping for a punt. The major difference between a long snap for a punt and a long snap for a placekick is that the placekick snap is nearly half as long (so the explosive use of the legs is not needed).

The long snapper's stance is the same as if he were snapping to a punter, but he'll have to make some adjustments because the target area is lower. The snapper aims directly through the holder's extended hand, which is over the point of placement and aligned with his back knee. This positioning of the hand, elbow, and knee creates a natural aiming point directly in line with the anticipated path of the snapped football.

The general point of placement for an extra point and field goal is 7 yards from the line of scrimmage. Recently, more teams are adjusting to a distance from 7 to 8 yards to enhance protection from the oncoming rush by maximizing distance and elevation of the kick.

Because the snap distance is nearly half what it is for a punt, the snapper needs to lower the flight path of the football. To deliver the ball on a lower flight path, he tilts the ball downward slightly to reduce the angle of the ball or moves his guide hand slightly down the ball. He can experiment by slightly lowering his guide hand until he finds a placement that allows him to keep the ball down. He should start by moving his guide hand down the football a quarter of an inch or less until he achieves the desired flight path of the ball.

Another way for the snapper to experiment is to tilt the football away from the forehead to lower the flight path. This tilts the wrist down a little and reduces the amount of whip action required of the wrist joint. The downward tilt also causes a slight straightening of the dominant arm, which reduces the elbow action as well.

Another way to lower the flight path is to lower the contact point when following through. When snapping for a punt, the snapper's arms usually make contact with the inner knee or inner thigh during the follow-through. Lowering this contact point might help the snapper keep the football down. When the contact point is lowered, the ball is released earlier, and thus lower.

Receipt of the Snap

At the exact moment the ball is snapped, two precise movements instantly follow. The holder's hand, which is at the point of placement, immediately rises to join with the other hand to catch the ball. As he sees the holder's hand rise, the kicker immediately leans, leading with his chest, to create the need for his initial step. This sequence of events—snap, raise of the hand, and forward lean of the kicker—should happen as close to simultaneously as possible. Orchestrated movement is key for optimally timing the kick.

As the snap is delivered, the holder extends his arms to meet the snap, brings both hands together with thumbs in, and catches the football with two hands (figure 10.13a). In this hand position, the holder's index finger on the left hand is near the point of the football as he secures the catch. After catching the snap, he turns his upper body until the elbow area of his left arm is stopped by the inside of his left leg. With the foot of the left leg securely on the ground, the inside of the knee creates a backstop

Figure 10.13 Receiving the snap: *(a)* holder catches the snap in two hands; *(b)* he turns his upper body and places the football on the ground; *(c)* he holds the football with his index finger and spins the laces to face the target.

that enables the holder to consistently position the football precisely on the ground (figure 10.13*b*).

The holder is facing the point of placement as he quickly brings the football to the ground directly in front of him. As soon as he sets the football on the ground, he slides his left hand toward the top of the ball while maintaining contact with it. Now only the index finger holds the football as he quickly spins the football with his right hand into place, if necessary (figure 10.13*c*) (the laces must be toward the target). Through quality repetitions, this entire process flows smoothly and becomes automatic.

Hold and Ball Position

The holder positions the football straight up and down with laces facing the target. The laces should not face the kicker. Soccer-style kickers might prefer to have the top end of the football tilted slightly away from the plant foot or, in other words, slightly toward the holder in order to obtain better contact with the sweet spot. Because the kicking foot is angled slightly at impact, the slight tilt of the ball creates an ideal spot for ball compression and control. This simple adjustment allows centrifugal force to create a more powerful vertical rotation of the ball. Vertical rotation allows a truer flight path and, thus, a more accurate kick.

When tilting the football back, the holder decreases the exposed portion of the sweet spot. An erect placement, which looks more vertical from the side, allows the kicker to see the entire football, enabling him to hit just under the ball's middle to get maximum height and distance. In some cases, kickers are so proficient at hitting the sweet spot that they might ask the holder to lean the football slightly forward to expose even more of the area of the football so they can obtain the most compression.

Unkickable Snaps and Blocked Kicks

Proper ball positioning is developed through repetition. The snapper, holder, and kicker work regularly together to develop consistency and confidence in one another. When a bad snap or mishandled ball, or a combination of the two, occurs, the kicker must adjust his approach as necessary (e.g., use a hesitation step)—or continue with his normal approach, confident that the holder will recover and position the football just in time. Regularly working with the holder and snapper gives the kicker opportunities to learn to adjust at the last second and execute an effective kick.

Everyone involved in the kicking game must be prepared for those times when something goes wrong. They must have a plan for every worst-case scenario that can happen in a game. Ideally, kickers, punters, and snappers should help develop game strategy with their coaches. This way they'll truly know how to respond for their team when faced with a serious challenge during a critical point of a game.

Unkickable Snaps

Most unkickable snaps are caused by bad snaps, mishandled balls, or both. When this happens, the holder instinctively positions the football at the very last moment to save the play or else abandons the play and attempts to run or throw a pass. Because he's well aware that a kick normally takes about 1.3 seconds to execute, the holder goes with his gut instincts and reacts in the way in which his team has prepared.

If there's any way to get the kick off, that's what should be done. The kick was the purpose of calling the play. But when an effective kick is highly improbable, there must be an alternative. The most common alternative is for the holder to try to salvage the play by yelling "fire, fire, fire!" This alerts the tight ends and wingbacks to run predetermined routes that spread out the field by taking them toward the corners and sidelines.

The holder can roll out to either side, depending on where the bounce of the football takes him. If the holder is right handed, it's best (though not always possible) to roll right. The kicker must react quickly and protect the first threat to the backside of the holder, which is opposite of the direction in which the holder rolls out.

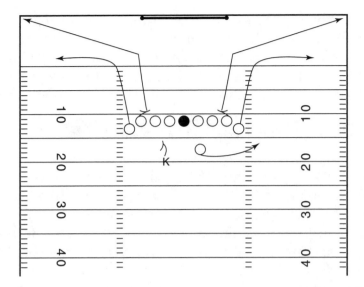

Figure 10.14 Routes run by tight ends and wingbacks during a botched attempt at a PAT.

The tight ends usually run corner or flag routes that take them to the corners of the end zone (figure 10.14), while the wingbacks run arrow or quick out routes that take them just across the goal line (for an extra point attempt) or the first-down marker (for a field goal), depending on the situation. If the unkickable snap occurs in field goal range, the wingbacks must make sure the depth of their routes put them in position to get the first down.

It's best to have a great athlete as the holder, especially one who can throw and run the football. In any case, in times of crisis the holder must make a good decision. If he can't find an open receiver, he must run with the ball or simply throw it away. If this is the last play of the game, the holder makes a play happen any way he can.

Blocked Kicks

One thing coaches can thoroughly impress on their players is to know the rules. In regards to blocked kicks, all players should know the following:

- A blocked field goal that's recovered behind the line of scrimmage may be advanced by either team.
- A blocked field goal that crosses the line of scrimmage may be advanced only by the defense.
- In college football, a blocked extra point can be picked up by the defense and returned to the kicking team's end zone for two points.

Some rules or variation of rules might change at certain levels of play. The only way to ensure that rules are current is to annually review the rulebooks and check for updates.

In the case of a blocked kick that doesn't make it past the line of scrimmage, the kicking team's top priority is to secure the football so they can either advance the ball or simply down it so it can't be advanced by the opposition. If a blocked field goal crosses the line of scrimmage, the top priority is to secure the football and down it. If the ball has been recovered by the opposition, the kicking team must ensure the football is downed, which might mean making a tackle.

The college rule for a blocked extra point states that the football can be picked up by the defense and returned to the kicking team's end zone for two points. So, in the event of a blocked PAT, the kicking team must secure the football and down it or make the tackle.

Fake Plays

When the kicker or punter is performing exceptionally well and there's no need for a fake PAT, field goal, or punt, that might be the best time to run one. This is especially true if an opponent is showing a weak spot that can be exploited, such as an overly aggressive rush that has produced some weaknesses in the interior alignment, a limited or very weak containment on the outside perimeter, or a tendency to ignore eligible receivers.

Whatever the reason for calling a fake play, a properly executed fake can be tremendously beneficial to the kicking team. If the kicker and punter are performing exceptionally, then the play should be more or less unexpected. If the play is performed to perfection, it provides a great opportunity for a big play. Even if it's close to being successful, the proper execution of the play will display its potential so that the next time the kicking team lines up in a similar formation and situation, the defense might play more tentatively in anticipation of another fake. They might not rush as aggressively or set up the return as effectively. Better yet, future opponents will have to take time out of their practice schedules to work on a play that you might not use for a long time (but they don't know that).

Once you use a fake play, it's wise to implement a similar version that's considered a fake of the fake or to come up with a new play altogether.

Kickers and punters can play key roles in fake plays by simulating their skills to perfection without kicking or punting the football. Because of the poor visibility caused by the interior linemen, the defense might have difficulty seeing if the football has been kicked or not. A momentary hesitation caused by the kicker or punter who's faking his performance might be all it takes to make the play successful.

11

Pregame Program

For success in competition, kickers and punters must develop a pregame program that's a concise culmination of their weekly workout routine. In this chapter we present drills and exercises that have proven effective in preparing kickers and punters to be at their optimal level of performance on game day. Through a methodical teaching progression, each player builds a solid foundation on proven strategies and learns to design his own pregame program based on this foundation.

Pregame Routine

The pregame routine is a blueprint for the kicker and punter to follow, preparing them mentally and physically to perform on the field. The pregame routine is not just a routine but a series of habits that develops through experience and proper training. Each habit has a purpose that prepares the kicker and punter for situations that arise in games. Successful kickers and punters create their own pregame routines, ones that best fit their individual and team needs.

Arrival at the Stadium

On game day, kickers and punters arrive at the stadium early enough to begin a warm-up routine that prepares them for competition. They establish a timeframe to warm up and stretch in preparation to join the snapper and holder on the field 70 to 80 minutes before kickoff. As they come together during this timeframe, they begin performing a series of kicks that simulate game situations. This progression of kicks systematically advances to incorporate kick and punt returners to prepare their skills as well.

For home games, professional kickers and punters arrive as early as three hours before kickoff. They go out on the game field in warm-up gear (no helmets or shoulder pads) as early as 2 ½ hours before the game to walk around the stadium, check out the field, and monitor wind conditions, especially in the areas where kicks and punts will be made. Around this same time, placekickers, punters, long snappers, and holders start their warm-up and stretch routine, which is necessary before any kicking or punting begins. After this, they return to the locker room, put on their helmets and shoulder pads, and return to the game field, ready to complete the kicking and punting warm-ups.

For away games, kickers and punters arrive the same time as everyone else because they're traveling with the team. Sometimes on the professional level, transportation is provided for earlier and later arrivals. Ideally, the coach plans well enough for everyone to arrive early. If not, the punter and kicker need to explain their objectives to the coach and ask for more time. When players take the initiative for the betterment of the team, the coach will likely be receptive. If he's not, the punter and kicker must do their best with what time they have.

Prestretch Warm-Up

These warm-up drills are designed to be done outside on the football field. In the case of extreme weather, the drills can be modified to be done indoors within limited space.

Stretching is often considered to be warming up, but it's not—it's simply stretching. To properly stretch, the kicker and punter need to warm up beforehand. The two basic ways to warm up before stretching are by loosening up and performing cardiovascular exercises. This part of the pregame routine can be done indoors or on the field.

To loosen up, players move around to get limber and warm up their muscles. The kicker and punter rotate areas of the body systematically from the head down: neck, shoulders, chest, arms and elbows, waist and trunk, hips, legs, knees, and ankles. This loosens up all the joints of the body.

The loosening-up exercises are simple: rotate the head; shrug the shoulders; cross the arms; twist the trunk; turn the hips; raise the legs. These exercises are done one at time or can be combined. Loosening up takes 5 to 10 minutes.

After loosening up, the kicker and punter jog, form run, or do calisthenics (any cardiovascular exercise that gets the heart pumping). By increasing cardiovascular productivity, the kicker and punter increase the body's temperature enough to break a sweat. The jog can be a simple lap or two around the football field or four running strides across the length of the field for 100 yards. This type of gradual warm-up raises the body temperature, increases blood flow to the muscles, lubricates the joints, and promotes initial flexibility for stretching. The warm-up also increases range of motion and minimizes risk of injury. Three to five minutes is enough for the athlete to break a sweat.

Static Stretching

Static stretching (stretching without movement) is effective and considered one of the safest methods of stretching. It's also one of the least fatiguing. Static stretching can complement dynamic stretching before or during competition, especially if an area of the body seems tight and needs a release. Static stretching is ideal for off days, at the end of practice, or as a part of a relaxation routine. By concentrating on releasing all tension in a specific area, muscles can relax better. This helps mental relaxation as well. Any individual stretch, or a variety of them, can be incorporated into the pregame warm-up as needed. They can also be performed throughout the game if additional stretching is needed to maintain flexibility for performance.

Static stretching increases range of motion. The simplest and most common way to stretch muscles is by lengthening them to their farthest point and then holding that position for 10 to 25 seconds in a static stretch. Athletes exhale at the start of the stretch, breathe in and out until relaxed, and then inhale to finish. Static stretching takes 8 to 10 minutes. If time allows, the kicker or punter might choose to take up to 15 minutes to make sure he's relaxed.

Many static stretching exercises are beneficial and can be tailored to meet individual needs. The kicker and punter focus on the muscles they'll use in their kicking and punting motions. They might begin by gradually proceeding with each stretch in a systematic way, starting with the neck and moving down the body.

Standing Static Stretches

1. Neck: apply steady pressure in each direction: backward, forward, to the right, to the left.

2. Shoulder: place one arm parallel across the neck and pull with the opposite arm while head is turned in the opposite direction of the shoulder being stretched.

3. Arm: place hand on same-side shoulder and pull elbow back with opposite hand.

4. Trunk: lean front, left, back, and right, holding each position in all directions.

5. Hamstrings: with legs together and knees locked, grab the ankles with both hands and pull nose to knees *(a)*. Next, stand with feet slightly wider than shoulder-width and knees locked. Grab ankles and pull down, touching the head to the right knee and then to the left knee *(b)*. Finish by reaching back through legs as far as possible *(c)*.

6. Hamstrings: stand with the right leg over the locked left leg. Grab ankles with both hands and pull nose to knees. Repeat the stretch with the left leg over the right.

7. Groin, quadriceps, and calves: stand with feet a little wider than hip-width apart. Turn torso to face right leg and lunge to the right, bending both knees and balancing on the left toe. Return to the initial position and turn to the left, repeating the stretch to the left side.

(continued)

8. Groin: stand in a slightly straddled position. Lean right, then left *(a)*. Rotate right, then left *(b)*. Grab right ankle, then left ankle *(c)*.

9. Quadriceps: stand with legs together. Lift right foot and reach back to grab foot. Pull foot toward butt. This stretch is also great for working on balance.

10. Sumo squat for quadriceps, back, and groin: stand with feet wide apart and toes turned diagonally outward. Squat, keeping heels in contact with the ground. The butt is lower than the knees. Use the elbows to push the knees out to the sides.

Seated Static Stretches

1. Groin: sit and pull the soles of the feet together. Use elbows to push down knees.

2. Lower back: sit with legs straddled and knees bent. Grab the inside bottom of feet and pull toward body.

3. Lower back: lie on back. Reach around legs and clasp hands together. Pull legs into chest.

4. Hamstrings: sit with legs together. Grab behind ankles with both hands and stretch torso over legs.

(continued)

Seated Static Stretches *(continued)*

5. Gluteus: sit up with legs together. Bend the right leg and place the right foot over the left knee. Place the left elbow on the right knee and turn to the right.

6. Gluteus: lie back. Keep head, shoulders, and elbows on the ground. Lift the right leg over the left leg and touch the ground with the right foot. Repeat to the left.

7. Quadriceps: lie on side and extend lower arm for balance. With opposite arm, reach for upper foot and pull toward butt.

Dynamic Stretching

Once the kicker and punter have warmed up enough to break a sweat and loosened up through static stretching, they can perform dynamic stretching (stretching with movement). This is a fast-track way to replicate the movements of kickers and punters, enabling them to kick-start their mobility. Dynamic stretching is vital to sport-specific motion and is best incorporated into the warm-up routine before training or competition. This form of stretching develops flexibility, enhances balance and coordination, improves mobility, increases strength, and improves full range of motion. Muscles can stretch further when the speed of motion, body momentum, and muscular action are used to improve stretching. This is a controlled and gentle form of stretching that takes athletes to the limits of their range of motion. One example of dynamic stretching is when kickers and punters warm up with form kicks—the swinging motion of the legs is a type of dynamic stretching.

These exercises cover an up-and-back distance of 10 to 20 yards. The stretch can begin on a yard line and cover 10 to 20 yards, or it can cover 10 yards, at which point the athlete strides out or sprints the final 10 yards.

Dynamic Stretches

1. High-knee walking: lift the knee as high as possible, using proper arm swing; simultaneously rise up on the toes of the opposite foot. Alternate knee pulls.

2. Walking lunge: place hands behind head. Exaggerate stride forward and land heel to toe. Extend legs until back leg is balanced on toes and back knee doesn't touch the ground. Bring the back leg through and continue.

3. Side lunge: keep body upright with hands on hips. Face to the right and lunge to the right by bending the right leg while rising on the toes and taking an exaggerated step to the right. Keep the left leg straight with the inside edge of the shoe touching the ground. Shift weight back and lunge to the opposite leg. Stand and pivot counterclockwise to the opposite side. Repeat and progress downfield.

(continued)

4. Backward lunge: place hands behind head, exaggerate stride, and step backward on toes, keeping knee off the ground. Once balanced, bring front leg through and continue.

5. Pretzel lunge: lunge and place the arm on the same side inside the knee, reaching around to grab the lead foot. The back leg remains straight. Keep the back knee off the ground. Try to pull the chest toward the ground with the other hand on the ground for balance.

6. Frankenstein walk: extend arms straight out, keeping hands at eye level. As you walk, kick each foot up to the hand on the same side as you go.

7. High-knee carioca: stand and face to the side, hips lowered and weight balanced on the balls of the feet. Step laterally with the lead foot and immediately twist the hips to bring the back leg ahead of the front leg. As the back leg moves forward, lift the knee in a high motion across the front of the body before putting it ahead of the other. Continue laterally by stepping with the front leg and bringing the back leg behind the body. Make sure the shoulders stay steady and square as the arms extend to maintain balance. A quick-step carioca uses the same body position and stepping pattern but no high-knee movement.

8. Power skips: skip forward, exaggerating the skip with a high-knee lift. With each leg lift, bring the opposite arm forward and up in an exaggerated movement.

9. Flutter kicks: skip forward and kick the leg straight out.

(continued)

10. Back pedal: stay low and begin to back pedal. Keep balanced by maintaining weight over the balls of the feet.

11. Butt kicks: lean body forward, staying on the balls of the feet. Quickly bring the heels toward the top of the buttocks while moving forward at a pace of 15 to 20 kicks for 10 yards.

12. High-knee running: lean backward slightly. Exaggerate the knee drive and lift the knees extremely high. Exaggerate the arm movement. Run with high knees for 10 yards, then sprint 10 yards.

Partner-Assisted Static Stretching

These exercises are done with a partner, preferably a coach, trainer, or teammate who knows how to apply pressure safely and effectively. These exercises can be done in the traditional static method or by using proprioceptive neuromuscular facilitation (PNF). This more advanced form of flexibility training done with a partner involves both stretching and contracting targeted muscle groups. Originally a form of rehabilitation, PNF is ideal for targeting muscle groups and is an excellent way to improve muscular strength, increase flexibility, increase range of motion, and prevent injuries.

Perform the technique with a contract-and-relax cadence. The athlete is placed in the targeted stretch position for 6 to 12 seconds and is then asked to contract the muscle by pushing or pulling in the opposite direction of the stretch. At the same time as the contraction, resistance is applied and held for 6 to 12 seconds. This is a form of isometrics, in which muscles are put under tension but not allowed to actually contract. The athlete contracts gradually, with no abrupt jerking motions.

After 6 to 12 seconds, the athlete relaxes, and the partner applies gradual pressure to stretch and lengthen the targeted muscles even further. Because of the resistance applied during the contraction, this technique enables muscles to relax more, increasing their ability to stretch. The athlete and his partner must be extremely careful when performing these stretches. Every stretch is done in a smooth and methodical manner.

Partner-Assisted Static Stretches

1. Hamstrings: lie flat on back with arms to the side and raise one leg. The partner braces the raised leg at the foot with the hand to the same side and places the opposite hand on the knee to help keep the knee locked. To help the athlete keep his leg flat on the ground, the partner places his own foot to the inside of the leg and his knee to the outside.

(continued)

2. Lower back: lie on back and bring knees to chest by clasping hands on the knees. The partner stands with his toes near the stretcher's buttocks and places his hands on the stretcher's feet. The partner pushes down to begin the stretch.

3. Groin: lie on back. Open legs to the sides, keeping legs straight. The partner stands with his feet to the sides of the hips, allowing his shins to support the legs in a straight position to the sides. The partner places his hands on the insides of the knees and gently applies pressure to begin the stretch. The partner must be careful and press lightly.

4. Hamstrings: from a seated position, legs together and knees flat, reach with both hands toward the outside of the ankles. The partner positions behind and presses against the athlete's back to begin the stretch.

5. Shoulder: from a seated position with legs flat and upper body vertical, extend arms back with thumbs up, keeping arms parallel to the ground. The partner holds the stretcher's hands and begins the stretch by bringing the arms toward each other.

6. Quadriceps: lie face down and turn head to the left, opposite the stretching leg. The partner kneels on his right knee and lifts the athlete's right leg, allowing it to bend at the knee. The partner positions his right hand just under the knee in a position that simulates throwing a shot. He then gradually pushes the knee up to begin the stretch while keeping his left hand on the buttocks area of the leg being stretched for support.

After warming up and stretching, kickers, punters, and snappers complete their kicking and punting warm-up with other specialists in the kicking game. Sometimes a kicker or punter arrives early enough to do some basic kicking and punting on his own before putting on the pads. If so, they need to be disciplined and not overkick by executing too many reps and fatiguing their legs. Any kicks or punts during this time must be basic and minimal, such as no-step and one-step kicks for placekickers or punt passes and short directional punts for punters.

Technique-Specific Warm-Up

This is the last phase of warming up prior to performing kicking and punting skills with snappers, holders, and return specialists.

Warming up and stretching through a systematic program that focuses on skills to be performed enhances the speed of the development and preparedness of the kicker and punter. This skill-specific approach allows players to effectively apply their training to game-day performance. The technique-specific warm-up is done on the football field.

Once the kicker or punter has warmed up and stretched, he continues the progression by doing drills more specific to the kicking and punting motions. This phase focuses on dynamic movements that complete the stretch of the muscles used in kicking by simulating the kicking motion.

Kickers do form kicks, and punters execute the escape gravity drill. The kicker and punter simulate the entire kicking and punting motion without a football, using a one-step and full-step approach. When he reaches his maximum follow-through, the kicker skips forward with his plant while the punter lifts up off the ground and moves forward, landing on his plant foot.

This basic dynamic stretching technique is to be done only after the kicker or punter has thoroughly warmed up and is preparing to kick or punt. This movement takes the muscles through a full range of motion to stretch the muscles further than previous drills to optimize the efficiency of the movement. This same movement is generally used on the sideline when a kicker or punter is about to perform during competition. They might even perform this movement after hustling into the game if there's time after a penalty or other delay.

It's common to see the punter hustle onto the field and quickly align only to find he has some extra time before everyone is set. He'll sometimes go through his approach and simulate punting the football while directing all his mental momentum toward the intended path of the football.

Kick and Return Specialists Warm-Up

This phase of warm-up begins 65 to 80 minutes before kickoff. The kicker and punter go on to the game field early enough to prepare effectively for the game ahead. Just as important, they need to help prepare the snappers, holders, and return specialists.

At the professional level, the punter is usually the holder. It's common for him to hold for the placekicker during warm-ups first before proceeding to warm up his punting skills. This efficient progression gives the placekicker time to complete his extra point and field goal warm-up before the return specialists take the field. Once the placekicking phase is complete, the return specialists arrive on the field just as the punter begins his warm-up. At the same time, the placekicker transitions from placement kicks to kickoffs. This allows the return specialists to warm up, receiving both punts and kickoffs. If a team has its punter hold for placement kicks, or if the punter also handles kickoffs, the format can simply be modified in a combination of ways to accomplish pregame goals.

College and high school teams often have more depth at special teams positions than the pros do, so more specialists are involved in the pregame warm-up. This means that some backup players must be incorporated into the warm-up to get repetitions. They then service the returners by providing them more repetitions. Although more athletes are involved, the starters can still maintain quality repetitions by ensuring that each drill is organized effectively. One way to do this is to allow both kickers and punters to perform warm-up drills at the same time. Placekicks, punts, and kickoffs are performed simultaneously, which involves the return specialists and back-ups, maximizing the use of the field and optimizing the time available.

During pregame, at the 60-minute mark before kickoff, each football team needs to be in its designated area of the field. Both teams have a section, traditionally from the end zone across mid-field to the 40-yard line, considered the long side of each opponent's side of the field. This distance may vary at certain levels of play. At the high school level, for instance, the field generally is split in half at the 50-yard line. At the professional level, and for some college teams, teams may have all the way to the 30-yard line on both sides of the field. This gives each team the necessary distance to perform punts and kickoffs. These areas need to be honored; everyone stays in their respective space.

For the kicker and punter to perform drills at both ends of the stadium, they need to go on to the field more than an hour before kickoff. Usually each team has access to both ends of the field as long as it is not within the 60-minute timeframe that designates specific pregame areas. Because the field normally is clear, this is a prime time to use the opposing team's end of the stadium for kicking. This practice is common at the professional level but more challenging to accomplish on the college and high school levels unless it's approved and coordinated ahead of time. Taking advantage of this opportunity gives the kicker a chance to gauge field and wind conditions, visualize references for aiming points, and determine adjustments that might be needed at either end of the field or both. It's not as important for the punter to be at both ends, primarily because goalposts are not a concern and he has enough room to punt both ways on the field within the assigned pregame area. If wind is a concern, the punter still has the opportunity to prepare in either direction.

Placekicking Kick Progression

The placekicker initially warms up with a series of one-step and full-step kicks at short range using a portable football holder. Meanwhile, the snapper and holder warm up and perform a few repetitions in anticipation of quickly joining the placekicker. After 4 to 5 minutes, they join together to begin a progressive number of short- to long-range kicks that vary from the right and left hashmarks. This sequence gives the placekicker the chance to work with his entire kicking unit while kicking from varying angles and distances. The specific number of kicks executed during the sequence is an effective way to ensure the placekicker doesn't overkick. The kicker knows that when the sequence of kicks is completed he needs to stop and save his leg for his kicks during the game. This is an ideal time for the coach to time the entire snap-to-kick sequence to ensure consistency and instill confidence.

The true holder should hold for the placekicker whenever he's available. When the holder is unavailable, the placekicker temporarily uses a portable football holder. This is a simple, progressive way for the kicker to quickly build to the full kicking motion. Table 11.1 summarizes the progression of the placekicker's warm-up.

Table 11.1 Placekicker Warm-Up Progression

1. Stretch	3. Snap-to-kick, snapper and holder timed by coach
Loosen up	Extra-point kicks (4)
Jog, cardio warm-up: break a sweat	Zigzag, phase one (6 to 8)
Static stretch	Zigzag, phase two (6 to 8)
Dynamic stretch	4. Kickoffs to returners
Technique-specific warm-up	Half approach (4)
2. Kicking progression	Full approach (4 to 8)
Form leg swings (3)	
One-step kicks (4)	
Full-step kicks (4)	

The placekicker begins with one-step kicks, kicking four kicks from the 10-yard line (extra-point distance). He then performs four full-step kicks from the 10-yard line.

After a brief warm-up, the snapper and holder join the placekicker to warm up as a unit. The coach begins timing every kick. The placekicker begins hitting his mark in order to be performing at his optimal level. As a unit, they perform four extra-point kicks from the 10-yard line.

Phase one of the zigzag kicks is next. The unit performs six to eight kicks, starting at the 10-yard line (professionals may start at 20-yard line) and left hashmark. The placekicker kicks a 20-yard field goal. Then he moves back 5 yards and to the opposite hashmark and kicks a 25-yard field goal. He continues to zigzag in 5-yard increments to his maximum distance. His range might vary because of wind direction or field conditions. The wind might be favorable going one direction and unfavorable the opposite. At this time during pregame the coach and placekicker determine the kicker's exact range for the game ahead.

The movement of each placement enables the snapper, holder, and kicker to establish a different distance and angle for every kick. This is an effective form of simulating gamelike conditions to prepare the kicking unit for competition. It's also a good way for the placekicker to determine his exact range on a given day based on field and weather conditions.

Executing six to eight kicks takes the kicker back about 45 to 55 yards. A younger kicker whose usual distance is less might need to kick twice at each hashmark to get in six to eight kicks during this phase of the warm-up.

Phase two of the zigzag kicks is next. The kicker repeats the sequence of phase one at the opposite end of the field, if available, or stays on the same end and reverses the sequence. He then decreases the distance of his kicks. He counts down six to eight kicks by using the hashmarks opposite of the ones used when he increased his distance. He then works his way back on the same yard lines but from the opposite hashmarks back to where he began the drill on the 10-yard line.

Now the placekicker moves to the designated side of the field (midfield to the 30-yard line) and begins kicking off to the return men positioned near the goal line. In the event a team has two kickers, the back-up place-kicker can warm up the kickoff returners while the starting placekicker and punter are performing their initial warm-ups. This way they can warm up and rotate effectively, ensuring the return men for both punts and kickoffs get quality repetitions.

Finally, the placekicker practices kickoffs to returners, executing four half-approach kickoffs, gradually warming up to a full approach. After warming up, he kicks four to eight full-approach kickoffs. At this point, he has completed his warm-up and joins the rest of the team as they come onto the field for team stretch. The kicker might want to try kicking a few more kickoffs just minutes before the game starts if he has the opportunity.

Punting Warm-Up Progression

Table 11.2 summarizes the punter's warm-up. The punter begins loosening up his leg by positioning on the 45-yard line on the right hashmark and performing three to five leg swings with no football.

Table 11.2   Punter Warm-Up Progression

1. Stretch	3. Snap to punt with snapper
Loosen up	Pooch punts right (5)
Jog, cardio warm-up: break a sweat	Pooch punts left (5)
Static stretch	Tight punts out of end zone (5-, 4-, 3-, 2-,
Dynamic stretch	1-yard lines)
Technique-specific warm-up	Directional punts
2. Punting progression	
Form leg swings (3 to 5)	
Pooch punts out of hands, no snapper (3)	

He then retrieves some footballs and pooches three punts out of his hands with no snap to the returners on the right side of the field near the numbers on the 10- to 5-yard lines.

Now the snapper joins in. The punter repositions back 5 yards to the 50-yard line. He pooch punts to the right five times to the returners. When finished, he and the snapper move to the opposite hashmark and pooch punt five more times to the left.

At this point the punter aligns deep in the end zone, keeping a 1 foot minimum distance from the endline, as the snapper sets up on the hashmark with the football on the 5-yard line. From this position, he punts as if simulating a tight-punt formation. Each succeeding snap is from 1 yard line closer, causing each snap to be closer to the punter (5-4-3-2-1 drill). (The ball moves from the 5-yard line to the 4-yard line and so on to the 1-yard line.) The goal is to punt the football straight ahead down the middle of the field with optimal hang time. The punter is timed hand to foot to ensure he gets the punt off in 1.25 to 1.3 seconds (or 1.4 seconds for a high school kicker). The punter keeps at least a 1 foot minimum distance from the back line of the end zone. This allows adequate room to catch the football, regardless of the distance of the snap, without inadvertently stepping on or past the endline.

Once the snapper completes the sequence (5-4-3-2-1), he stays on the hash mark and moves the football up to the 10-yard line. He's now in normal snap-to-punt distance as he works on more directional punts. He places the football toward the near sideline outside the numbers. If there's room on the field, he and the snapper might move at 10-yard increments downfield while continuing to directional punt six times based on the situation and field position. For example: 10- to 20-yard lines: drive punt (straight down the hashmark with optimal hang time and distance); 30- to 40-yard lines: directional punt (to a point outside the numbers); 50- to 40-yard lines: pooch punt (or aim for the corner). Once the punter has completed each punt he turns around (at the opposite end of the field) and repeats the sequence. This enables him to work both left and right hashmarks as well as punt in both directions (in case there's wind).

If there's no room at the other end of the field, the punter stays on the 10-yard line and executes the drive and directional punts first. He then moves out to midfield (50-yard line) and turns around to work on pooch punts and corners. Once this is completed, he goes to the opposite hashmark and reverses the sequence (pooch, corner, directional, drive). Either way, the punter can work both hashmarks in both directions on the field. This lets him punt in all situations and also to determine the wind effects (if any).

Game-Day Strategy

Normally, after the kickers, punters, and return specialists have warmed-up during the pregame, the rest of the team comes onto the field for a team stretch. Unless directed by a coach to perform other responsibilities, such as kick to a returner, every kicker and punter needs to be with the team for stretching. This is another opportunity for the kicker and punter to get involved and feel unity with the team.

Once the team stretch is over, the kicker and punter meet with the special teams coach or the head coach and go over the field conditions, the effects of the wind, range, team strategy, and so on. At this time, the kicker and punter might be able to get a few additional reps to stay loose.

Some teams like to conclude pregame warm-ups with special teams after the offense and defense complete their warm-ups. Other teams prefer only to review personnel to ensure proper substitution. The following game-ready kicks and punts are optional and can be modified for any team. They can be performed quickly before heading into the locker room for the last time before kickoff.

Some of these game-ready kicks are done with a blocking team and some without. The placekicker and punter kick and punt the football. If a blocking unit is used, there's no rush—only initial movement when the ball is snapped. Emphasize protection and coverage. Teams might want to add the block and return teams to review personnel as well as individual assignments.

1. Extra-point kick: one kick by the extra-point and field goal team. Simulate the play.
2. Field goal kick: one kick with the extra-point and field goal team. Simulate the play.
3. Pooch punt: one pooch punt with the punting team toward the end zone. No blocking team. Returners are optional. The punt team covers to the end zone, then are in position for the next and last play: the tight punt.
4. Tight punt: one punt out of the end zone. No blocking team. Returners are optional.

Some teams might use the punt out of the end zone as a way to bring the entire team together before heading back into the locker room before the start of the game. Once the football is punted and caught by the return man near midfield, the team gathers around the returner. They then break it down before heading into the locker room.

Staying Loose on the Sidelines

For the kicker and punter to stay loose on the sidelines, they must stay mentally in the game. They need to be totally aware of every situation throughout the course of action. A change of possession, a gain or loss of field position, or a score could occur at any time, requiring them to perform immediately. During these times, the kicker and punter must stay alert, be in their designated area on the sideline, and have their equipment (tees and helmets) in an easily accessible location.

Don't Overkick

The kicker and punter shouldn't continually kick or punt during the football game. This is exactly how punters and kickers can overkick, leading to fatigue and the technique problems caused by fatigue. They stay mentally focused on the game and each situation that arises and warm up only when appropriate.

Most of the time, it's easy to predict when the kicker or punter will be needed during the game because of the team's position on the field. But sometimes it's not. During the unpredictable times, the kicker and punter need to use common sense and maintain the preparedness they developed through their pregame warm-up. Game-day kicking is unlike practice; the game can last more than four hours. So they need to pace themselves.

The goal for the kicker and punter is to execute their skills optimally every time they step on the playing field. Kicking and punting the football are skills that require momentary exertion and precise technique. These skills take less than 1.4 seconds to perform. A punter or kicker exerts more energy by jogging onto the football field and getting lined up than he does when actually kicking or punting.

The kicker and punter always strive to produce the result that best helps their team win. To do this, they learn not only how to practice but how to be game-ready. All the practice, drills, and effort are done to develop optimal performance during the game. Once they reach this level, they must learn to maintain optimal performance.

If the offense is struggling during a game and have few opportunities to score, the kicker might want to kick some balls into the net from time to time and maybe stretch to stay limber.

The punter needs to stay ready on the sideline regardless of field position. He should occasionally pick up a football and execute some drops on the sideline. This is a simple way to help him focus and be prepared without wearing out his leg. He might have to punt after any three downs of a series, so he should head to the net occasionally, particularly on first down, to punt a few balls into the net. On second down, he should take a few snaps from the snapper. On third down, he should stand on the sideline by his coach. At this point, the punter and coach will know what type of punt to use based on field position and field conditions discussed during pregame.

One of the biggest challenges, particularly with young, inexperienced kickers and punters, is overkicking, especially leading up to and during game day. Sometimes kickers and punters kick and punt too much, causing their muscles to fatigue. The body naturally compensates for the fatigue and adjusts the kicking or punting motion to accommodate the weakness, causing a technique change. Through muscle memory, the body records this adjustment and repeats it.

The kicker and punter can maintain optimal performance on the sideline by developing a plan during the game to stay loose and maintain flexibility. Even after pregame warm-ups, the kicker and punter maintain their game-ready preparedness until kickoff. They can kick a few balls into the net, work on drop drills, and maybe work off some nervous energy with additional stretching.

During the game, the kicker and punter must always be ready on the sideline. They pay attention to down and distance as well as field position. The kicker knows that when his team crosses the 50-yard line, they are heading into field goal range. He might want to kick a few balls into the net. As the team progresses downfield, he should work with the snapper and holder on the sideline, if they're available. The closer the team moves toward the goal line (especially on third down), the kicker needs to be on the sideline very near the coach who decides when he's to go into the game. Ideally, both are on the sideline aligned with the closest point from which the kicker would kick. This enables the placekicker to hustle into the game at the shortest and quickest distance to arrive at the point of placement. This strategy is especially important when every second counts and a game-winning kick is needed.

The closer to the goal line his team gets, the greater the chances of a field goal or an extra point. In the case of a field goal or extra point, the placekicker who also handles kickoffs must be prepared to return to the sideline after the kick to gather his tee in order to kick off after a score.

12

Special Teams Preparation

Special teams preparation is more than just evaluating the opponent. It involves evaluating your own team as well, identifying strengths, weaknesses, and tendencies in every facet of your special teams squad. This information enables the formulation of a game strategy and can be incorporated into your team's objectives for practice planning. If you're a coach, you'll tailor your weekly practice checklist to include goals for your special teams to prepare optimally for the upcoming opponent.

From film breakdown to game-day adjustments, everyone on the team needs to contribute in preparing the special teams for game-day competition. Kickers and punters particularly need to be involved. They provide an extra set of eyes that prove invaluable because of their unique perspective. By involving every player, coaches can develop team unity and make players want to be a part of the special teams unit.

Protection Packages

The kicker and punter must have an overall understanding of the team's protection packages regarding various phases of the kicking game. They must be able to quickly anticipate and identify last-second adjustments that alter alignments, cause a delay in the snap, create a need to change direction of a kick, or allow the kicking team to attack a weakness by changing the play and running a fake.

The kicker and punter have primary responsibility to kick and punt the football in ways that best benefit the team. Of course, their first priority is to get the kick off without a block. After that, the kick requires accuracy and, usually, distance, whereas the punt requires optimal hang time and precise placement. If they can handle these responsibilities, it's not important that kickers and punters know specific details regarding blocking assignments of the protection. They have enough to deal with.

Placekicking Protection

When kicking a field goal with the football spotted on the hashmark, the kicker follows the exact same procedure as usual to determine the point of placement. Because of the increased angle of the kick, especially on the high school and college levels because the hashmarks are wider apart, the placekicking unit might need to adjust and align in an unbalanced protection. Some teams designate the 20-yard line as the determining point for where they alter their usual protection.

In an unbalanced alignment, a tackle or end shifts over from the short side of the field to line up on the wide side, leaving only the guard and end or tackle on the short side outside the center (figure 12.1). An extra man is now aligned outside the left tackle on the wide side. This simple adjustment lengthens the line of protection, taking away the angle of the edge rushers from the wide side of the field and allowing the kick to better travel over the center of protection.

Shifting to an unbalanced protection takes away the advantage the outside rushers have because of the increased angle of the kick. The typical flight of a football from a straight, down-the-field kick, such as an extra point, takes the ball directly over the center. Thus the ideal protection is

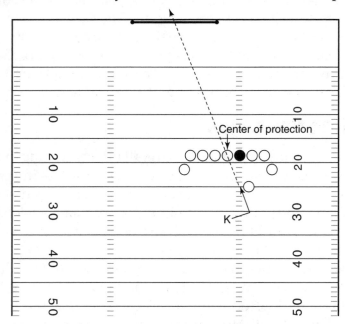

Figure 12.1 Unbalanced protection on a field goal taken from the 20-yard line or closer.

the center point directly in line with the flight path of the football. When the kick is made from either hashmark, the angle increases as you get closer to the goal line. This means the angle of the kick moves toward the wide side of the field, taking its flight path outside the center and closer to the edge of the protection where outside rushers are coming from.

In theory, widening the edge of protection by shifting a tackle from the other side compensates for the angle of the kick and adjusts the center of protection to align with the new flight path of the ball. When a kick is attempted from the hashmark, the flight path of the football needs to angle toward the center of the field to reach its target.

The placekicker might need to slightly adjust the point of placement over to ensure the center of the protection is within the unbalanced alignment. This needs to be coordinated with his coach. It can be done by setting his spot very slightly toward the wide side of the field. The adjustment should actually be quite subtle and unnoticeable.

Punt Team Protection

Punters, especially at the professional level, sometimes adjust their alignment in a slightly offset position to compensate for the direction they step during their approach. This offset pre-positions them to be better aligned within their punt protection by the time they complete their approach and make contact with the football.

For instance, when attempting a punt toward the right, a punter might adjust his stance slightly to the left by aligning his inside leg with the snapper's outside foot. He may want to open up slightly toward his intended target or, preferably, disguise it. This adjustment is so subtle the snapper should have no problem with it, but this simple modification allows the punter to receive the snap, complete his approach, and successfully punt the football to the right, the desired direction, while maintaining a safe position well within his protection.

Figure 12.2 Punter offsetting slightly left to punt right.

The punter should always be prepared to direct the ball to a specific zone to minimize the coverage area and allow the cover team to quickly blanket the return man. When the ball is placed on or near a hashmark, he should take advantage of the closest sideline. When the ball is in the middle of the field or when there's an overload and he feels too much pressure from the outside, he needs to consider punting the ball straight downfield with maximum hang time and maximum distance. By punting straight downfield, the punter stays within the center of his blockers and therefore maximizes protection.

When punting out of the end zone, the punter considers his distance from the line of scrimmage. If the scrimmage line is inside the 5-yard line, he's in a tight punt situation, with less distance than normal separating him from the oncoming rush. The more inside the 5-yard line the football is spotted, the less room he has to take his normal steps during his approach to punt the football downfield. Even though the punter is closer to the oncoming rush, the distance of the snap and the snap time decrease, meaning the football gets to the punter more quickly.

The best way for a punter to approach a tight punt is to shorten his steps to cover less distance. He needs to practice this technique and allow it to develop naturally to maintain a quick, rhythmic get-off time. This technique enables him to use his natural stepping approach, whether two steps or two and a half steps, which simplifies the adjustment and maintains consistency with his usual pattern. The best way to accomplish this is by practicing the optimal stride, or block point, drill.

Responsibility Following Kicks and Punts

If there's a possibility of a return, kickers and punters typically become safeties after kicking or punting the ball. Their responsibility is to cover downfield, maintaining a 20-yard cushion behind the coverage team and aligning with the return man so they can mirror his lateral moves. Kickers and punters commonly play too deep. A 20-yard distance behind the coverage team allows a good vantage point to see the return develop and determine what the ball carrier will do.

When there's a return, the top priority of the kicker or punter is to prevent the return man from getting past him. The best way to accomplish this is not to let the return man get to him in the first place. To do this, he executes a strategically placed kick or punt with optimal distance and hang time. This gives the coverage team time to blanket the return man and minimize or eliminate the return. On the kickoff, it's often best to kick away from a particularly talented return man who poses a runback threat or to squib the football along the ground. When punting to a strong return man, the punter might direct the ball toward the sidelines or out of bounds to avoid a potentially long runback. By punting away from the returner, the punter also causes the returner to leave his area in order to field the punt. This challenges him. Having to move from his area and make the catch on the run sometimes distracts the returner, causing a poor decision or a mishandled football. Even if the returner does successfully field the punt, he may still be too far away from his blockers.

If the return coverage breaks down and the return man heads upfield, the kicker or punter must respond by running toward the return man and closing the gap between himself and the runner. As the return man continues upfield, the kicker or punter maintains a position that enables him to alter the return man's course or slow him momentarily so someone can tackle him. The kicker or punter might need to assist in making the tackle or, in rare cases, go for the solo tackle himself.

As an example, let's look at a sideline or wall return. The kicker or punter watches the return develop and anticipates the route of the return man. Virtually unnoticed, he moves to fill in the wall or pocket opposite the return man. His objective then becomes maintaining leverage in the inside-out position and attempting to invite the return man to get near the sideline so he can be forced out of bounds. If the return man decides to cut back, the kicker or punter is in good position to make the tackle, get a piece of the runner, or force him further inside, enabling other players to tackle him. An assertive kicker or punter always challenges the return man. This challenge might be the difference between a stop and a score.

To develop their skills at playing the safety position, kickers and punters need to get involved with the team and learn how to tackle in the open field. The defensive secondary is the best group to practice with. They are the resident open-field tackling experts on the team and can provide the edge that makes the difference.

The kicker and punter should also participate in tackling drills, especially any drills that work on open-field tackling. They'll develop basic tackling fundamentals, and their teammates will respect them for participating in these tough drills. Most important, they'll learn skills that keep them safe during the tackle.

Breaking Down Upcoming Opponents

At most levels of play, coaches will have detailed scouting reports and sometimes game films on upcoming opponents so they can effectively prepare their special teams. This information provides a blueprint for practice sessions.

Studying Opponent Game Film

Before studying the game films of opponents, develop a checklist to follow. This list helps establish a consistent collection of information. Use it to focus on the upcoming opponent and to analyze the ways their previous opponents approached and responded to them.

Kickers and punters need to focus on the following:

Kickoff-Return Team

- Alignments: regular and onside
- Types of return
- Return positions: right, left, or middle
- Best return men
- Number of returns
- Average yards per return
- Longest return
- Strengths, weaknesses, special tendencies, and timing

Extra Point and Field Goal Blocking

- Alignments
- Blocks: right, left, or middle
- Strengths, weaknesses, special tendencies, and timing

Punt Return and Punt Blocking

- Alignments (including gunners)
- Tight punt
- Spread punt
- Types of return (who do they substitute from the sideline?)
- Middle, sideline right, or sideline left
- Best return men
- Number of returns
- Average yards per return
- Longest return
- Punt blocks (rushers and aiming points)
- Shifts
- Strengths, weaknesses, special tendencies, timing

Evaluating the Return Man and Defense

When evaluating the return man and defense, first determine their tendencies. Create charts for punt and kickoff returns. Note the type and direction of returns as well as the frequency of each. Completely analyze each return man, including his capabilities, his method of carrying the football, and his decision-making skills. Chart the opponent's tendencies related to the types of kick and punt blocks they use. This information is crucial in determining what to expect and how to prepare your kicking game.

Preparing the Weekly Game Plan

When preparing weekly game plans, coaches should incorporate special teams into the normal practice schedule. It's common for holders, kickers, punters, snappers, and return specialists to come out early and warm up to ensure they're prepared when practice begins. They need quality repetitions during both unit work and full-team work.

Coaches should ensure kickers and punters are involved in every aspect of the practice schedule. When they're not kicking (and they should not be kicking for the entire practice), they need to be somewhere doing something. They could be doing ball drills, working with the secondary on open-field tackle drills, or working on drops (punter) or onside kicks (placekicker). Whenever a period ends, the kicker and punter need to be headed somewhere with a direction and a purpose. Coaches need to have a section on the daily practice schedule to guide the kickers and punters throughout every practice. They should have a checklist and work on every type of kick or punt that may be needed during a game. This will ensure they are prepared for anything! If the coaches don't initiate this, the kickers and punters should take it upon themselves to stay busy.

The kicking game tends to be the last phase worked on in practice as well as the last practiced during the week. Often it's even the last phase installed when practice begins in the fall. If it's always last in the minds of coaches, it will probably remain last in the minds of players. This is one of the main reasons why it's extremely important to incorporate special teams into your team's normal practice routine. This emphasis sends a message to the players of the importance of the kicking game.

Think about it. A football game always begins with a kick. So why not practice the kicking game in regular intervals during practice? This is the way it happens during a game. If you're a coach, consider the positive message you convey about the importance of your kicking game if you start a practice with a kickoff.

Players sometimes feel they're being punished if they have to come to practice early or stay late, which they must do if the kicking game is worked before or after practice. By working the special teams during practice, coaches eliminate this mind-set. Holders, kickers, punters, snappers, and return specialists usually want to work more anyway as a unit to get the quality reps they need.

Timing Kickers and Punters

Regardless of the situation—type of rush, angle of the kick, and so on—the kicker must kick the extra point or field goal within the same timeframe. There should be no change. Even when he's kicking out of his range, the kicker must still get the football off within his optimal time.

It's impossible to overemphasize the importance of timing to kicking and punting the football. Kickers and punters must consistently hit their mark. By establishing and consistently hitting this mark, they develop consistency.

One of the greatest mistakes coaches make when working with kickers and punters involves timing. Some coaches don't time them at all, some don't time them enough, and some time them improperly, which is even worse. Coaches must understand that optimal timing enables the kicker to establish a rhythm, develop consistency, and enhance his performance.

If a kick or punt is nearly blocked, and the time of the kick was optimal, clearly the concern is not the kicker's or punter's timing. The problem might be the trajectory of the kick or poor protection. To irrationally speed up the kicking process and change the rhythm of the kicking unit is a major mistake. Too many times the kicker is blamed when the way to correct the problem is to improve the protection.

Kickers and punters must be timed properly. Coaches can't approach timing kickers and punters with a track meet mentality, where the fastest time is always the best. For the success of kickers, punters, special teams, and the team as a whole, kickers and punters should strive for optimal timing in the kicking game.

As we've stated earlier, optimal timing for kickers (snap to kick) is 1.3 to 1.4 seconds for high school kickers and 1.25 to 1.3 seconds for college and professional kickers. For punters, optimal timing (hand to foot) is 1.3 to 1.4 seconds for high school punters, and 1.25 to 1.3 for college and professional punters. The total get-off time (snap to punt) is 2.1 to 2.2 seconds for high school punters, and 2.0 to 2.1 seconds for college and professional punters.

To prepare a weekly game plan, first evaluate and review your team's most recent game and thoroughly study your upcoming opponent. Use film breakdowns to determine tendencies and abilities of the opponent's personnel. Also analyze the tendencies of your own team. Examine recent games and practices. Break your team down to discover weaknesses so you can anticipate how your opponent will attempt to exploit them.

Analyzing Practices and Films

Kickers and punters should be accountable for their performances during practice. Much of this accountability comes from timing and recording a certain number of kicks and punts each day the kicking game is practiced. This could be as few as 10 kicks or punts daily. Always be sure to time the snap-to-kick time because this information is useful for coaches and motivational for members of the kicking unit. Timing each kick or punt leads to developing an optimal rhythm that translates to optimal performance.

Individual filming and analysis is necessary for the development of kicking and punting skills as well as long snapping and holding skills. In order for the kicker and punter to fully understand the fundamentals of kicking and punting, they must be able to analyze themselves. Today's game features high tech equipment with high definition quality that can record athletes like no other equipment before. Athletes have at their fingertips computer laptops that can display every minute detail of their performance in ultimate clarity. This allows them to isolate, frame-by-frame, every movement made during their entire kicking and punting motion.

The off-season is a great time to film and brush up on fundamentals to improve technique. During preseason, the kicker and punter should take advantage of filming in order to polish their developed skills, especially as they work more with the holders and snappers. Finally during the season, filming can be done as needed. Coaches should use a twofold approach; the kicker and punter should be filmed when they are experiencing technique challenges and when they are performing at their best. When they are having challenges, filming can provide a visual quick fix. When they are performing at their best, filming will capture their optimal technique for a future visual reference.

Filming need not be done all the time, particularly during the season, but it does need to be done. Kickers and punters, along with the entire kicking team, are filmed each week during games. Even when filming is done through a wide-angle lens to capture each play, there is still enough detail to view individual performances and for the trained eye to evaluate.

Kickers and punters should be coached so thoroughly that they learn to coach themselves. At some point they can adjust and correct things on their own most of the time. They need to have confidence in the coach as well as the coach needs to have confidence in them. Just because they miss in practice or during a game doesn't mean they need to be filmed, analyzed, and rebuilt. The skill of kicking and punting the football should be approached with the mind-set that no one is perfect, but they had better be very consistent.

Occasional miskicks will occur. When one happens, coaches and players should not overreact by overanalyzing the kick on the sidelines or on film the following week. Yelling about or dwelling on the miss likely will make things worse by putting undue pressure on the kicker as he prepares for the next kick. Just as important, kickers and punters should not throw temper tantrums, throw helmets, make any negative gesture, or do anything that displays disgust. This only makes them and their team look bad. It's best to simply hustle off the field, eliminate the thought, and move on, especially on game day. Most importantly, the kicker and punter are never to blame anyone for not performing well, even if someone really does deserve it. They will gain more respect and support from their teammates for simply being quiet. The snapper knows when he had a bad snap and the holder knows when he had a bad hold. They don't need to be told or blamed. They will not always be perfect. The kicker and punter should be athletic enough to consistently make up for any imperfect snaps or holds and still get the job done. The kicker and punter must stay focused on their performances throughout the game and be timed constantly. They should not be coached on technique during games. At this point, they mainly need to be encouraged.

Developing kickers and punters until they can coach themselves means teaching them to identify when to make technique adjustments and when not to. Just because a kick or punt is off the mark does not mean any techniques need to be changed. They may simply have been off the mark. Once this has been identified, they need to focus on successfully making the next kick.

During Super Bowl XXXVI, Adam Vinatieri missed a field goal attempt and had a second attempt blocked, both during the first quarter. Later in the game, he still had the confidence to kick a game-winning field goal near the end of regulation. Kickers must retain confidence in their abilities even after a miss or two. For placekickers, lost confidence leads to loss of focus, which leads to another missed kick.

Even after kickers and punters learn to self-coach, they need to receive or seek feedback from their position coach, especially regarding their performance. The only other coach that should say anything to them is the head coach. Other position coaches need to coach their players and not coach the kickers. The head coach can say what he wants because he is the head coach and the kicker and punter are on his team. Kickers and punters must be prepared, especially during games when tensions are high, for the head coach to say anything at anytime. Kickers and punters need to be respectful and deal with it. They should remember the head coach cares about them and believes in them or they wouldn't be the starters on his team.

The kicker and punter should approach practice as if it is game day and every kick and punt counts. In this way, performance in practice transfers to game performance. If kickers and punters are continually timed, charted, and involved in practice, they will produce in games.

Weekly Practice Countdown to Game Day

Table 12.1 presents a plan consisting of proven information used by pro and college players to guide the kicker and punter through a week of preparation leading up to game day. This plan is designed to systematically progress athletes to enhance strength, maintain power, and develop the endurance to perform optimally, during games and throughout the season. The key to this plan is to do heavy legwork (kicking) early in the week and then taper off as game day approaches.

Table 12.1 Weekly Practice Plan: Countdown to Game Day

Day	High school	College	Professional	Kicking intensity	Special teams emphasis
Day 7	Saturday	Sunday	Monday	No kicking	No kicking
Day 6	Sunday	Monday	Tuesday	No practice	No practice
Day 5	Monday	Tuesday	Wednesday	Heavy kicking	PAT/FG/punt and kickoff coverage
Day 4	Tuesday	Wednesday	Thursday	Heavy kicking	PAT/FG/punt and kickoff return
Day 3	Wednesday	Thursday	Friday	Moderate to light kicking	Review all special teams
Day 2	Thursday	Friday	Saturday	No kicking	Mental repetitions and review
Game day	Friday	Saturday	Sunday	Game day	Game day

Kickers and punters can modify this plan as necessary to suit their individual and team needs. Every athlete is different; some have needs others don't have. It's up to the kicker and punter to take the initiative to work with their coach and develop a personal practice routine that's tailored to meet their needs.

13
Coming Through in the Clutch

Coming through in the clutch is all about being prepared to perform. Kickers and punters develop until they reach a level at which their skills have become habits that are second nature to them. At this level, they can respond confidently to any situation during a game.

In this chapter we cover mental-training techniques that build on the resources kickers and punters already possess. If you're a kicker or a punter, you'll learn to incorporate these positive moments naturally into every kick or punt, maximizing the efficiency and effectiveness of your training as well as your game-day performance.

Training Visualization and Imagery

Many kickers and punters use visualization regularly while training and during competition. This mental exercise is a powerful technique that can be easily incorporated into everyday practice drills and game-day performances. Kickers and punters who use visualization gain a competitive edge through improved mental awareness and confidence.

Visualization involves producing a vivid positive mental image of what you want to accomplish. It's a visual image of an ideal performance as seen through the kicker's or punter's eyes. By adding imagery, you feel and hear as well as see what is being visualized.

Visualization and imagery are often considered the same, but visualization is exactly what it sounds like it is—seeing. Imagery goes beyond just seeing and uses the imagination to feel the emotion of an accomplishment and hear the crowd cheer the outcome. Visualization and imagery are often used together. Imagery sets itself apart as more of a meditative exercise that requires more time to perform than visualization, but imagery can be used fairly quickly prior to performance.

Building a Mental Plan Into Your Routine

The skills of kicking and punting are based on directing a kicked or punted football at a target or toward a particular position on the football field. To accomplish these objectives, the kicker or punter first aligns in a precise position to effectively direct the flight of the ball. Throughout the alignment process, the kicker or punter uses natural aiming points and landmarks as reference points. Each time they refer to these positions on the football field, they have an opportunity to set an immediate goal and visualize the football reaching that target. Whether they realize it or not, they are constantly preparing to succeed by first seeing the results of their efforts before they ever kick or punt the ball.

Kickers and punters can incorporate visualization and imagery techniques into their everyday routines in many ways. This is a natural approach to the mental aspect of the game and should be incorporated as part of the skill-training process. These techniques can effectively increase the kicker's and punter's abilities to perform under pressure by increasing their confidence. Through gamelike experiences, kickers and punters use these techniques to maximize the efficiency and effectiveness of training and give them the edge they need to perform at an optimal level.

Every time the kicker or punter aligns in position to kick or punt and focuses on his reference points, he should quickly visualize the flight path of the football going directly to the target. For example, the placekicker has the opportunity to visualize when he's determining his point of placement, when he's toeing the line to determine his vertical alignment, and when he checks his target from his stance.

The placekicker can develop the ability to read his mechanics by seeing and feeling his body position (kinesthetic feel) during the post-kick check phase to learn the precise path of the football. He develops this technique so thoroughly that he anticipates the exact location of the football simply by evaluating the reference points of his body.

See Through Your Eyes

When kickers and punters perform imagery and visualization, they should do so from their own perspective. That is, they should "see" through their own eyes. They shouldn't view a kick or imagine the sound of a crowd from some faraway place, such as the press box or the bleachers, but through their own senses.

As his eyes ascend, he'll be able to extend the arm on the side of his kicking leg upward in a direct line toward his target, pointing as if he were touching the football in flight.

As part of their pregame preparation, the kicker and punter should check the field surface, assess weather conditions and wind direction, and study the general layout of the facility. This is especially important before away games. They should identify certain landmarks or stationary objects to use as aiming points and become familiar with the environment. The pregame is also an excellent opportunity to align on various spots of the field and simulate game situations in order to visualize successful kicks and punts. This active form of imagery can be done anywhere on the field.

Attentional Focus and Distraction Elimination

Getting properly aligned provides a great opportunity for the kicker or punter to focus his attention on his target and then ensure every step of his alignment aligns precisely with his target. This process is the basis of kicking and punting a football in a precise direction.

The routine of alignment requires focused attention that also serves to eliminate distraction. The alignment routine gives the kicker or punter something constructive to do when the game is on the line and the kicker or punter must focus solely on the kick or punt.

As the kicker or punter runs onto the field, he should

- know the game situation and focus on the official's spotting of the football at the line of scrimmage;
- locate his target according to the placement of the football and precisely align in a position that ensures optimal direction and placement of his kick;
- check his target once he's in his stance and quickly visualize a successful kick, which can be a simple positive affirmation toward where he'll direct the football, before acknowledging his readiness to the holder or snapper; and
- keep things simple by limiting his thoughts, allowing him to focus entirely on performing at the optimal level he has prepared for.

The progression of running into the game, determining his target, aligning precisely, visualizing the objective, and performing optimally demands total concentration. The entire process requires attention to details and allows the disciplined kicker and punter to eliminate outside distractions.

Enduring the Opposition's Icing Attempts

When the game is on the line and a pressure kick is coming, you can expect the opposing team to try to disrupt the kicker's focus by calling a time-out to delay the kick. This is known as icing the kicker. The opponent wants to make the kicker consider the magnitude of the kick. The delay also provides an opportunity for opposing players to do a little taunting by reminding the kicker of the enormity of the situation. They might even throw out a few personal barbs to try to create negative thoughts that anger or frustrate the kicker.

Whatever the case, the kicker has a multitude of mental weapons to shield himself from a barrage of verbal attacks. First, to be prepared and game-ready, he should always strive to develop his skills until they become second nature. He should be so confident in his performance that he doesn't have to think—he simply responds.

He should plan to succeed by practicing the situation. He rehearses and practices the last-second kick and the kick-with-the-game-on-the-line scenarios throughout the season during a weekly regimen. He approaches every kick as if it were a game winner. It doesn't matter if it's a PAT in the first minute of the game, a 45-yard field goal in the middle of the second quarter, or a chip-shot kick early in the second half. He routinely approaches each kick as if the game depended on his success. This way, he can approach a true game-winning kick as if it's just another kick.

He identifies his target and aligns accordingly. The alignment routine requires focused attention that also serves as a remedy to eliminate distraction. He also focuses on the finish and on performing his mechanics optimally. By aligning properly and finishing properly, he allows the fundamentals to be executed effectively. This in itself demands total concentration.

He sticks with his routine. The act of running onto the field to perform the kick is a routine every kicker is accustomed to. An opposing team trying to ice the kicker might call time-out after the kicker finds his target and aligns in his stance. With approval from the coach, the kicker should consider running back to the sideline and standing next to the coach, just as he did prior to running into the game to make the kick. After the time-out, he gets approval from the coach and then goes back into the game, just as he did the first time he went onto the field. This is a great way to keep active during the time-out without standing on the field and thinking. More important, the kicker sticks to his usual routine.

He separates himself from the opponents. When the time-out is called, the kicker is usually 9 or 10 yards away from the opposing team. This is too close because he'll clearly hear any verbal barbs directed his way.

Instead, he should immediately walk away to establish separation and allow some of the crowd noise to block out the onfield banter. He might talk to a teammate or take the chance to visualize the upcoming kick.

He thrives in the moment. This is exactly the kind of situation he has prepared for. He develops the mentality to embrace the challenge. This is a moment he has played in his head over and over. Not only is he prepared, he is thankful for the opportunity.

He talks with either the holder or the coach about something insignificant or what needs to be done after the kick is made. For example, while on the sideline during the icing time-out, the coach might say, "After you make the kick, make sure that on the kickoff you kick a deep squib kick down the middle of the field, and tell everyone we need an all-out effort to cover." With these words, the coach provides a powerful message about his confidence in his kicker.

Dusty Mangum, who began his college football career as a walk-on for the University of Texas, is best known for a 37-yard game-winning field goal as time expired in the 2005 Rose Bowl. Moments prior to Mangum's kick, head coach Mack Brown told the senior, "You're the luckiest human being in the world because your last kick at Texas will win the Rose Bowl." The kick made Mangum an instant celebrity and a legend in the storied history of Texas football.

Finally, the kicker repeats a positive mantra—*finish to the target, fluid and smooth, focus on the finish*. He stays positive, waits for the time-out to end, and then calmly kicks the ball through the uprights.

14

Conditioning for Kickers and Punters

In football today, highly trained coaches specialize in developing strength and conditioning programs specifically for individual athletes. Although this position-specific specialized training is seen mostly at the professional and college levels, more high school teams are benefiting from this expertise. An increasing number of players are taking the initiative to seek this guidance in the private sector as well.

Although this expertise is available, the athlete must continue to work out and train with his team first to develop the basic overall strength that all football players need. Before doing skill-specific exercises or specialized training, athletes need basic technique and strength training. The player must communicate with his coaches about any specialized training outside of the football program. In no way should a player's specialized training interfere with or be a substitute for training time with teammates.

Teamwork, unity, and work toward a common goal always takes precedence. Often kickers and punters are excluded or treated differently, which negatively impacts team unity. Kickers and punters should work with the rest of the team during practice, especially for conditioning. They need to be involved in everything that involves the team. If this philosophy is not in place, the kicker and punter must take the initiative to make it happen. The respect and support they will gain by working in the trenches with their teammates is immeasurable.

Strength and conditioning training complement the kicker's and punter's performance by enhancing the skills and techniques they have developed. First kickers and punters must develop proper kicking and punting techniques. This is the key to developing leg speed and power. Only then will strength and conditioning training enhance the kicker's and punter's performance. Proper weight-lifting techniques must be taught to reduce the risk of injury and maximize the impact of strength training on performance.

Kickers and punters are a lot like golfers in the mechanics of their skills. When hitting a golf ball, golfers rely on increased club head speed to increase performance and power through the ball. In football, kickers and punters increase overall performance and power through the ball by increasing leg speed. It's not how strong the kicker, punter, or golfer is that matters—it's how fast he brings his foot or club head through the ball. To kick farther and punt higher, the kicker and punter must create leg speed.

Consider that golfers are not typically big, strong, physical men, yet they often hit golf balls a great distance, much farther than a much bigger and stronger athlete could. They have attained tremendous muscle coordination that enables them to produce phenomenal acceleration with their swings. The same principle is at play with kickers and punters. Some kickers and punters are not the big, strong, physical men you might find at the linebacker position, yet they are far superior in kicking and punting a football because they have enhanced leg speed. The way to increase leg speed is to develop the techniques and skills that will create it.

Remember that force equals mass times acceleration. The faster a kicker or punter accelerates his leg swing, the more force he applies to the football, and the farther it travels. Simply developing strength might make a kicker or punter stronger, but it won't maximize his leg speed through the football. In fact, a kicker or punter who trains specifically to increase strength could actually slow his leg speed. The kicker and punter must effectively develop strength, transfer it into power, and then apply it to sport-specific movements.

In-Season Training and Conditioning

The in-season program in this chapter (table 14.1) has been used by professional and college players and has been proven on the field. It complements team workouts, encouraging the kicker and punter to take initiative to make the most effective use of their time.

This program guides the kicker and punter through a week of preparation leading up to game day. The systematic progression enhances strength, maintains power, and develops endurance for performing

Table 14.1 In-Season Training and Conditioning Program

Month	Resistance training	Days per week	Cardiovascular conditioning	Days per week	Skill training	Days per week
August	Maintenance	2 or 3	With team during on-field practice	3 or 4	Technique and game-ready drills	4 or 5
September	Maintenance	2 or 3	With team during on-field practice	3 or 4	Game-ready drills	3 or 4
October	Maintenance	2 or 3	With team during on-field practice	3 or 4	Game-ready drills	3 or 4
November	Maintenance	2 or 3	With team during on-field practice	3 or 4	Game-ready drills	3 or 4
December	Transition period; active rest and recovery					

optimally throughout the season. In-season strength training is about maintaining the gains in strength and power developed during the off-season. The quantity and intensity of workouts are reduced. This maintenance phase enables athletes to maintain performance levels throughout the season and begin their off-season workouts at a higher level than the year before.

This plan lays a foundation for the kicker and punter that they can then adjust, modify, and build on. Every athlete is different and has certain needs that others don't have. However all football players, including kickers and punters, need total-body strength.

Countdown to Game Day

During the season, practice quality, not quantity. Practice harder early in the week and then taper off as game day approaches in order to have fresh, fast, and powerful legs. Follow a countdown of days prior to the football game, beginning with day 7 and ending with day 1 (game day). This way, regardless of the level of play, the progression will be similar. Figure 14.1 shows off-field training during the countdown to game day; figure 14.2 shows on-field training.

Off-Field Countdown to Game Day

Day 7: Saturday (high school), Sunday (college), Monday (professional)

Objective   Work out with team; active recovery day.

Warm-up
- Properly loosen up joints.
- Jog, cardio warm-up: break a sweat.

(continued)

Static and dynamic flexibility

- Prepare muscles for training.
- Maintain optimal flexibility and range of motion.

Resistance training

- Maintain optimal total-body development of strength, power, and endurance.
- Focus on total-body lifting (emphasis on legs).
- Low number of sets and high number of reps (example: 2 or 3 sets $\times$ 8 to 12 reps).

Cool-down

- Active recovery: static stretching.

Day 6: Sunday (high school), Monday (college), Tuesday (professional)

Objective   Active rest and recovery day.

Day off

- No kicking practice.
- No resistance training.
- No cardio training.

Day 5: Monday (high school), Tuesday (college), Wednesday (professional)

Objective   Maintain optimal power and performance.

Warm-up

- Properly loosen up joints.
- Jog, cardio warm-up: break a sweat.

Static and dynamic flexibility

- Prepare muscles for training.
- Maintain optimal flexibility and range of motion.

Resistance training

- Maintain optimal total-body development of strength, power, and endurance.
- Focus on upper-body lifting (chest and back).
- Perform three sets of 10 repetitions (3 $\times$ 10).

Cool-down

- Active recovery: static stretching.

Day 4: Tuesday (high school), Wednesday (college), Thursday (professional)

Objective   Maintain optimal power and performance.

Warm-up
- Properly loosen up joints.
- Jog, cardio warm-up: break a sweat.

Static and dynamic flexibility
- Prepare muscles for training.
- Maintain optimal flexibility and range of motion.

Resistance training
- Maintain optimal total-body development of strength, power, and endurance.
- Focus on upper-body lifting (arms and shoulders).
- Perform low number of sets and high number of reps (example: 3 sets × 10 reps).

Cool-down
- Active recovery: static stretching.

Day 3: Wednesday (high school), Thursday (college), Friday (professional)

Objective   Maintain optimal power and performance.

Warm-up
- Properly loosen up joints.
- Perform cardio training.
- Jog, cardio warm-up: break a sweat.

Static and dynamic flexibility
- Prepare muscles for training.
- Maintain optimal flexibility and range of motion.

Resistance training
- Maintain optimal total-body development of strength, power, and endurance.
- Focus on total-body lifting (light leg work).
- Perform low number of sets and high number of reps (example: 2 or 3 sets × 8 to 12 reps).

Cool-down
- Active recovery: static stretching.

(continued)

Day 2: Thursday (high school), Friday (college), Saturday (professional)

Objective   Maintain optimal power and performance.

Day off
- No off-field work.
- Review and walk-through with team.

Game day: Friday (high school), Saturday (college), Sunday (professional)

Objective   Optimal performance day. Win battle of field position and win game.

On-Field Countdown to Game Day

Day 7: Saturday (high school), Sunday (college), Monday (professional)

Objective   Work out with team; active recovery day.

Warm-up
- Properly loosen up joints.
- Jog, cardio warm-up: break a sweat.

Static and dynamic flexibility
- Prepare muscles for training.
- Maintain optimal flexibility and range of motion.

Skill development
No kicking the day after a game.

Conditioning
- Perform 20 to 30 minutes of aerobic training.
- Train to maintain endurance.

Cool-down
- Active recovery: static stretching.

Day 6: Sunday (high school), Monday (college), Tuesday (professional)

No kicking; active rest and recovery day.

Day 5: Monday (high school), Tuesday (college), Wednesday (professional)

Objective   Heavy kicking day, intense drill work.

Warm-up
- Properly loosen up joints.
- Jog, cardio warm-up: break a sweat.

Static and dynamic flexibility
- Prepare muscles for training.
- Maintain optimal flexibility and range of motion.

Drill work
- Focus on technique.
- Situational kicking and punting.

Special teams
- Extra points and field goals.
- Punt and kickoff coverage.

Kicking intensity
- Volume determined by needs of individual.
- Kick with purpose only to fatigue to maintain proper form.

Conditioning
- Perform 20 to 30 minutes of aerobic and anaerobic training.
- Train to maintain endurance, speed, power, and agility.

Cool-down
- Active recovery: static stretching.

Day 4: Tuesday (high school), Wednesday (college), Thursday (professional)

Objective   Heavy kicking day, intense drill work.

Warm-up
- Properly loosen up joints.
- Jog, cardio warm-up: break a sweat.

Static and dynamic flexibility
- Prepare muscles for training.
- Maintain optimal flexibility and range of motion.

(continued)

Drill work
- Focus on technique.
- Situational kicking and punting.
- Mark checklist to ensure every game-day situation has been covered.

Special teams
- Extra points and field goals.
- Punt and kickoff returns; punter and kicker simulate opponent.

Kicking intensity
- Volume determined by needs of individual.
- Kick with purpose only to fatigue to maintain proper form.

Conditioning
- Perform 20 to 30 minutes of aerobic and anaerobic training.
- Train to maintain endurance, speed, power, and agility.

Cool-down
- Active recovery: static stretching.

Day 3: Wednesday (high school), Thursday (college), Friday (professional)

Objective   Very light kicking; review day.

Warm-up
- Properly loosen up joints.
- Jog, cardio warm-up: break a sweat.

Static and dynamic flexibility
- Prepare muscles for training.
- Maintain optimal flexibility and range of motion.

Drill work
- Situational kicking and punting.

Special teams
- Review all special teams.
- Punter and kicker simulate opponent.

Kicking intensity
- Very light kicking.
- Save reps for special teams period, if needed.

Conditioning
- Light conditioning to rest legs.
- Perform 5 to 10 minutes of anaerobic training.
- Train to maintain endurance, speed, power, and agility.

Cool-down
- Active recovery: static stretching.

Day 2: Thursday (high school), Friday (college), Saturday (professional)

Objective   No kicking; review and walk-through day.

Warm-up
- Properly loosen up joints.
- Jog, cardio warm-up: break a sweat.

Static and dynamic flexibility
- Prepare muscles for training.
- Maintain optimal flexibility and range of motion.

Skill development
No kicking; special teams review and walk-through with team.

Conditioning   None.

Game day: Friday (high school), Saturday (college), Sunday (professional)

Objective   Optimal performance day. Win battle of field position and win game!

In-season off-field training schedules normally are more flexible since they aren't affected by the time constraints of on-field practicing. Often various times during weekdays are available for individual, small group, or team workouts. These times can be scheduled around classes. The kicker and punter should work with the coach to schedule weight lifting on days they will not kick or will have only light kicking. The coach may even consider scheduling upper-body lifts on kicking days. If the kicker and punter must lift weights on the same days they kick, they should kick or punt first and then work out with weights. This will keep the legs fresh and avoid fatigue that may adversely affect the kicking and punting motions.

The maintenance training plan includes days of active rest. During active rest, athletes are encouraged to get involved in a sports activity outside of football, something they enjoy, to eliminate the stresses on the mind and body associated with preparing for a game. Possibilities include swimming, golfing, or walking. Obviously the athlete needs to choose an activity that carries an extremely low risk of injury, especially during the season.

Maintenance training will help the kicker and punter maintain optimal levels of performance and stay fresh throughout the season. Focusing on intense workouts early in the week and gradually reducing intensity as game day approaches is key to performing optimally on game day.

Kicking and punting require precision technique. Because of muscle memory, punters and kickers tend to repeat the same technique over and over. To perform each technique optimally and consistently, the athlete must be properly rested. Remember that the entire kicking or punting motion takes less than 1.4 seconds. If the muscles are fatigued, the body might try to compensate by adjusting the motion. If the body compensates for fatigue by altering the kicker's motion, he might end up repeating that altered motion and throw his technique off until his muscles have been retrained.

Kickers and punters must listen to their bodies and learn to determine the exact moment when they start to feel fatigue. When they do, they need to back off and rest. Even when performing optimally, kickers and punters need to pay close attention to their bodies. They might want to keep kicking because everything feels good and they're getting tremendous results. But as they continue to kick, they can start to fatigue, leading to breakdowns in performance. Once they are fatigued, they start to overkick as their bodies try to compensate for the fatigue. Kickers and punters need to avoid having their muscle memory store an altered motion. The only memory of muscle movement they want to record is optimal motion.

Increasing Center, Holder, and Kicker Efficiency

The best way to increase efficiency and optimize the performance of the kicking unit is to consistently time the snap-to-kick sequence. Accomplish consistent timing and effectiveness by having the kicker, holder, and snapper work together extensively. This is critical to determining optimal timing and developing tempo among the unit. Set aside time regularly to chart snap-to-kick times. Remember that the total time from snap to kick should be 1.25 to 1.4 seconds for high school players and 1.25 to 1.3 seconds for college and professional players. Charting the snapper, holder, and kicker motivates them to focus on the task at hand. Frequently timing kickers helps them develop proper rhythm and improve consistency.

Increasing Snapper and Punter Efficiency

Consistently timing the snapper and punter is the best way to increase efficiency and optimize performance. Although individual timing is helpful, timing is most useful when the snapper and punter work together. Total time from snap to punt should be 2.0 to 2.1 seconds for college and professional players. The center snap takes about 0.75 to 0.8 seconds, and the punter's handling time is 1.25 to 1.3 seconds, for a total of 2.0 to 2.1 seconds. High school players can attain this time as well because they align closer to the line of scrimmage, so the snap doesn't travel as far. A snap-to-punt time of 2.1 to 2.2 seconds is acceptable for high school players.

The snapper and punter must develop proper rhythm to improve the consistency of the punt. It's possible to punt too quickly. The effectiveness of the punter is altered when he hurries, and rushing places the football in the hands of the opponent too soon, giving the returner more time and separation from the coverage team. When a snap is slow or off-the-mark, the punter must know that his job is to make up for lost time. He must be athletic enough to handle any snap effectively and make the punt.

On game day, use a stopwatch to assess the success of the special teams and the outcome of the game. Time every kick to confirm consistent get-off times and identify problems that might arise in protection. For instance, if a punt was close to being blocked, but the punter's get-off time was ideal, the problem was with the protection. This information can then be relayed to the coaches and players involved, allowing the problem to be addressed and corrected. Coaches should never assume the punter is the problem. Time punts and hold everyone accountable for the outcome.

Off-Season Training and Conditioning

In football today, kickers and punters must do more than just practice their skills. They must train and condition throughout the year, using well-designed workouts to improve sport-specific performance, prevent injury, and increase longevity in the sport. To do this effectively, they need to progressively achieve their maximum physical abilities in strength, power, speed, flexibility, and endurance through a period leading up to the first football game. This preparation allows kickers and punters to achieve peak performance at the right time. Players then train to maintain this level of performance throughout the season.

Off-season training starts with postseason rest and continues with winter, spring, summer, and preseason workouts. Each workout period leads to the next in a progression that prepares the athlete for the next stage. No secret formula exists to determine the exact course. Programs may vary, and many exercises will work. The programs presented here will help the athlete understand specific objectives related to strength training and conditioning. This knowledge will enable the athlete to be more proactive in his development as a player.

When a team makes it to playoff or bowl games, in-season workouts can be extended. Kickers and punters will stay in the maintenance phase with their teammates. Younger or less-experienced athletes can get an early start in the postseason by learning proper strength-training techniques and developing a base of strength on which to build.

Postseason Rest

The postseason begins with a transition phase, a time for active rest and recovery. Immediately after the season ends, kickers and punters should take a physical and mental break from the game for at least one month. This gives the body and mind time to recharge after a long, hard season. During this active rest and recovery phase, athletes are encouraged to participate in safe activities such as basketball, tennis, swimming, and golf—any activity that they enjoy and that eliminates the stress to the mind and body associated with football. Active rest allows athletes to physically and mentally recover from the stress of training and competing while maintaining their level of fitness.

Winter Workout

Traditionally winter workouts start in January after Christmas break and run through late March. Prior to the winter workouts, athletes have a chance to actively rest and recover after the season. Now they are ready to focus on resistance training and conditioning. This three-month training period (table 14.2) usually ends just before spring break with an assessment period to measure physical gains and improvements. Kickers and punters should have reached their peak physical performance levels and be ready for on-field spring practices after spring break.

During the winter workout phase, kickers and punters should take additional time off from kicking and punting, as professional players do. Players should do little, if any, kicking in January, only two days a week in February, and then at least three days a week in March in preparation for spring practice or minicamp. Kickers and punters benefit from this much-needed rest from their sport-specific movements. Any kicking or punting during this timeframe should be minimal. Off-season kicking camps that emphasize the fundamentals are useful for gaining advanced training. At these camps, players can focus on technique development through quality repetitions, complemented with film and video analy-

Table 14.2 Winter Conditioning Program

Month	Resistance training	Days per week	Cardiovascular conditioning	Days per week	Skill training	Days per week
January	Basic strength	3 or 4	Endurance, speed, agility	3 or 4	Technique drills, video analysis	1 or 2
February	Strength development	3 or 4	Endurance, speed, agility	3 or 4	Technique drills, video analysis	1 or 2
March	Maximum strength	3 or 4	Endurance and speed	3 or 4	Explosive drills	2 or 3
	Power phase	3 or 4	Power (plyometrics)	1 or 2	Technique and game-ready drills	2 or 3
Last week	Fitness testing, followed by one week off before spring practice starts					

sis. Kickers and punters should avoid kicking or punting after strength and conditioning workouts. If they choose to include kicking and punting repetitions during winter workouts, they should kick prior to any strength or conditioning workouts or on off days, only when their legs are well rested.

Off-season goals for kickers and punters include developing maximum strength, power, speed, endurance, and flexibility that will transfer effectively into the sport-specific movements of kicking and punting. A progressive order of training will accomplish this. A simple way to break down each workout phase is to split each phase into a minimum of four-week timeframes. During each week, athletes work out either three days (usually Monday, Wednesday, and Friday) or four days (Monday, Tuesday, Thursday, and Friday, which often is referred to as a four-day split) (figure 14.3). Each phase of the workout can be modified to fit athletes' schedules. These phases can be extended, if necessary, from four to six weeks to accommodate needs at different levels of play.

Resistance Training

In January, athletes begin the first phase of resistance training: basic strength. This is a light to moderate total-body workout that slowly builds volume and intensity. The objective is for the athlete to learn proper lifting techniques while determining his base strength. Developing proper technique is key as this will give the athlete a solid foundation on which to build strength in the near future.

This four-week period gradually prepares the body for more demanding workouts to come. The goal is to develop the total-body, overall strength that every football player needs. A circuit training program

Monday
- Lower-body resistance training
- Conditioning: endurance training

Tuesday
- Upper-body resistance training
- Conditioning: speed training
- Skill training: kicking and punting optional

Wednesday
Plyometric training

Thursday
- Lower-body resistance training
- Conditioning: endurance training

Friday
- Upper-body resistance training
- Conditioning: speed training
- Skill training: kicking and punting (optional)

Saturday
Skill training: kicking and punting (optional)

Sunday
Off day: no practice

Figure 14.3 Sample four-day split winter workout.

that focuses on strength exercises will accomplish this goal. Beginners should start with simple exercises that use body weight or medicine balls. Athletes then can advance to using free weights, such as dumbbells and barbells, as they gain strength and learn proper technique. Include basic lifts such as bench presses, squats, cleans, and overhead presses. These exercises are common for football players.

Once the athlete develops proper lifting technique and determines his base strength, he is ready to begin a new four-week phase of resistance training that increases intensity as the athlete increases strength and power. The key to a good progressive, off-season program is to wisely adjust intensity levels and training volume to avoid overtraining and burnout. Intensity is gradually increased over two or three weeks by reducing repetitions and increasing weight. In general, the athlete performs three to five sets of 6 to 12 repetitions of each exercise. By the third week, the athlete will peak. At this point, he can taper workout intensity for a week by lessening the weight and increasing the repetitions.

After this tapering-off period, intensity gradually increases again so the athlete finishes the remaining weeks at a higher level. If the program is divided into four-week timeframes, the athlete may simply allow the transition into the next period to serve as the program modification that prevents overtraining or burnout. It is wise to modify workouts by including a variety of exercises that work the same muscle groups but in different ways.

After developing proper weightlifting technique and gaining strength, kickers and punters are ready for the next phase of training: maximum strength. The main objective of this phase is to prepare the body for training of the highest intensity: power training. Intensity increases in each workout over three or four weeks by minimizing repetitions and maximizing weight. In general, the athlete performs three to five sets or one to four repetitions of each exercise.

To train for maximum strength, athletes must be explosive in their efforts to perform each lift. This type of training recruits fast-twitch muscle fibers, which are key to developing explosive power. This type of power, important for all football players, is key in developing the power and leg speed needed to enhance kicking and punting techniques. For a kicker or punter, a fast leg is a powerful leg.

To convert strength gains into sport-specific power, athletes must enter a power phase that consists of maximum strength training complemented with power training. In power training, the athlete incorporates speed into strength training. One of the most popular ways to train for power is plyometrics, also known as jump training.

Plyometrics

Plyometric exercises don't require weights or machines. Athletes use their own body weight as they perform fast, explosive movements. These specialized exercises are more advanced and should be administered by a coach. Since most athletic movements are plyometric to some extent, it is wise to incorporate this type of training into football drills. Athletes should be careful not to overdo plyometric training, restricting it to one or two days a week during the power phase of off-season conditioning. Plyometric exercises should be performed before any conditioning or heavy resistance training in the weight room. An athlete who is fatigued prior to plyometric training risks altering proper technique, preventing the gains in explosive power that will enhance leg speed.

Whereas heavy resistance training focuses on the internal working of the muscles, plyometric training, through lighter resistance, focuses on the coordinated actions of separate muscles and muscle groups that work together. For example, compare a squat to a plyometric jump. The squat is a controlled, isolated movement that focuses on the legs. The plyometric jump is an explosive movement that involves the legs, arms, and core. Both exercises require similar vertical movements, and they complement each other. The plyometric exercise, however, helps increase leg speed due to the explosive nature of the movement.

Complementing maximum resistance training with plyometric training develops vertical power that enhances jumping ability and horizontal power that enhances sprinting. Both types of power enhance the leg speed of the kicker and punter since the upward and forward movements are similar to the kicking and punting motions.

During this training phase, skill-specific drills are included to enhance the development of leg speed during the kicking and punting motions. The one-step drill for kickers (page 88) and the rocker step drill for punters (page 165) are examples of good skill-specific drills for this phase. Both drills focus on proper technique and leg explosion through the football.

Core Training

Core training is crucial for the kicker and punter because all powerful and explosive athletic movements originate from the center of the body. The core consists of many muscles that run the length of the torso and stabilize the spine and pelvis. The core provides a foundation for the movement of the extremities. A strong core enables a secure, stable plant step prior to the kick and a faster, more powerful leg swing through the football.

The four actions of the core to consider during core training are trunk flexion, trunk extension, side movement, and stabilization. Sit-ups and crunches are examples of trunk flexion. Exercises that arch the back are trunk extension exercises. Side movements, such as a rotation exercise with a medicine ball, train the internal and external obliques. This motion is also a fundamental part of the soccer-style kick. Stabilization is the foundation of all movements.

Common core-strengthening exercises use dumbbells, stability ball, medicine balls, and kettle bells. Some exercises that use only body weight can be effective in developing core strength. Some weight-room exercises may indirectly train the core as well. The key is for the kicker and punter to incorporate core training into each workout to specifically address the need to develop core conditioning.

Cardiovascular Conditioning

To enhance the strength and power developed through strength training and apply this force consistently on the playing field, the athlete must improve his cardiovascular conditioning. By strategically incorporating sprint, agility, and distance running into his workout program, the

Video Analysis

For the kicker and punter to completely develop and refine their technique, they must invest the time and money, if necessary, in video recording and stop-action analysis. In recent years, tremendous advances in technology have led to good digital cameras and video analysis software. An athlete can review his technique with high-definition clarity, viewing in detail every minute movement of the kicking process or punting motion. This self-coaching opportunity is priceless. Some computer programs even have a split-screen function that allows the athlete to compare his recent technique with prior film sessions so he can track his development and progress. He can compare himself to other athletes, including professionals, synchronizing his motion to the other athlete's. He will be able to compare exactly each movement of the kicking or punting motion.

Video analysis should be done early in the off-season as the athlete begins the process of developing and improving his technique. To allow sufficient time to improve technique between filming sessions, the athlete should use video analysis at least once every two to three weeks, no more. This also gives the athlete time to feel comfortable with any technique adjustments so his movement is natural.

By comparing himself with other athletes, the athlete is not trying to mimic a certain kicking or punting style. Instead he reviews the successful methods of other kickers or punters to find the common denominators that can be applied as he develops his own individual style.

athlete will make sure he is prepared to endure the rigors of competition. Running and conditioning drills should simulate the requirements of game-day performance.

Football consists of quick bursts of speed, stop-and-go movements, sudden changes of direction, and swift agility. These intense movements are inherent in anaerobic training that is geared toward speed and power. This type of training prepares the athlete for maximum muscle activity over brief periods of time. For the kicker and punter, this type of cardiovascular training is applied toward the acceleration and explosive movement of the leg during the kick or punt.

The other type of cardiovascular training essential for football players is aerobic, or endurance, training. Aerobic training prepares the athlete for activities of long duration, enabling him to maintain a high level of performance throughout a game.

Kickers and punters should train to recover quickly during brief periods of complete rest or less-intense exercises. This simulates game conditions in which a kicker or punter is called on to execute a specific play at full speed and then jog back to the sideline to wait for the next opportunity. A highly trained athlete will recover more efficiently during these intervals and be prepared for the next play.

The well-conditioned athlete blends both anaerobic and aerobic training. As with resistance training, the intensity and duration of cardiovascular training should increase gradually in a strategic progression that enables the athlete to peak for competition.

Spring Practice

When on-field spring football practice starts, athletes usually transition to a maintenance phase (table 14.3). This period also provides a natural transition for high school athletes who participate in spring sports. The quantity and intensity of workouts are reduced. Instead of resistance training three or four days a week, athletes perform resistance training only two or three days to maintain strength and power gains and performance levels. The number of sets and amount of weight are also reduced as repetitions are increased.

An athlete who does not maintain the gains he made during the winter will revert to where he started. Therefore even during spring practice, kickers and punters must enter a maintenance phase of training. This will enable athletes to maintain their performance throughout the spring and take their gains into the summer workout program.

In the second month of the spring workout, athletes return to working out three or four days a week and focusing on increasing strength. Since they have maintained their gains from their winter workouts, these athletes will be able to increase strength even more. Intensity increases during this four-week phase as athletes plan to peak just as the season begins. Athletes must remain aware of their bodies and watch for signs of overtraining and burnout.

Table 14.3 Spring Conditioning Program

Month	Resistance training	Days per week	Cardiovascular conditioning	Days per week	Skill training	Days per week
April	Maintenance	2 or 3	With team during on-field practice	3 or 4	Game-ready drills	3 or 4
May	Strength development	3 or 4	Endurance, speed, agility	3 or 4	Technique drills	2 or 3

Summer, or Preseason, Workout

The summer workout continues the phase of increasing strength started at the end of the spring workout (table 14.4). Throughout the initial month, the focus shifts to maximum strength and then enters a power phase. The main objective is to prepare the body for high-intensity training. Intensity increases over three or four weeks as repetitions are minimized and weight is maximized. Athletes typically perform three to five sets of one to four repetitions of each exercise. Athletes need to be explosive when performing each lift.

To convert strength gains into sport-specific power, in July athletes enter a power phase that consists of maximum resistance training complemented by power training. During preseason training, kickers and punters transition from plyometric exercises to more skill-specific drills to enhance the development of leg speed.

Table 14.4   Summer, or Preseason, Conditioning Program

Month	Resistance training	Days per week	Cardiovascular conditioning	Days per week	Skill training	Days per week
June	Strength development, maximum strength (power phase)	3 or 4	Endurance, speed, power (plyometrics)	3 or 4	Explosive, technique, game-ready drills	3
July	Maximum strength (power phase)	3 or 4	Endurance, speed, skill-specific power	3 or 4	Explosive, technique, game-ready drills	3 or 4
Prior to season	Strength, speed, and quickness testing					

Skill Training

Kickers and punters should learn the fundamentals of kicking and punting so thoroughly they are able to coach themselves. A strategic progression of drills designed to develop skills will lead to game-day readiness. Each drill should begin with individual technique warm-up and progress to isolate parts of the kicking and punting mechanics. Kickers and punters develop and master each movement before combining them to complete the entire sequence. Drill work enables kickers and punters to develop consistent technique without wearing out their legs. Focus on quality and not quantity.

268 Football Kicking and Punting

Each drill must have a purpose. Drills that focus on warming up, developing techniques, and enhancing performance can be used during the off-season and preseason. As the season approaches, kickers and punters should focus primarily on warm-up drills and drills that simulate game-like situations. Kickers and punters should practice with the holders and snappers whenever possible. Timing is essential to develop accountability, so the entire kicking and punting processes should be timed during practice and games.

Flexibility training, discussed in chapter 11, is a key aspect of skill development. Improvements in flexibility promote a full range of motion. Stretching helps improve sport-specific movements and prevent or minimize injuries. Incorporate stretching into the warm-up routine before and during training and competition, and use stretching to cool down after each workout or game. Stretching muscles fatigued from intense training or on-field performance will enhance flexibility and reduce or prevent muscle soreness.

Stretching exercises increase flexibility, develop full range of motion, improve mobility, and enhance balance and coordination. In combination with technique development and increased power, flexibility improves leg speed. Combining proper technique, power of movement, and a full range of motion enables the kicker or punter to develop a fast leg that will impart tremendous force into the football.

Index

Note: The italicized *t* and *f* following page numbers refer to tables and figures, respectively.

A

alignment
    and field conditions 64-66
    kickoffs 34-39, 36*f*, 39*f*
    placekicking 6-11
    punting 107-108, 108*f*
Alignment Drill 78
approach
    adjustments for conditions 64-66
    kickoffs 40
    placekicking 9, 14-19
    punting 110-129
Arm Position Drill 81
artificial turf 62-63
attentional focus 245
Australian end-over-end drop punt 142

B

Bad Hold and Mishandled Snap Drill 100
Bad Snap Drill 183
Bag Drill 82-83
Balance Drill 167
Ball Drill 175
Ball Drop Drill 162-163
ball position 19-20, 20*f*, 202-203
Blindfolded Punt Drill 173
blocked kicks 204-205
Block Point Drill 169
body position
    placekicking 12-13, 12*f*
    punting 108-109, 109*f*

C

cardiovascular conditioning 264-266
Chute Drill 168
classic drive kicks 48-49
cleats
    detachable 62, 74
    in rain and snow 73-75
clutch performance. *See* mental preparation

Coffin Corner Drill 177
coffin corner punts 137-138, 137*f*
cold temperatures 75-76
conditioning
    about 249-250
    in-season 250-258, 251*t*
    off-season 259-267, 261*t*, 266*t*
conditions. *See* field surfaces; weather
        conditions
confidence 3
control, ball 3-4
core training 264
crosswind 68-70, 68*f*, 69*f*, 143

D

deep kicks 47
depth
    punting 107-108, 108*f*
depth of setup
    placekicking 8-9
detachable cleats 62, 74
directional kicks 46
directional punting 134-135, 134*f*
drag kicks 49-50
drills
    placekicking game-ready 98-104
    placekicking with football 85-97
    placekicking without football 78-84
    punting game-ready 176-184
    punting with football 160-175
    punting without football 156-159
drive step 17-18

E

Escape Gravity Drill 158-159, 221-222

F

Fade Punt Drill 170
fair catch 152
fake field goals 59-60, 205

Field Goal Punt Drill 172
field goals
    about 53-54
    angle of kick 55*f*
    blocked kicks 204-205
    differences from kickoffs 37-38
    fakes 59-60
    long-range attempts 58-59
    optimal height 56-57, 57*f*
    optimal range 57-58
    placement point 54-56, 54*f*, 55*f*, 56*f*
    target zone 54*f*, 56*f*
    timing 56
field surfaces
    approach and plant adjustments 64-66
    artificial turf 62-63
    field turf 63
    indoors 64
    natural grass 62
    poor maintenance of 63-64
    practice for 61
field turf 63
film analysis 239-241
focus 13, 14, 27
follow-through
    drill for kickoffs 44-45, 44*f*
    kickoffs 42-43, 43*f*
    placekicking 24-27, 26*f*
    punting 128-129, 128*f*
football sweet spot 21-22, 22*f*
foot impact
    and control 3-4
    kickoffs 41-42, 41*f*
    placekicking 20-21, 21*f*
    sweet spot impact 21-22, 22*f*
form kicks 221

G

game-day strategy 226-227
goalposts, and angle of kick 55*f*
grass surface, natural 62
Guy, Ray 156

H

hang time
    kickoffs 29, 34, 45, 71, 72
    punting 135-136, 136*f*
Hang Time Drill 176
headwind 67-68, 67*f*, 143
Hentrich, Craig 142
high-bounce kicks 48

high school
    kickoff point 31
    teeing up 63-64
holding/holder
    blocked kicks 204-205
    fake field goals 59-60, 205
    hold and ball position 19-20, 20*f*, 202-203
    placement point 197-198
    receiving snap 201-202, 202*f*
    and snapper 200
    technique 198-200, 198*f*, 199*f*, 200*f*
    timing 14, 238
    unkickable snaps 203-204, 204*f*

I

icing attempts 245-247
impact with ball
    kickoffs 41-42, 41*f*
    punting 125-127, 125*f*, 127*f*
indoor field surfaces 64
intended target 68-70, 68*f*, 69*f*

J

jab step 15-17

K

kickers
    film and practice analysis 239-241
    mental preparation 243-247
    responsibilities after kicks 234-235
    weekly practice countdown 241*t*
Kickoff Hurdle Drill 44-45, 44*f*
kickoffs
    about 29
    alignment 34-39, 36*f*, 39*f*
    approach 40
    deep kicks 47
    differences from field goals 37-38
    directional kicks 46
    disguising types 49
    follow-through 42-43, 43*f*
    follow-through drill 44-45, 44*f*
    foot impact with ball 41-42, 41*f*
    hang time 45
    headwind 68
    onside kicks 47-50, 49*f*
    placement point 31-32, 32*f*
    plant step 35, 37, 41
    purpose 46
    responsibilities following 234-235
    situational kicks 45-47

sky kicks 51-52
specialty kicks 50-52
squib kicks 50-51
stance 40
target zone 29-31, 30*f*
teeing up 32-34, 33*f*

L

Last-Second Kick Drill 101
laterals 50
leg swing
    placekicking 20-21, 21*f*
    punting 123-125, 123*f*, 124*f*
Lift Drill 85
Line Drill 84, 166
Line Kicks Drill 92

M

Mangum, Dusty 247
mental preparation
    attentional focus 245
    and icing attempts 245-247
    routine plan for 244
    visualization and imagery 243, 245

N

No-Step Drill 86-87

O

off-season conditioning
    about 259-260
    cardiovascular conditioning 264-266
    core training 264
    plyometrics 263-264
    postseason rest 260
    preseason practice 266*t*, 267
    resistance training 261-263
    skill training 267-268
    spring practice 266-267
    winter workout 260-261*t*
offside 51
One-Step Drill 88-89
onside kicks 47-50, 49*f*
opponents, breaking down 235-237
Optimal Stride Drill 169
Out of the End Zone Drill 180

P

path to ball, placekicking 13-14, 13*f*

placekicking
    about 3-4
    alignment 6-11
    angle of approach 9
    approach 9, 14-19
    ball position 19-20, 20*f*
    body lean 12-13, 12*f*
    depth of setup 8-9
    follow-through 24-27, 26*f*
    foot impact position 20-21, 21*f*
    foot pivot 9-11, 10*f*
    foot position 20-21, 21*f*
    hold 19-20, 20*f*
    leg swing 20-21, 21*f*
    path to ball 13-14, 13*f*
    placement point 5*f*, 23
    postkick check 27-28
    pregame routine 223-225, 224*t*
    protection packages 232-233, 232*f*
    ready stance 11-13, 12*f*
    sideline preparation 227-229
    target zone 4*f*
    timing 23-24, 238, 258
    trajectory 22-23
    two-step approach 19
placekicking drills
    with football 85-97
    game-ready 98-104
    without football 78-84
Placement Drill 179
placement point
    field goals 54-56, 54*f*, 55*f*, 56*f*
    kickoffs 31-32, 32*f*
    placekicking 5*f*, 23
Plant Foot Balance Drill 95
plant step
    adjustments for conditions 64-66
    kickoffs 35, 37, 41
    placekicking 18-19, 18*f*, 23, 26
    punting 123-125, 123*f*, 124*f*
plyometrics 263-264
Pooch Punt Drill 181
power 3
precise target 68-70, 68*f*, 69*f*
pregame routine
    dynamic stretching 214-218
    kick and return specialists warm-up
        222-223
    partner-assisted static stretching 219-221
    placekicking kick progression 223-225,
        224*t*
    punter warm-up progression 225-226, 225*f*

pregame routine, *continued*
    routine and warm-up 207-209
    static stretching 209-214
    technique-specific warm-up 221-222
proprioceptive neruomuscular facilitation
    (PNF) 219
protection packages 231-234, 232*f*, 233*f*
Punt After a Safety Drill 182
punting
    about 107
    approach 110-129
    blocked kicks 204-205
    depth and alignment 107-108, 108*f*
    follow-through 128-129, 128*f*
    football alignment 117-121, 119*f*
    hand positioning and grip 115-117, 116*f*
    impact with football 125-127, 125*f*, 127*f*
    leg swing 123-125, 123*f*, 124*f*
    meeting the snap 114
    postpunt check 130
    pregame routine 225-226, 225*f*
    protection packages 233-234
    receiving the snap 114-115, 115*f*, 145-146
    releasing football 121-123, 121*f*, 122*f*
    responsibilities following 234-235
    sideline preparation 227-229
    stance and body position 108-109, 109*f*
    stepping patterns 110-114, 112*f*
    timing 129-130, 196-197, 238, 258
punting adjustments
    approach adjustments 145-148, 146*f*
    challenging returner 152-153
    drawing offsides 153-154
    from end zone 147
    kicking away from return 149-152, 150*f*,
        151*f*
    learning from previous game punts
        148-149
punting drills
    with football 160-175
    game-ready 176-184
    without football 156-159
punting situations
    coffin corner 137-138, 137*f*
    conditions compensation 143-144
    directional 134-135, 134*f*
    distance and hang time 135-136, 136*f*
    distance driving 144
    hang time 132-133, 133*f*
    objectives 131-132
    out of endzone 138-140, 139*f*
    pooch punts 140-143, 141*f*

Punt Pass Drill 164

R
rainy conditions 73-74
range, field goal 57-59
Range Finder Drill 102
Rapid Fire Drill 171
ready stance, placekicking 11-13, 12*f*
Redirect Drill 178
resistance training 261-263
return men
    challenging 152-153
    evaluating 237
    kicking away from 149-152, 150*f*, 151*f*
Rocker Step Drill 165

S
shoes
    detachable cleats 62
    kicking shoe 63
    for rain 73-74
    for snow 74-75
    turf shoes 63
Side Angle Drill 93
situational kicks 45-47
Skip Step Drill 94
sky kicks 51-52, 68
snapping/snapper
    approach and setup 188
    arm position 190
    body position 192*f*
    feet positioning 189*f*
    football placement 191-192, 192*f*
    hand placement 190-191, 190*f*, 191*f*
    motion 193-194, 193*f*, 194*f*
    placekicking 14, 200-201
    snap timing 107-108, 129, 194-197, 238
    stance 189-190, 189*f*
    unkickable snaps 203-204, 204*f*
Snap to Kick Drill 103
snap-to-kick time 56
snowy conditions 74-75
Soccer Ball Punt Drill 174
soccer-style kicking 3-4
special teams
    breaking down opponents 235-237
    film and practice analysis 239-241
    kick and return specialists warm-up
        222-223
    protection packages 231-234, 232*f*, 233*f*
    responsibilities on 234-235

weekly game plan 237-239
weekly practice countdown 241*t*
specialty kicks 50-52
Spot Drill 98-99
spring practice 266-267
squib kicks 50-51
stance
    kickoffs 40
    placekicking 11-13, 12*f*
    punting 108-109, 109*f*
Stance and Reception Drill 160-161
Stance and Start Drill 79
stretching
    dynamic 214-218
    partner-assisted static 219-221
    static 209-214
sweet spot impact 21-22, 22*f*
swirls and gusts 72-73, 73*f*

T

Tackling Practice 184
tailwind 70-72, 71*f*, 143
target zone
    crosswind 68-70, 68*f*, 69*f*
    field goals 54-56, 54*f*, 55*f*, 56*f*
    kickoffs 29-31, 30*f*
    placekicking 4*f*
tee height 18*f*, 32
teeing up
    high school 63-64
    kickoffs 32-34, 33*f*
timing 238, 258-259
    field goals 56
    placekicking 23-24
    punting 129-130, 196-197

toeing the line 8
torque 3
touchbacks, punting 138-140, 139*f*
trajectory, placekicking 22-23
Trajectory Drill 90-91
turf shoes 63, 74

U

Upright Drill 96-97

V

Varying Conditons Drill 104
Vinatieri, Adam 61
visualization and imagery 243, 245
Visualize Punt Drill 157
Visualize the Kick Drill 80

W

weather conditions
    about 66
    cold temperatures 75-76
    practice for 61
    punting 143-144
    rain 73-74
    snow 75
    wind 66-73, 68*f*, 69*f*, 71*f*, 73*f*
windy conditions
    about 66-67
    crosswind 68-70, 68*f*, 69*f*
    headwind 67-68, 67*f*
    punting 143-144
    swirls and gusts 72-73, 73*f*
    tailwind 70-72, 71*f*
winter workout 260-261*t*

About the Authors

Coming out of the University of Southern Mississippi, **Ray Guy** was the first pure punter ever to be drafted in the first round of the NFL draft when the Oakland Raiders selected him in 1973. Guy was a key member of three Super Bowl-winning Raiders teams: Super Bowls XI, XV, and XVIII. During his career, Guy played in a record 207 consecutive games, averaged 42.4 yards per punt for his career, had 210 punts inside the 20-yard line, led the NFL in punting three times, had a  streak of 619 consecutive punts before having one blocked, had a record 111 career punts in postseason games, had five punts of over 60 yards during the 1981 season, and never had a punt returned for a touchdown. Guy was selected to seven AFC Pro Bowl teams, and in 1994 he was named the punter on the National Football League's 75th Anniversary Team.

Guy was also an outstanding punter and placekicker at Southern Mississippi. During his senior season, Guy recorded a 93-yard punt while leading the NCAA with a 46.2 yard average. As a placekicker at Southern Mississippi, he kicked a then-record 61-yard field goal. Guy was also a starting safety in college and intercepted a record eight passes. He was a consensus All-American, which included being named to the prestigious Walter Camp All-America Team. After his senior season, Guy was named Most Valuable Player of the annual College All-Star game, in which an all-star team of college seniors played the current Super Bowl champion.

Guy has been inducted into both the Mississippi and the Georgia Sports Halls of Fame, the National High School Sports Hall of Fame, the College Football Hall of Fame, the American Football Kicking Hall of Fame, and he was the first pure punter to be nominated for enshrinement in the Pro Football Hall of Fame. Guy was known for punts with a high hang time—sometimes as long as six seconds—and once punted the ball with so much hang time that the opponents pulled the ball and had it tested for helium.

As the cofounder and director of the Ray Guy Prokicker.com Academy, **Rick Sang** is a veteran with over 29 years of experience establishing kicking instructional programs at colleges and universities across the country. This program has produced two Lou Groza Award winners, numerous college All-Americans, and several NCAA and NFL record holders. A former college coach, he was a member of both Eastern Kentucky University NCAA Division 1AA national championship teams (1979 punter and receiver, 1982 kicking coach) and a kicking coach for Arizona State's 1986-87 PAC-10, Rose Bowl, and Freedom Bowl championship teams. During his coaching career, he had a punter win

an NCAA national net punting title and a kicker set a record of five field goals in one game. He is a member of the American Football Coaches Association and the Greater Augusta Sports Council.